CHE'S CHEVROLET, FIDEL'S OLDSMOBILE

CHE'S CHEVROLET

FIDEL'S OLDSMOBILE

On the Road in Cuba

RICHARD SCHWEID

The University of North Carolina Press

Chapel Hill and London

27.50

10/04

Set in Mrs Eaves, Bureau Grotesque,
and Cezanne types by
Tseng Information Systems, Inc.
Manufactured in the United States of America
Page vii photograph by John Newcomb

The paper in this book meets the guidelines for
permanence and durability of the Committee on
Production Guidelines for Book Longevity of the
Council on Library Resources.

Library of Congress
Cataloging-in-Publication Data
Schweid, Richard, 1946–
Che's Chevrolet, Fidel's Oldsmobile : on the road
in Cuba / by Richard Schweid.
p. cm.
Includes bibliographical references and index.
ISBN 0-8078-2892-0 (cloth : alk. paper)
1. Automobiles—Cuba. I. Title.
TL33.C83S38 2004
388.3'2'097291—dc22
2004000617

08 07 06 05 04   5 4 3 2 1

For Carlos Bosch,

a loyal friend, as well as

an extraordinary journalist

and filmmaker, who first

brought me to Cuba,

and for my favorite biochemist,

Carmen Martínez Gómez,

who helps light the way

El Encanto
IETO
RENACIMIENTO
ARTE y MODA
VIVERES FINOS
DULCES y HELADOS
LAS COLUMNAS
LOS PRECIOS FIJOS

CONTENTS

Chapter 1. Locomobiles and Model T's 5

Chapter 2. *Tudores* and *Fordores* 52

Chapter 3. Buses and Trolleys 96

Chapter 4. 1957 Chevys 135

Chapter 5. Che's Chevy and Fidel's Olds 172

Bibliography 217

Acknowledgments 227

Index 229

CHE'S CHEVROLET, FIDEL'S OLDSMOBILE

Gulf of Mexico

Santiago de las Vegas
Gaunajay
Bahía Honda
Artemisa
Consolación del Sur
Pinar del Río
San Antonio de los Baños
Bejucal
Regla
Havana
Santa Cruz del Norte
Cárdenas
Camajuaní
Sagua la Grande
Remedios
Madruga
Matanzas
Jovellanos
Güines
Unión de Reyes
Colón
Santa Clara
Nueva Paz
Bolondrón
Cruces
Palmira
Placetas
Batabanó
Nueva Gerona
Bay of Pigs
Cienfuegos
Ranchuelo
Trinidad
Isle of Pines
Santa Fé

Caribbean Sea

Atlantic Ocean

Caibarién

Cabaiguán
Sancti-Spíritus
Morón
Ciego de Ávila
Júcaro
Nuevitas
Camagüey
Puerto Padre
Gibara
Vertientes
Martí
Banes
Victoria de
las Tunas
Holguín
Sagua de Tánamo
Antilla
Mayarí
Baracoa
Alto Cedro
Manzanillo
Bayamo
Palma Soriano
San Luis
El Caney
Guantánamo
Sierra Maestra
Santiago de Cuba
Siboney
Daiquirí
Caimanera

LOCOMOBILES & MODEL T'S

One of the first things most visitors to Cuba note is the absence of advertisements for anything other than the Revolution. The relatively few billboards to be seen stand at the entrances to towns or at important urban junctions. They carry short, punchy, revolutionary exhortations in bright letters—social realism in advertising. Some call on the Cuban people to set their sights on the future, and others pay homage to heroes of the Revolution like Fidel Castro Ruz and Ernesto "Che" Guevara de la Serna, the Argentine physician who fought beside Castro and later died trying to organize a revolution from the mountains of Bolivia. While Castro and Che are known around the world, others extolled in signage are less well known outside Cuba; but they gave their lives for the Revolution, and their names are familiar to any Cuban over eight years old—patriots like Camilo Cienfuegos, Abel Santamaría, Frank País, and José Antonio Echevarría. Rather than learning brand names, every schoolchild learns a long list of Cuba's heroes.

Numerous North American heroes of the Cuban Revolution, however, remain unsung, and they *do* have brand names—names like Chevrolet, Ford, Studebaker, Chrysler, Rambler, Cadillac, Plymouth, Dodge, and Buick. Unsung, but not unknown, they have served the Revolution tirelessly, and continue to do so on a daily basis, carrying its loads, transporting its people. Che Guevara had a Chevrolet, and Fidel Castro's favorite car after the triumph of the Revolution on January 1, 1959, was an Oldsmobile, although he has long since graduated to a Mercedes with a driver. A 1951 Chevrolet carried Fidel's brother Raúl Castro Ruz to an assault on the Moncada military barracks in Santiago de Cuba in 1953. The attack failed, and both Fidel and Raúl Castro went to prison, but the Revolution had begun. Less than seven years later, Castro would fly victorious from Santiago de Cuba, at the eastern end of the island, to Havana and would then ride from the airport into the city in a Willys Jeep.

Like images of Che Guevara and Fidel Castro, whose faces or silhouettes adorn walls in nearly every home and office, the cars built in Detroit and sold to Cubans fifty, sixty, or seventy years ago have become emblematic. A photo of a 1957 Chevrolet Bel Air in front of an arched colonnade means Havana and Cuba all over the world, much as does Che's image on scores of products from T-shirts to postcards. Detroit's cars have been absorbed into the extensive iconography of Cuban history.

Present-day Cuba reveals a remarkable mixture of influences that seem to come in roughly equal parts from Africa's west coast, Spain, and the United States. Cubans have combined Europe and Africa, the Catholic Church and Santería's pantheon of deities, in approximately equal amounts, all leavened with a big dose of North American money, manners, and cultural values, in a tropical climate, with the whole loaf iced by a revolution. The island is somewhere unlike anywhere else. For Cubans, the irony of depending for much of their automobile transport on pre-1960 cars built by the enemy merits little more than a shrug of the shoulders.

In the very center of old Havana, white and gleaming in the sun stands a full-scale, two-block-long replica of the United States Capitol called El Capitolio Nacional. The National Capitol was initiated in 1929, under the government of Gerardo Machado, and it took 5,000 workers more than three years to complete the project. It looms domed and familiar over the Paseo Martí. The huge expanse of marble serves as the heart of Cuba, as the one in Washington, D.C., does for the United States. It is the beginning of everything, the alpha of national identity. An imitation two-carat diamond is sunk into the marble floor directly under the center of the dome. This is point zero—the distances between

Havana and other places along the 750-mile length of the island are measured from this spot. Outside, at the bottom of the long rows of marble steps descending to the sidewalk, are parked long lines of pre-1959 American cars. The sight of sixty or seventy 1950s cars from the States, parked in ranks in front of an exact replica of the U.S. Capitol, in the middle of Fidel Castro's Havana, is an odd sight, indeed. On any given day, some of the automobiles parked there are makes that have been declared extinct on the streets of the United States: Packards, Plymouths, Studebakers, Nash Ramblers, Kaisers, Henry J's, Willys Overlands, Edsels, and De Sotos. To say nothing of the "muscle cars," the 1954 Ford station wagons, and the 1957 Chevrolet Bel Airs. Havana's residents, *Habaneros* as they call themselves, can still enjoy a sighting of the sleek curving lines of a Studebaker or the boxy, functional design of a Rambler, cars built by automobile companies so long disappeared from the commercial map of the States as to be unknown to a majority of living North Americans. These endangered species in the streets surrounding El Capitolio are working cars, not pampered, garaged collectibles like the few of their ilk that still exist stateside. They are *ruteros*, taxis that run fixed routes beginning at the foot of the Capitol's steps and fanning out along the broad avenues and main thoroughfares of the city. All day long, crossing the chewed-up streets of Havana under a broiling sun in heavy traffic, they carry as many humans as can be squeezed in: three in the front seat and five behind is the minimum. The number of passengers who can be accommodated is often higher, as rudimentary seats are welded in place to fill any open space, and many of the cars Detroit produced in the 1950s had plenty of open space. Havana has its share of hills as well as terrible heat and corrosive, wet salt air blowing in from the sea. It is not a climate conducive to keeping an automobile in good working condition.

Many of these cars are what Cubans call *cacharros*, a term of semi-endearment, semicontempt, more or less equivalent to the English word "jalopy." These cars are like old people. They have liver spots of discolored paint, an inability to retain their fluids, and a coughing ignition that makes it hard for them to get started in the morning. Still, they

El Capitolio (Biblioteca Nacional José Martí, Havana)

· · ·

hunch over and keep on going. Most of these *cacharros* have been seriously altered as they aged, have undergone the equivalents of organ transplants and joint reconstructions, with a great number of them adapted to burn diesel fuel, much more economical than high-octane gasoline. After many years of coexisting with big, old North American cars and newer, smaller models from the Soviet Bloc, plenty of Cuban mechanics have learned to combine an original Detroit engine with a diesel model out of a Volga or a Moskvich or a Lada, encouraging relations between the USA and the USSR long before the Cold War ended. Few are the parts of a car that Cubans have not learned to adapt or duplicate.

In the summer of 2002, gas was selling for seventy-five U.S. cents a liter (almost $3.00 a gallon), while diesel was going for fifteen to twenty cents, and most people paid less than that since they bought their fuel on the ample black market. From refinery to gas station, all along the way are people with siphons. Where there are lots of state-owned vehicles and the gasoline to keep them running, some of the fuel will find its way to cars being put to private use. Often the easiest way to find black-market gas or diesel is to pull into a Cupet, the state-owned filling station, and ask the attendant where you can find something cheaper than what he is pumping.

The converted Soviet diesel engine works for a while, but it wears out motors, transmissions, drive trains. It is a modification that sentences a car to a slow but certain death. Everyone knows the drawbacks to diesel, so a lot of cars still have their original engines. If it is financially possible, people prefer not to install a diesel. A *rutero* does not afford that luxury. With the car running back and forth all day, filled with passengers, it must be adapted to hold down costs any way possible.

New, factory-made spare parts have not been available for North American cars in Cuba since the United States stopped doing business with the island in October 1960. Nevertheless, knowledgeable observers estimate that some 60,000 such cars are still on the streets, most of them in the island's two largest cities, Santiago de Cuba and Havana. Somehow, they keep on running, despite the blockade. When asked how it is possible to maintain so many cars without factory-made parts, most

Cubans will just shrug and say something offhand, invoking what has become the real national slogan in five decades of revolutionary life: *hay que resolver*, it has to be resolved, a solution has to be found. If a car has to have a part replaced, *hay que resolver*. In a country where the whole point is to keep cars running as long as possible, the number of vehicles available to be cannibalized for parts is steadily declining. The daily newspapers *Granma* and *Juventud Rebelde* have no ads, classified or otherwise; no one publishes an old car newsletter; there are no junkyards; no parts houses exist. News of an old car being dismantled or sold usually arrives through the same media that carries other real news pertinent to a person's life in Cuba: *Radio Bemba*, *bemba* being Cuban for lip. *Radio Bemba*, word of mouth, lip-to-ear. That's where the market for brake shoes and transmissions and front ends operates, and the casual mention of an old car stored away somewhere is enough to justify spending a day following up on such a *Radio Bemba* tip.

For many of these old cars, life was not always such a struggle. Originally, they were owned by members of the middle and upper class. Like the majority of the Cuban people themselves during the 1950s, these automobiles served the rich, toiled in an economy with its roots sunk deep in sugarcane and the United States, an economy built on the backs of people condemned to grinding poverty. Cadillacs and their drivers waited all night outside glittering casinos, while not far away people bedded down on the sidewalk. But car ownership in Cuba was not entirely limited to the rich during Detroit's glory years of design. Chevys graced many a middle-class life, and even secretaries and clerks in Havana or Santiago de Cuba were able, using the credit that was readily available, to buy a Ford. Certainly, a majority of Cubans did not make enough to own a car, but Detroit reached out even to them. Those without steady work, or any work, could ride a bus for five cents. These, too, were most often built in Detroit and shipped to the island.

The history of motor vehicles in Cuba, up until the Revolution, is a microcosm of the history of relations between the United States and its island neighbor ninety miles to the south. The United States and Cuba were so close during the first half of the twentieth century that they

*Aging but still on the road, a Ford station wagon helps
move Cubans and their belongings in December 1990.
(Courtesy of the photographic archives,* Bohemia, Havana)

• • •

were practically joined together at the waist, knit together at the eyebrows. Cubans were fascinated with North American consumer culture
and provided a busy market for all things modern and yankee, *yanqui.*
Likewise, its huge neighbor to the north had an ongoing fascination
with Cuba. Politicians in the United States have long been trying, with
lesser or greater success, to impose their will on Cuba, and for the first
sixty years of the twentieth century, huge fortunes flowed out of Cuba to
the United States, as they had to Spain in the preceding century, while
dollars flooded back in to line the pockets of the island's privileged.

After the Revolution, vehicles, like housing, had to be placed at the
disposal of the new regime and the people of Cuba. Outwardly, the
island's cars and trucks deteriorated, rusted, were rewired and rebuilt,
not unlike the spectacular buildings of Havana, but they were deemed to

be serving a greater good—the people they carried had learned to read and write, and, by 1998, their society had a lower infant mortality rate than that of the United States. The cars, like the buildings, were called on to make sacrifices, required to accommodate more people: the comfort factor was severely reduced in favor of utility and assuring that everyone had a little bit of something. Like Cuba's crumbling housing stock, some of the cars and trucks could not take it and collapsed, but others have stayed the race.

The face of Eastern European or Soviet communism was drab, second-best, and gray—safe, if unexciting. Cuba has never been that way. Life in Cuba is colorful; pleasure and passion are cultural keynotes, and the island's vegetation is lush, exuberant, and tropical. Its architecture is colonial, and Cuba is, first and foremost, a Caribbean country. To gauge the effects of the totalitarian communist regime that is the cult-of-the-personality Revolution in Cuba today, it is more instructive to look to life in the rest of Caribbean Latin America than to other vanished communist economies. It is not hard to see what Cuba would be like now if it were not for the Revolution. Just look at its neighbors, former Spanish colonies like Nicaragua, Guatemala, Honduras, El Salvador, Mexico, and the Dominican Republic, all places where being poor can kill you, where there is a bone-crushing, hope-extinguishing level of poverty. This sort of privation has not existed in Cuba since 1959. There have been hard times, lean times, long periods when there was not enough to go around, but people have not moved en masse to raise their children and their children's children at garbage dumps. It is true that people are not free to travel or to live uncensored lives. The Revolution treats Cubans like children, not permitting them to grow up and make choices for themselves. Real children in Cuba, however, all go to school, and adults have medical attention for their families and can keep a roof—albeit, a humble one—over their heads. None of their more "democratic" neighbors have quite figured out how to accomplish this, and Cubans are proud of these achievements.

Most Cubans will manage to get by, but they will never, in their whole lives, have enough money to buy a car. There is no formal credit system, and the only way to get a car is to buy one for cash, unless its owner is prepared to offer a private payment plan. The government has given many thousands of Soviet cars to Cuban professionals, government workers, managers, and military officers to use for life, but they cannot be sold or even inherited. They belong to the state. Pre-1960 Detroit models can be owned by individuals. They are given a paper called a *traspaso*, which allows the cars to be bought and sold privately, but as the pool of vehicles has grown smaller, the prices that must be paid for them have reached levels far out of most people's reach. For the few Cubans who inherit a car, only rarely can they afford fuel for it. Gasoline is too expensive to buy on a Cuban salary, even on the black market.

The near impossibility of ever owning private transport chafes, because Cubans like cars and they start wanting one early in life. Just look at Santiago de Cuba's Plaza de Marte on any mellow Saturday evening. As the light fades and the day cools, the park fills with small kids wheeling miniature tin cars around, many of them grinning fiercely, pedaling furiously. In the center of today's Plaza de Marte is an obelisk, dedicated to José Martí and others who died in the 1898 War of Independence from Spain. At the foot of the obelisk, a rail-thin man in a well-washed, sky-blue *guayabera*—the four-pocket loose shirt favored by many older Cuban men—has tricycles, pedal cars, and scooters that he rents for twenty centavos, equal to a penny, for ten minutes to parents and their little kids. Also among the wheeled traffic for hire along the plaza's sidewalks on a Saturday evening are wooden carts with benches built on their long sides. Each bench can hold four small children, and the cart is pulled around the plaza by a goat. The keeper walks alongside and encourages the goat, if he sees the need, with a switch. The cart circulates through the plaza at a leisurely pace, and the toddlers sit in the back wide-eyed and laughing with pleasure.

Santiago de Cuba is the capital city of the province with the same name in the Oriente, as the eastern part of the country is known. It is Cuba's second largest city, with nearly a half million inhabitants. Founded in 1522, Santiago de Cuba was the island's first capital, serving in that capacity until 1601. It is more Caribbean than is Havana, with more dark-skinned Cubans, hotter and more tropical, with a slower, more relaxed pace of life. The Plaza de Marte, in the eastern part of downtown Santiago, is at the end of a long, long hill leading up from the port. The plaza was the parade ground for the imperial Spanish military in the nineteenth century, and it is also where firing squads carried out sentences of execution.

The goat carts roll past wooden park benches, a number of which are tacitly reserved for male debaters, under the acacia trees. A knot of men is always gathered around them, and the men do not even look up from their animated discussions of current events or sports as the carts pass by. The debaters are often eloquent and display a surprising level of awareness of international events, which would not be found among random groups of men in most other countries. These guys all know where Namibia is, and they can place Lithuania on the map in a moment. What they can't do, of course, is travel to these places or be audibly critical of the Revolution. The enemy is ever at the gate, and the security apparatus is everywhere. Then again, they might say, things are complicated. Life always demands a trade-off. Many of the men knotted up around the debaters' benches, listening and speaking, are Afro-Cubans. They know full well how it is in other Caribbean countries where there is no limit to how far poor, dark-skinned people can fall when things go wrong. The older men remember when it was that way in Cuba.

An older woman with polished brown skin, wearing a white dress and a white cloth wrapped around her head, walks by selling roasted peanuts in white paper cones, singing out her wares, *"Maní, maní."* There is a sweet, relaxed air to the plaza as the goats placidly pull cartloads of toddlers around while their mothers watch smiling, as little kids' eyes gleam while they pedal tricycles around people's legs, lampposts, and benches.

Without cars, Cubans living in both the city and the countryside are condemned to spend a lot of their time coping with public transport, and getting from one place to another takes a lot of energy. To understand why, it is necessary only to wait for a bus, for instance, down on Santiago de Cuba's Avenida Jesús Menéndez, the flat, six-lane road that runs by the train station and along the port. A lot of people do wait here daily for buses that go to, say, the Plaza de Marte on the other side of Santiago, up some terrifically long, steep hills. They wait at a bus stop in brain-burning heat under a steamy, searing sun. In half an hour of waiting on Jesús Menéndez, it is possible to watch virtually the entire history of human transport pass by: carts with benches on them, bigger versions of those built for the goats in the Plaza de Marte, these carrying up to eight full-sized adults and pulled by a beat-down, dragged-out donkey or a trudging horse with ribs outlined beneath its skin; bicycles with one person on them, and others serving as rickshaws, a platform built behind for two passengers; motor scooters with a man, woman, and child riding pillion; big, solid, workhorse motorcycles from the vanished Soviet Bloc with sidecars ample enough to hold a family; a 1949 Packard, a huge, squat beast with a hood longer than the entire length of most of today's cars; a variety of compact, rectangular, utilitarian Eastern European brands, cars like Ladas, Skodas, Fiat Polskis; and two oxen pulling a cart laden with cane stalks. Almost every kind of transport imaginable goes by. Except buses. And they, of course, are what most people standing, watching the traffic pass are waiting for, in polite and proper order. The buses cost about two cents to ride. When people arrive at the bus stop, they always call out, *Quién es el último?* (who is last?). Whoever it is answers, so the newcomer knows whom to follow when, after forty-five minutes, a bus finally does pull up. However, since only as many can get on as get off, the bus being inevitably packed to capacity, those for whom there is not room will have to wait another forty-five minutes or so for the next bus as they move up slowly in line. There is nothing so painful as watching a young mother, with deep circles under her eyes and the deadweight of a sleeping two-year-old draped over her shoulder, wait at the bus stop for an hour and a half under a punishing sun. Nothing so painful, that is, except for having to wait there with her.

─────────────

The first car to reach Santiago de Cuba appeared in May 1902, the same month in which the first stone was laid for the obelisk in the Plaza de Marte. It was a Locomobile, built by Locomobile & Company in New

Advertisement for Germán López's Locomobile dealership, Havana's first.
By 1905, López had competition from at least a dozen other brands of car.
(Biblioteca Nacional José Martí, Havana)

· · ·

York City and brought to Santiago, according to Carlos E. Forment's exhaustive daily chronicle of the city in the early twentieth century, by a man named Charles Brooks y Galo on his return from a long trip to the United States.

"The car had only two seats in the center of the vehicle, moved by a steam engine and steered by a lever," writes Forment. "The wheels had broad strips of wire like a bicycle wheel, producing a lot of noise as they turned. The only route it could take was Marina Street, turning at Nepomuceno to Enramadas until the parade grounds of Marte, because that was the only gravelled road at the time. The Locomobile went very slowly; the street urchins made fun of it and sometimes threw stones, believing it to be a carriage possessed by the devil."

In 1902, Santiago de Cuba had a population of 42,000, and was a city where the well-off were well off indeed. The English painter, Walter Goodman, who spent some five years there toward the end of the nineteenth century, as a young man, in 1895 published a book describing daily life for those who had money and those who did not. His words evoke a languid life of tropical leisure for Europeans and well-to-do Cubans, a life lived a great deal in the large, open, shaded patios of the high-ceilinged, wooden, colonial houses, each merchant family with its retinue of dependents and domestics. The entire city had an annual budget of only about $200,000, which did not allow much expenditure for public works, and the streets were not in good shape, according to Forment, who depicts "dirt streets that became rivers of mud when it rained or mountains of dust during the long dry spells."

Not until 1904 did a second car appear in Santiago de Cuba, one owned by Pepe Grinasy, a young pharmacist. It was a Fiat. No further sign of cars is to be found until 1907. On September 18 of that year, Forment relates,

> The popular politician Germán S. López, now working as a sales agent for automobiles, arrives from Havana, bringing two of them, one driven by himself and the other by a mechanic he has brought named José Geli. These cars are the latest in fashion, in mechanical technology and in speed . . . although we have to report that López was not able to sell one. However, he announced that he would bring other cars to Santiago that could serve as buses to establish a regular service for passengers to Canel, Cubitos, Dos Bocas, and San Vicente. But it was a lie! It was nothing more than a dream. The disastrous state of our unpaved streets and the impassable highways did not recommend the use of automobiles, with everyone preferring to use carriages pulled by horses.

The city's first garage opened in 1907, according to Roberto Pérez Mirabent, transport historian and director of the National Transport

Museum, an automotive museum in the Bacanao Biosphere Reserve about fifteen miles east of Santiago de Cuba. At forty-three, Pérez is a solidly built man with gray hair and a trim gray beard. He cares for about three dozen old cars on permanent display under sheds outside the museum, ranging from a 1912 Model T Ford to the late singer Benny Moré's 1958 Cadillac. Inside the museum are glass cases containing over 1,500 miniature model cars, a private collection assembled by a Spaniard named Fermín Fernández Hurtado, who fought on the side of the Republic against Franco's forces in Spain's civil war. In 1985, he donated his collection to Cuba, and the transport museum, built around it, opened in 1986.

Pérez has made an extensive study of the history of motoring in Santiago de Cuba. He explained to me, when I visited his home in 2002, that the early auto mechanics were horse and buggy experts who branched out when the new-fangled cars arrived. "The first mechanics worked on both cars and carriages. They replaced the strips of rubber on the wooden wheels of carriages, and they could work on auto bodies and do some engine work."

On May 30, 1909, less than two years after he had given up trying to sell his two cars and shipped them back to Havana, Germán López returned to Santiago, with another pair of cars. They were Fiats, as identified by Carlos Forment, who notes that López was able to sell them both. A market was beginning to form, and motorized traffic was becoming more common.

It was increasingly recognized that a car was not only a piece of sporting equipment, but could also generate revenue. "In 1913, we find references to the first taxi stand," Pérez told me. "It was at the Plaza de Marte. There were fourteen cars stationed there, different makes. They made trips in town and went to such nearby places as El Moro, San Juan, Vista Alegre, El Caney. Beyond the Plaza de Marte in those days were various *fincas*, open land without houses."

When a businessman from Des Moines, Iowa, who signed himself "M. Tuttle," wrote the governor of the province in 1915, asking for the numbers of cars registered in the cities and towns, the governor's count revealed the extent to which cars had gained in popularity. There were 133 automobiles registered in Santiago de Cuba, 47 being driven by private citizens, including 5 Fords, 5 Hupmobiles, 4 Fiats, 9 Studebakers, 13 Overlands, 3 Buicks, a Dodge, a Peerless, and a Chalmers. Another 78 cars were available for hire, owned by different businesses, including 47 Fords, by far the most popular brand for use as taxis, and 9 Chevrolets. In addition to these workaday vehicles, more automotive revenue was generated by parts and accessories shops, gas stations, garages, dealerships, and all the ancillary businesses that surround cars like pilot fish around a shark. The wave of automobiles had spread beyond the provincial capital to smaller cities and towns. In Manzanillo, there were 22 registered cars, 18 in Guantánamo, and 4 in Bayamo.

The year 2002 marked a hundred years since Charles Brooks y Galo drove that first Locomobile ashore. The members of the old car owners association in Santiago de Cuba hold an annual rally, and since the one for 2002 was set to coincide with the centennial year of cars in Santiago, it was accompanied by high expectations. Although the club is not quite as large as either of the two in Havana, it is active and has about fifty members who meet once a month to exchange news, talk about parts sources, drink and eat. Many *Santiagueros*, as Santiago's residents are called, claim that there are more old cars in their city than in Havana, because Havana is so hard on cars. They will tell you that the torrential rains in Havana, combined with the salt spray off the ocean, pit and corrode undercarriages, engines, gaskets, rings, pistons, valves, and fuel tanks. After a hard rain in Havana, cars move through the streets with great wings of water fanning up from beneath their wheels. In truth, while there are certainly a lot of old cars in Santiago de Cuba, it is unlikely that there are more than in Havana. After all, Santiago's population only approaches 450,000, while Havana's is 2.2 million; additionally, the hills of Santiago are steeper than those of Havana, the days are uniformly hotter, and although there is no salt water hanging in the air as there is along Havana's seaward avenues, abundant tropical rain falls in the deep, abysmally humid cane country of the Oriente. Even if Havana does have more cars—and numbers of currently registered cars are virtually impossible to pry loose from the Cuban government—the streets of Santiago de Cuba are full of head-turning relics from the 1950s.

Roberto Pérez has been organizing the annual rally since 1997, the first year enough gas was available to make it feasible following the brutal shortages of the so-called "Special Period in a Time of Peace." The Special Period was announced by Fidel Castro in 1990 after the fall of the Soviet Union, and it lasted until 1996, when the economy began a slow, halting recovery. The old car rally is held in June, and in this centennial year the event was affiliated with a Caribbean business fair being held on the grounds of the Herredia Theater, across from Santiago's Plaza de la Revolución. The initial elaborate plans for the rally, unfortunately, had to be scaled back. Oil shipments from Venezuela were temporarily halted as part of a failed coup attempt (supported by the United States) there, and gasoline was in even shorter supply than usual. The rally route normally runs out to the museum in the Bacanao Park and back, but this year the parade route was restricted to a drive in formation through the city. Each participating car received forty free liters of gas, ten gallons or so—not even a fill-up.

Roberto Pérez wore a perpetually worried expression during the days approaching the rally. Finally, the day comes, and thirty-nine cars fall in line, as opposed to the fifty for which he had hoped. He attributes the shortfall in vehicles to the fact that some car owners could not get off work—it was a Monday, midday. Some of the drivers, talking among themselves, mention a list of other gripes, like reduced gas allotments; resentment over a replica Model T, which is being allowed in the parade despite being actually made of plastic with a Volkswagen engine, got up to look like an old Ford for tourists to ride in; and the new Peugeots being allowed to drive right up front in the rally, because the company is one of its primary sponsors this year, along with Cristal, the national beer.

I ride with Frank, one of two Afro-Cuban drivers in the rally, in his 1953 white Chevrolet with a red interior. It is a solid workhorse of a car, rounded, a rock, much like Frank himself. He drives the Chevrolet as a taxi for tourists to make a living. His daily post is the taxi stand opposite the Parque Céspedes, Santiago de Cuba's most central park, bordered on one side by the Cathedral and on another by City Hall and on a third by the Grand Hotel, at the heart of Santiago's tourist traffic. Frank has agreed to cede me the shotgun seat in the Chevy, up front with him, for a couple of bottles of Cristal and a dollar. His car is one of the few at the rally that daily earns its keep; most of the club members' vehicles see only moderate use. All of the cars must contain at least 90 percent original parts to qualify for inclusion. In Cuba, the members of old car clubs represent a tiny fraction of the people who drive such vehicles, most of whom need their cars to keep running so they can make some kind of living and who modify them any way they can to keep them going.

The turnout of cars may be a disappointment to Roberto Pérez, but to a non-Cuban like myself it still provides an astonishing panorama. Here, parked along the edge of the Hotel Meliá Santiago, are some cars I had not, in this life, expected to see again with their rubber on the road. Such as a 1949 red Buick Special convertible, of which, its owner tells me proudly, only 108 were ever made. This one, originally painted green, was bought new in the States as a birthday present and brought over on the ferry from Miami. Since 1972, it has been kept in a garage. Chrome script on its side identifies it as being equipped with Super Dynaflow, and it has a rolled-and-pleated red interior. There is another Buick, this one from 1958, with enough room between the front and back seat for a person to stretch out full length and a chrome ashtray and cigarette lighter set into broad padded armrests on either side of the black leather back seat.

The owner of an impeccable, gray 1951 Studebaker Champion—an older, thin white man—tells me that he got it from his father, who bought it from the guy who bought it new. The Champion has an automatic transmission, and the rearview mirror is mounted on the dashboard. It also has neat little screened side vents just in front of the doors on either side, which open for extra ventilation. "The original owner was already an old guy in 1984, and one day he fell out of an avocado tree and broke some ribs, and after that he couldn't get under it to work on it, so he sold it to my father. This car runs like a top. I go to Siboney with five liters of gas, and have some left over when I get back."

Another car with an ingenious ventilation system is the red 1956 Ford Thunderbird convertible parked at the top of the Meliá's driveway, set to lead the parade. It has wind wings on the front windshield to deflect the air from passengers when the top is down and covered vents in the front fenders that can be opened to let the air in when the top is up. The dual exhaust pipes end in discrete slots in the back bumper. It gleams.

Departure time is scheduled for 10:00 A.M., but Roberto wants to wait a bit and see if anyone else turns up. At 10:30, the drivers gather round a club member, on the sidewalk by the hotel, for their marching orders. It is time to get on with it. The member reviews the route, and then there are a few words about maintaining a proper distance between cars from a motorcycle cop wearing a sharply creased, dark blue uniform, high-polished black leather boots, and a gleaming white helmet. He will lead the parade on its route through Santiago to the zoological park and back. "Let's avoid a repeat of last year," says a driver—Frank tells me there were two minor collisions in last year's rally that had somewhat marred the spirit of the event.

"*Mira qué linda*," he says, look how pretty, as the line of thirty-nine cars sets off, winding around the Plaza de la Revolución to head toward the city center. In the back seat, Frank's four-year-old daughter has big, beguiling brown eyes and a shy smile. The car came from the factory with a cord stretched across the back of the front seats. It gave people in the back seat something to grasp and pull on when they wanted to get out of the car. It is frayed, but Frank still has the original cord in place for the convenience of his backseat passengers. All the drivers are wearing green baseball caps and green knit golf shirts, both with the Cristal beer logo on them. The police go out in front and hold up traffic for the procession, lights flashing, sirens wailing. The parade route winds through many of the city's neighborhoods. This, of course, means up and down a lot of hills. Santiago is a hilly city, which virtually ensures that some car, at some point, will overheat toiling up a steep hill under a 95-degree direct sun, trying to keep up with the car in front and ahead of the one behind.

"Look how everyone comes out to watch," says Frank, pressing the button by his window that he has rigged so he can blow the horn with one finger. The parade winds downhill to the waterfront, along the Avenida Jesús Menéndez, and back uphill to the city. Indeed, people do come out to watch, or they stop what they are doing and turn to see us pass by. Skinny guys in ragged pants and torn T-shirts with fifty-pound sacks of rice on their backs stop to smile at us indulgently from underneath their loads; schoolkids pack a balcony in their neatly pressed Pioneer uniforms, each with a red kerchief knotted at the neck, and wave shyly; four shirtless, muscled young men kneeling on the sidewalk working on a tire, a collective repair of a *ponche*, a puncture, all look up; a thin old guy driving a cart half filled with mangos pulled by a mule with ribs even more prominent than its master's, eases over to the curb to watch us pass; a big man with a machete scar from beside his eye to the edge of his lip, working under the upraised hood of a 1953 De Soto, raises his head to regard us; large women rocking languidly on their porches turn their gaze our way; all the usual denizens of Santiago's streets stop what they are doing to watch us go by.

As we climb the steep hill of Bartolomé Masó Street, right behind the Cathedral, the gray 1954 Ford directly ahead of us boils over. It is driven by a young guy, a mulato, as Cubans call people of mixed European and African origins, who come in many shades of brown. He told me his father had passed the car on to him. He has what looks like a newly minted wife riding next to him, elegantly dressed, skin the color of caramel. She is thin, young, wearing a wide-brimmed black hat with a veil and a lovely, bright yellow sleeveless dress that looks brand new. The Ford overheats going up the hill. The young guy jumps out as traffic behind him, starting with us, begins to back up on the incline. He raises the hood and disappears in a big cloud of steam, which dissipates into the air around him. From a nearby shop, he returns with a bucket of water. "Start the car," he yells at the woman, who scoots over from her shotgun seat to do so, somehow contriving to immediately drop the

Ford-o-matic transmission into reverse. Frank begins honking frantically as the car lurches backward, toward us, and a woman crossing the street on foot just in front of us is nearly run down. The young woman in the Ford brakes just in time to avoid a disaster; her companion fills the radiator with water; and we are all in motion again, Frank's tank of a Chevrolet careening through the streets to catch up with the front half of the parade. Rounding the Plaza de Marte at full gallop, he leans his finger on the horn button, passing the Studebaker Champion on the ascent of Aguilera Street with its hood up. Later, while all the cars wait at the zoo for the line to re-form before returning to the starting point, the Studebaker turns up and takes its place. Over the rumble of our Chevy's idling engine, monkeys scream and parrots screech. As we turn in to make a circuit of the park, led by the '56 T-bird, we pass a plaque with a bronze relief set in one of the cement columns marking the entrance, showing the United States' eagle with arrows in its claws, *E Pluribus Unum* written over it.

Havana had cars before Santiago de Cuba, of course. It is forever the capital city, always ahead of its eastern country cousin in revenues, riches, hustles, and hypes. Habaneros consider themselves the island's trend-setters, and by the time that first Locomobile was circumscribing its limited route in Santiago, toiling uphill on Marina Street toward the Plaza de Marte in 1902, a score of cars were already cruising the streets of the capital. The first one was a Parisienne, brought from Paris by José Muñoz in 1898, where he had been sitting out the War of Independence. The car had an engine that ran on benzene and generated two horsepower, capable of covering more than seven miles in an hour. Muñoz had paid $1,000 for it, a lot of money in those days, even though the company had also bestowed on him the title of Cuba's exclusive agent for La Parisiennes.

People did not rush to purchase them, although they did watch in amazement whenever Muñoz passed by in his. It was reported that when he first displayed his horseless carriage during Carnival in 1898, onlookers thought it was a joke. "Is it true," asked a lady, "that it runs by itself?"

"Forget that idea, señora; don't be ridiculous," a man beside her is supposed to have answered. "Don't you see that there's a guy from Galicia inside it pushing?"

Muñoz's car was still running well three years later, according to an article in the December 10, 1901, issue of the popular illustrated weekly magazine El Fígaro: "Señor Muñoz has the good taste to be accompanied always by his distinguished wife, adding to the car's attraction by her attractiveness, which she communicates to everything she touches. It cost a thousand pesos and remains in good shape."

The second car to be seen in Havana was built by Rochet & Schneider in Lyon, France. It was bought there in 1899 and shipped back to Cuba by the Havana pharmacist Ernesto Sarrá. It cost him $4,000, but in return for its higher price, it could go twelve miles an hour, twice as fast as the trains of its day. It was driven by a two-cylinder, eight-horsepower engine. The steering wheel was in the back seat on the right-hand side; there was seating for one passenger beside the driver and for three more in the front seat. It had a belt transmission, which had a bad tendency to slip out of place. Sarrá had to stop every few hundred meters to put it back on track. Despite these inconveniences, as El Fígaro reported in 1901, he "made rapid and frequent excursions on the highways near to Havana in the company of friends."

The first Sarrá drugstore had been opened in 1853, and by 1899, when Ernesto bought his first car, the Sarrá family operated twenty-nine drugstores in Havana, as well as chemical and pharmaceutical laboratories. In addition, according to Luís Sexto, writing in Juventud Rebelde, he was a slumlord and a loan shark. Whatever he was, he cut a sharp figure in the Rochet & Schneider.

A letter published in a stateside magazine, The Horseless Age, in December 1899, explained a joint Havana–New York business venture, the Havana Automobile Transfer Company, which shipped four Haynes-Appersons to Havana in November of that year. The company's purpose was to run regular bus routes, two along the coast and two to inland

Pharmacist Ernesto Sarrá at the wheel of his Rochet & Schneider, which he brought to Havana in June 1899 (Biblioteca Nacional José Martí, Havana)

• • •

towns, according to the letter. "We are now fairly started and in working order, and I am pleased to state that the results thus far obtained are beyond my expectations," the company's director, Ramón Williams, wrote to the New York magazine from Havana. "The inhabitants are wild at the advent of our machines, and at first we had considerable difficulty in moving about the city. The boys in the streets and others as well would climb on the machine until we had to call upon the police to clear the roads for us."

Despite its fast start, the enterprise must not have prospered, because there is no mention of the Havana Automobile Transfer Company in any of the standard histories of motor-driven vehicles in Cuba. These invariably follow the lead of Fernando López Ortiz's essay, "50 Años de Automovilismo," which appeared in a special issue of his magazine, *El Automóvil de Cuba*, in May 1951, marking fifty years of auto enthusiasts banding together. López Ortiz asserted that the third car to appear in Havana arrived in 1900, another Parisienne, but this one more powerful than that of Muñoz, and totally enclosed, so that it could be used as a delivery truck. It made daily delivery rounds for H. de Cabañas y Carvajal cigars and cigarettes, which were manufactured by Guardia and Company. This Parisienne was the first vehicle bought locally for the purpose of daily labor, the first car actually to replace a horse toiling through the city's streets with the day's deliveries. The fourth person to bring a car to Havana was Rafael Arazoza, editor of the newspaper *La Gaceta*, who brought two Locomobiles from New York.

Next to arrive was an electric car manufactured by Woods Electric Automobiles, bought by Francisco de P. Astudillo, who was fire chief for downtown Havana and had a reputation for knowledge in the mechanical sciences, according to a December 1901 article in *El Fígaro*: "This automobile is electric, not unusual given the enthusiasms of its owner, and it can go 12 miles per hour and is one of the most elegant, light and simple of all those circulating in Havana."

The magazine was a strong promoter of the automobile. In June 1901, *El Fígaro* had convoked a gathering of Havana's existent score of cars, which all got together for a drive along the Malecón, the broad avenue and seawall that runs along the city's curving seaward edge. It was the first organized automobile event in Cuba.

The December article recorded the glorious three-year history of cars in Cuba and predicted a rosy future. "The automobile, once it is bought, does not have expenses. Its upkeep is so economical that it satisfies the most prudent, and for this the government has decided to consider sub-

Photograph accompanying an article about the first parade of automobiles
along the Malecón in the December 10, 1901, edition of El Fígaro.
(Biblioteca Nacional José Martí, Havana)

. . .

stituting automobiles for the present means of locomotion used by the branch of Public Works for road inspection. It will not be surprising, therefore, if in a restored Cuba, the elegant, rapid and most modern carriage will be lord and master of Havana.''

A former war correspondent who had covered the 1898 war for the *New York World*, Silvester Scovel, agreed. He went into business as the Cuban representative of the cars being made by the White Sewing Machine Company in Cleveland, Ohio. The White, with its simple, gasoline-driven engine, was the fastest car yet to hit Havana's streets. Its earliest fans were two brothers, Honoré and Dámaso Lainé, who each bought one from Scovel. Honoré was a veterinarian, and Dámaso was a physician who had once attended the daughter of the North American general Leonard Wood when she was ill with diphtheria. The only garage in the city was the space holding the spare parts that Muñoz had brought for his Parisienne. Convinced that cars were the coming things, the Lainé brothers opened a garage on Zulueta Street, for which they hired a full-time mechanic. Later, they bought out Scovel's agency and sold Whites as well.

At the beginning of 1902, there were as many as two dozen automobiles in Havana. Fernando López Ortiz, editor and publisher of *El Automóvil de Cuba*, which was published monthly between 1916 and 1961, wrote in his automotive history: "By the end of 1901, all the moneyed [Havana] families began to import automobiles, like Don Luis Marx, opulent tobacconist who brought a Rochet & Schneider, and Don Gustavo Bock, who imported a Dion Bouton and a Panhard Levassor."

European cars, all. North American automobile manufacturers had some trouble getting established commercially. In December 1904, *Motor Age* reported from Havana: "There are a few Whites and some Oldsmobiles, but American machines generally are not in favor owing to the failure of some early samples, three of which by the way were owned by the United States ambassador [Herbert Squiers], who, despite his hard luck, is still intent on discovering a car on which he can depend. Demonstrations will be necessary before our cars can be marketed satisfactorily."

In 1905, two years before he brought the first Fiats to Santiago de Cuba, Germán López acquired both the Fiat and Locomobile dealerships in Havana. Upon his return to Havana after serving in the U.S. Coast Guard as a mechanical engineer, he joined forces in an economic venture with Rafael Arazoza, the editor of *La Gaceta*, who had brought the first two Locomobiles to Havana. They opened a garage, the Havana Automobile Company, where a half-dozen cars could be worked on at once. A photo of Germán López, relaxed in a rocking chair in the garage's office, shows a man in his mid-thirties, lean, with the thick, wavy dark mustache favored by many of his contemporaries, well dressed, the kind of man who is at ease in white linen shirt and pants, as he wears in the photo, or in evening dress. His hat, a straw boater, rests on a small table beside the rocker.

By 1906, the growing number of cars was making its presence felt. The first fatal car accident in Cuba occurred in that year, according to an article in a July 1998 edition of *Granma*. Remarkably, the president of the Republic, Tomás Estrada Palma, was a passenger in the back seat at the time of the accident. He had lunched at a *finca* outside of Havana and accepted a general's offer of his car and driver to carry him back to town. The driver's name was Luis Marx, and there was speculation that he had been drinking. On the other hand, the pedestrian he struck and killed at the busy Havana intersection of Monte and Angeles Streets, a clerk named Justo Fernández, was said not to have looked both ways before he stepped into the street. Whatever happened, it seems to have affected the president, who shortly thereafter instituted the first requirement for driver's licenses.

The original president of the board of examiners that issued the licenses was Ernesto Carricaburu, who was President Estrada's normal driver, and who was a founder and president of the first Cuban drivers' association. When he left the president's service, he drove for generals and other high-ranking officials. He spent a lifetime in a variety of automobile-based businesses and was one of the earliest believers in the potential of the auto. He was an enthusiastic race car driver, and in 1905, Carricaburu set a world speed record, when he reached fifty-three miles per hour in a Mercedes. In September 1911, he put his name in the record books again, driving the 108 kilometers between Havana and Matanzas in an hour and twelve minutes.

The streets of Havana were passable, as were those of most of the island's cities, if there was not a lot of rain; but in the countryside there were virtually no roads. In 1908, an American journalist from Detroit named Ralph Estep teamed up with the Packard Motor Company to take a car to Cuba. Once there, he and his companions covered 313 miles from Havana to Sancti Spíritus in nine days, three gringos and an interpreter in an open Packard. Estep related that many of the mountain passes were so narrow "we were forced to run with one wheel on a sloping side wall and the other on the crest of the deepest rut."

They nicknamed the car *El Toro* (the Bull), and that was also what Estep titled his thin book about the trip, published the year after by the Packard Company. He and his companions spent a lot of time clearing rocks. "Scorpions under just about every rock," he wrote. Estep and his party covered all kinds of terrain, almost all of it challenging to the Packard. As Estep recalled:

There are more kinds of trail in a half day's journey in Cuba than there is in going from Hell's Gate to the Golden Gate. A comparatively level stretch of red dirt, strewn with boulders, suddenly leaves

*Tomás Estrada Palma (in the back seat, far right), president of Cuba from
1902 to 1906. At the wheel is his chauffeur, Ernesto Carricaburu, who would later
own Havana's first taxi fleet. Note the bicycle–chain drive train visible beneath the car.
(Biblioteca Nacional José Martí, Havana)*

• • •

"Those who arrived, 1912" read the lines written on the photo, evoking an arduous journey over a primitive road system. (Biblioteca Nacional José Martí, Havana)

* * *

off in a tract of grass. . . . In some places there is nothing to follow but a path through high growing sugar cane. In other places, unless the ground is seamed with deep ruts by the continuous travel of heavy ox carts in wet weather, the only thing which signifies a traveled path will be the country stores. Some of these are in board houses. Most of them are merely thatched huts. They all keep a little supply of vile liquors and canned meats. At some of them it is possible to buy oranges and bananas.

By 1913, there were over 4,000 motorized vehicles in Cuba, according to Fernando López Ortiz. A taxi ride between any two places in old Havana cost twenty cents. The European automobiles were still popular, with Mercedes, Lancia, Hupmobile, Fiat, Renault, and Benz all repre-

The ten Fords purchased by Ernesto Carricaburu in 1914 for Havana's first taxi fleet represented the largest number of cars imported into Cuba at the same time up until that date. (Biblioteca Nacional José Martí, Havana)

sented in numbers. However, cars manufactured by North American companies also could be seen on Havana's streets early in the century, including Oldsmobiles, Locomobiles, Overlands, Cadillacs, Dodges, Whites, Chalmerses, Packards, and Chevrolets. Many of the cars were open, and drivers put small mentholated cloths in their ears and noses to protect against the dust and smoke of the city.

It was Ford's Model T that changed the European–North American sales balance and made Detroit's cars the most popular in Cuba. Eventually, nine out of every ten cars sold there were from the States. The first Model T, with its three pedals for two speeds of forward and reverse, was called a "Foot 'n Go" in Cuba, and that contracted to *fotingo*, which is what all Model T's were nicknamed. They had a hand lever for a brake and a manual throttle on the steering post, first appearing on the streets in 1913, selling for a price of $550. The next year, the price went down to about $400. As Ford's assembly line rolled them out, they were easier and easier to sell, until by 1916 a new Model T could be bought for $365 in Cuba.

In 1914, Ernesto Carricaburu bought ten of them to begin Havana's first fleet of taxis. His purchase of ten cars was a hefty boost to the newly named exclusive Ford agency in Cuba, Shumeway & Ross, which belonged to Lawrence Ross, one of the city's premier auto dealers.

At the close of 1916, E. C. Sherman, Ford's foreign manager, wrote to N. A. Hawkins at the company's Dearborn, Michigan, headquarters, praising Ross and his seventeen subagencies. "We now have a good live Ford dealer who maintains a suitable garage for giving proper service to

Locomobiles and Model T's : 33

all Ford owners in every town of importance in Cuba, in fact, we are the only concern who have any kind of a sales organization throughout the entire island. Most of the other automobile manufacturers are only represented in Havana and one or two other towns such as Camagüey and Santiago."

Sherman's report goes on to describe the market Ross served:

Cuba's population is about 2,500,000 of which about 80% are poor negroes and it is estimated that over 50% of the entire population cannot read or write. . . . There are not more than about 2,000 miles of roads in all Cuba on which automobiles can travel all year round. The means of travel throughout the island, except by railroad and possibly in the vicinity of Havana and Santiago, is by mule or horse-back over trails, which are as a rule too narrow even for two-wheeled ox-carts which are extensively seen in all of Cuba, let alone automobiles.

The lack of roads restricts the use of the automobile, except in and around the larger towns. Very little touring is done. Over 80% of the cars we have sold in the entire island are used in the rent service. One or two persons can ride practically any place in Havana in a Ford car for 20 cents. The Fords on the street are kept in splendid condition, which is a very good advertisement for the car.

Sherman informed Hawkins that Ross would contract for 3,382 cars in 1917, and summed up driving conditions: "The streets in Havana are mostly very narrow with barely enough room for two cars to pass one another. . . . There are, of course, a few fairly wide streets including the Malecon and Prado which are the two principal streets in Havana. After five o'clock in the afternoon there is a continual stream of automobiles, mostly Fords, running up and down these two streets as this is the time of day when the people, mostly Cuban women, go automobile riding."

In addition to touring or taxiing, cars were used for sport in those early years. Auto racing was immediately popular in Havana. People began racing cars virtually as soon as they began driving them. The first race was held in July 1903, according to Fernando López Ortiz, organized by garage owner and White driver Honoré Lainé to celebrate the founding of the Havana Automobile Club, whose president, Enrique J. Conill, drove a Mercedes. Five cars participated, each driven by a man accompanied by his wife or sister, including one driven by Herbert Squiers, the first U.S. ambassador following the 1898 War of Independence from Spain, whose wife was in the passenger seat. The winner of the race was Honoré's brother, Dámaso Lainé, driving a French car called a Darracq.

The second race, in 1905, was a grander affair, organized to celebrate the automobile club's new affiliation with the International Association of Automobile Racing, and famous drivers were invited from foreign countries. The race was to San Cristóbal and back. It covered 99.33 miles, and, notwithstanding the international competition, it was won by a Cuban, none other than Ernesto Carricaburu, driving Conill's Mercedes. It was during this race that he set his speed record of fifty-three miles per hour.

In 1907, races were run on a track for the first time in Havana, at La Sierra, a new horseracing track that would also come to host auto racing two or three times a year. In one such race, a popular Cuban driver named Losado was killed, although his assistant, riding shotgun, was thrown free and escaped uninjured, while in another race on the same track a car overturned, killing both driver and assistant.

Racing has traditionally been used as a marketing device by automobile companies to impress their brand names on racing fans. As more and more cars sold, more races were held. Havana became a stop on the international racing circuit. In 1912, cars began running on a racetrack in Havana's Almendares neighborhood. Champion of the track was a man named Rodolfo Lusso who had served as mayor of Remedios at the turn of the century, moved to Havana, and set a new Cuban speed record of 55.4 miles an hour in a Marmon.

Such were Lusso's successes that after he retired he stayed on in Havana, and opened a garage in 1916. "Lusso did not have fewer triumphs as a practical technician," wrote Fernando López Ortiz in *El Automóvil de Cuba*. "Many times, he applied his notable knowledge of mechanics

Since cars have existed, they have, occasionally, killed people. Whether one is racing or simply driving, car accidents can prove fatal. (Biblioteca Nacional José Martí, Havana)

• • •

to winning cars driven by other drivers, but this knowledge also served him when he opened the best garage in Cuba. It was a time when doing general repairs meant dismantling the body, taking apart the whole engine to the last piece. The reconstruction of those European cars did not mean using those pieces, or spare parts, but that Lusso made them in his garage, and it did not matter if they were gears, or pistons and their rings."

In Santiago de Cuba, racing was no less popular. In 1915, the province's department of public works issued a memorandum recommending a minimum of thirty days advance application for permission to hold a race:

> The sporting clubs have the tradition of occasionally celebrating, particularly on patriotic holidays, motorcycle and bicycle races and now automobile races, submitting applications to obtain the corresponding permission. . . . These are always events that are dangerous, and more so when you are dealing with machines like motorcycles or automobiles whose mass and speed are driven by mechanical means, so that the danger is greater than with the force of animals. . . . When a road is used as a racetrack, it is necessary to see that the road is in a convenient place and is in condition to celebrate the races and also to set hours, more time than necessary, so that stress is not put on those personnel whose services are required.

In 1918, *El Automóvil de Cuba* had slick paper and forty-eight pages, with plenty of advertising. Its reporting was almost entirely about national and international auto racing. While Havana and the international circuit dominated the news, the magazine always managed to include racing results from Santiago de Cuba, along with a few notes about the city's auto-related businesses. Their number was growing. In 1914, Ford had sold eight *fotingos* to garage owner Alberto González, who used them to establish Santiago de Cuba's first taxi fleet. In November 1916, a total of 260 cars could be found in Santiago, of which 110 were Fords, according to Ford's foreign department manager, E. C. Sherman. He wrote the Dearborn office that he looked to the coming year with optimism:

Rodolfo Lusso (with a firm grip on the tiller) in a 1901 Oldsmobile, setting out
from Remedios on a trip to Caibarién, just under six miles distant on the coast.
The car was reported to have reached speeds of fourteen miles an hour.
(Biblioteca Nacional José Martí, Havana)

• • •

World champion driver Bob Burman in his Benz racing car during a 1906 tour of Cuba
(Biblioteca Nacional José Martí, Havana)

• • •

"Conditions in Santiago very good as it is quite a tourists town and everybody is making money this year on account of the good sugar crop and the prospect of there being a high price for sugar."

Not long after parading around Santiago in the passenger seat of Frank's Chevrolet, I got a chance to parade around again, this time on foot and in the frenzy of *la conga*. Santiago de Cuba's conga is the forebear of all the "conga lines" of Europeans and North Americans dancing across the floor, hands on the waist of the person in front, a dance that first became popular during the 1920s. Ordered and simple enough for even bad dancers, it is danced at French soirées and London dance parties, or in the way we danced a conga line at a Saturday night party celebrating a friend's bar mitzvah in Nashville, Tennessee, where I learned it as an awkward Jewish teenager. A far cry indeed from the real thing in the streets of Santiago, surrounded by people dancing incredibly rhythmically, thrusting pelvises and hips that seem to be mechanically powered, sweating copiously beneath the glare of a tropical sun. Conga bands are formed by neighborhood and invariably are made up of young Afro-Cubans.

In bygone times, crowds of Afro-Cubans dancing with abandon in the streets was a sight to arouse fear in the lighter-skinned breasts of the well-to-do, and congas were only rarely permitted in public. In a book published in 1934, called *Cuban Popular Music*, Emilio Grenet, a Cuban dance teacher who lived in Paris, wrote about the conga: "Since the advent of the Republic, the conga had an element of political propaganda. . . . The lowest social classes made up these conga lines in which the rhythm was converted into a delirious obsession. Only during election campaigns was it permitted to hold these popular processions in which a gala was made from the crudest and most primitive displays."

My part in the conga begins on a Sunday morning when my friend Richard Neill, who is in Santiago studying music, asks if I would like to go with him to his conga practice. We spend a couple of hours sitting in the diminutive living room of a small cement house with a twenty-year-old musical wonder, Carlos, the director of the conga from the San Agustín neighborhood, whose father was the director before him. They work during the baseball season, coming to every home game at the Guillermón Moncada baseball stadium, keeping the crowd happy, keeping the team animated, rewarding every good play, run scored, strikeout pitched with their lively beats. They also play in the streets during the summer on June 24, the day of Saint John; at various festivals; and during Carnival, held near the end of July. There are three kinds of drums played in most congas and Carlos—Carlitos to his friends—can play them all, as well as the Chinese cornet, an oboelike instrument, which is essential to a conga and looks like a *shenai*, the Tibetan reed instrument. The other instrument in a conga band is bells, and current conga groups all use brake shoes held in one hand and struck with a steel rod in the other to provide a piercing, ringing beat. Carlitos can also play such nonconga instruments as saxophone and piano, and just about anything else that crosses his path. His conga is made up of young men from his marginal neighborhood, and he takes his director's job extremely seriously.

In his tiny living room, he assigns me to play bells and shows me how to heft a rusty, heavy, old brake shoe, which looks like it probably came out of a mid-1950s Chevy, gripping it with my thumb over one edge, balancing it on my left palm and beating rhythm with a short, thin length of steel pipe, to make a ringing, resonant clang. It is a simple enough rhythm that he taps and sings for me a couple of times, but I lose it every few minutes, and each time I do his thirteen-year-old cousin sitting next to me, playing a flawless *batá* drum, is kind enough to lean over as soon as I miss a beat and count it out loud for me, "tee-tee-*pah*-pah-pah," with a slightly dismayed look on his face, as if he can't quite believe even a gringo geezer could have so much trouble with something that comes naturally to anyone in his family old enough to count to ten. Five of us are playing, another half-dozen young guys looking in through the bars of the windows, drawn perhaps by the unusual makeup of the group. My friend Richard is over six feet tall, with a shaved head and the slightly pink skin of the Englishman he is, while I am plainly just too damn old to be here, probably the first fifty-plus *yanqui* Jew ever to play in a conga. Certainly in this one. The sweat pours off us; the little room is an oven, but it's cooking with rhythm. I finally get it and sustain the beat for a while. A delightful sauna of a morning, shirts soaked by the time we leave.

After we finish, Carlitos kindly invites me to play in the conga on the day of Saint John, and, flattered, I accept. The baseball season is just winding up, and with Santiago de Cuba already eliminated from the national playoffs, attention has turned to the summer's busy schedule of congas, beginning with Saint John and continuing with the Festival of the Caribbean at the beginning of July and Carnival at the end. These are days and nights when the band is in the streets, competing with groups from other barrios, and this is the season when they really want to shine. It is one thing to provide a throbbing background beat for a baseball game, another to move people to abandoned dancing in the street. It is the latter that has been the traditional function of the conga, and it is still the one by which a conga band's quality will be judged.

Everyone shows up for this first street event of the season knowing that Carlos considers it to be particularly important. We gather in the early afternoon in a small, shadowy room where everyone is taking *traguitos*, "little swallows," from the bottles making the rounds, taping their fingers, adjusting the reed of the Chinese cornet and trying it with occasional blasts, nervously tapping out waiting rhythms on drum skins, taking more *traguitos*. It is 2:00 on a Saturday afternoon when we finally step out of the practice hall into the furnace heat outside, where it is 95° with a cloudless sky. Most of the foreigners in Santiago de Cuba are sitting in the shade of the terrace at the Hotel Casa Grande on comfortable wicker porch furniture, watching the Parque Céspedes below, and sipping *mojitos*, the delicious iced concoction of rum, soda, and mint for which Cuban bartenders are justly famous, enjoying the breeze generated by the large overhead fans. I, however, am standing under the blazing sun drinking from an unlabelled plastic liter bottle. My companions in the band call it rum, but that is being generous. Whatever the ingredients, which I would just as soon not know, it bites like a mean dog and stings like a fire ant going down, but it seems to help against the heat.

A strong police presence is waiting in the street for things to get under way. The police are in pressed gray uniforms, and their function is to protect the musicians, using their hard rubber batons to keep the spectators and dancers up on the sidewalk. As we pass the bottle around, one of the young *batá* drum players explains to me that congas are dangerous: people take advantage of the crowds and bodies packed together to avenge old grudges, and there are almost always stabbings during the parades. It was worse before the Revolution, when people wore masks at Carnival, says Carlitos's father. Sometimes, even these days, if a person cannot find whomever he wants to stab, he gets carried away and settles for someone else, anyone else—whoever has the bad luck to cross his path at that moment. And the blades are so thin and sharp that sometimes people get stabbed and don't even know it until they fall down on the sidewalk weak from blood loss. I ask for another pull on the anonymous bottle.

We start out under the merciless sun, in the humid glare of early afternoon, and within ten minutes I am drenched, soaked with sweat, inside the rhythm and moving to the music, which is playing right behind my head. There are two sets of musicians, the first team and their substitutes, and we, the substitutes, lead the way down the middle of the street, dancing as we go. Both our line and the musicians behind us are flanked by a moving wall of police who do not let people off the sidewalk. It will not be long before the second string is called on to step up and play—this heat will wear anyone down—but right now the musicians are fresh and wailing. Somewhere in the middle of the three-hour circuit through the streets, Carlitos hands me one of the brake drums and, at least, I do not embarrass either myself or the band.

It is not a pretty sight to watch the police swing their truncheons at the legs of onlookers whose exuberance brings them stepping off the sidewalk and into the street; but when I see a cop lift up a young guy's shirttail and relieve him of a screwdriver sharpened to a wicked point and hidden in the waistband of his pants, my indignation toward them lessens considerably. I have a rush of gratitude for the young, strong musicians at my back. The music is under, over, and around it all, Carlitos playing the Chinese cornet, the two big drums and the smaller *batá* filling the air with beat, the men and women on the sidewalk dancing furiously, the street packed wall to wall, police swatting at people's legs with their hard rubber batons to move them back. As the afternoon wears on, the police grow more relaxed about isolating the band, and soon there are women in our midst. One, who appears to be in her mid-thirties, tall and strong, latches on to my arm and insists that I dance with her. I decline, but she persists. I cannot dance well, and in Cuba, where people dance with breathtaking grace, I do not set foot on the dance floor. My usual plea when Cuban women ask me to dance—and they do, they do—is tapping my chest to indicate a weak heart. This time, that ruse will not serve, since I have been dancing by myself like a fool through the streets for the past two hours. She starts to pinch the roll of fat around my stomach, pinch it hard, saying she's not going to stop until I dance with her. The police move her back to the sidewalk, she is suddenly erased from my field of vision and, once again, I am surrounded by the music, wrapped, enveloped in the rhythm, the smell, the exudation of all our sweating bodies, a sweet, dusty animal smell, accompanied by the huge booming of the big drum, the pounding of the *galleta*, the *campana*'s sharp clanging, the piercing wail of the Chinese cornet. It takes nearly four hours for the line to roll along its circuit of the city.

———

Daily travel across Santiago is a much more mundane experience, fueled by necessity, not ecstasy, but it can sometimes take nearly as long. Every day tides of people move back and forth across the city. Public transportation plays a critical role in many of their lives, and in how well or poorly the city functions as a whole.

Santiago de Cuba inaugurated an electric trolley system, a *tranvía*, on February 8, 1908. The Santiaguero historian Carlos E. Forment has painted the scene, noting that everyone who was anyone in the city turned up that morning, including "a select group of women," all gathered in the garage of the Electric Light and Traction Company of Santiago de Cuba. The company was owned by Cubans, one of whom was Eduardo Chibás, a wealthy Santiaguero with large sugarcane holdings, whose son, also named Eduardo, would grow up to lead an important political party, the Cuban People's Party, or Ortodoxos, and be a primary influence on Fidel Castro's political formation.

The streetcars had been built in Philadelphia by the J. C. Broll Company and shipped to Santiago. The inaugural morning was taken up by speechifying and ceremony, until, Forment reports, the mayor slowly opened the key that allowed the steam to flow from the boilers to the generators. "From this moment, the fluid of civilization flowed out through all the streetcar cables in the city!" he enthused. At 2:00 P.M., the streetcars were opened to the public for a free ride. That afternoon, and the next day, some 38,000 passengers tried out the trolleys. The inaugural festivities ended with a concert by a military band in Céspedes Park and a display of light bulbs forming the Cuban flag on the front of City Hall.

Havana had had horse-drawn streetcars as early as the middle of the 1800s, and the first electric trams were running by 1901. That year they carried some 12.2 million passengers, and by 1910 the *tranvías* transported 45 million passengers a year, according to Berta Alfonso Gallol's *Los Transportes Habaneros*. Unlike Santiago's, however, Havana's trolleys were not locally owned. The company that owned them was in the hands of a group of North American, French, and Canadian investors, led by a former U.S. consul-general in Cuba, Frank Steinhart, who took over the Havana Electric Railway, Light & Power Company from an investment group in Montreal.

"Frank Steinhart, because he was a North American, always got, from each [Cuban] government, the necessary support for the best development of the business," wrote Aurelio Arizala in 1950, in *Verdades vs. Mentiras*, his small history of the bus-owners' cooperative in Havana. The business, Arizala continued,

produced an unending stream of gold fed by trolley revenues, extending even to the modest employees onboard, those mustached conductors and motormen of days gone by, many of whom were able to become happy owners of their own piece of city land.

But, the satisfaction of the Habaneros was not complete, because soon they began to feel the consequences that accompany any monopoly. They suffered the same lack of attention as they do now with telephones and electricity. Big groups of people waited patiently on the corners for a streetcar to pass, in the morning to go to work and in the late afternoon to go home. The number of vehicles was insufficient, and the patience of the Habaneros never had an opportunity to flood over into protest against that powerful company, the very legal name of which, painted on both sides of the vehicles [in English], proclaimed its North American origin and, therefore, the obligation to respect it.

The first buses, shipped down from the States, bore little resemblance to later aerodynamically designed models, wrote Arizala. "However, those [buses] that look like rolling chicken coops to us today, brought transport to distant places, at great cost to and enormous sacrifice by their owners, leaving here a spring, there a wheel, establishing new routes, which the Havana Electric, with great egoism, did not want or intend ever to provide to the Habaneros."

The streetcars have been gone a long time, and the buses that replaced them in both Havana and Santiago in the early 1950s are, themselves, now gone to scrap. Buses, and the fuel it takes to run them, are in short supply. Time after time, in cities and towns, it has been private initiative that relieved some of the pressure on the public transport system. Officials have been reluctant to amplify the system with private enterprise but have had to do so.

As the Special Period was lightening up in 1996, and limited supplies of gasoline began to arrive from here and there, the government decided to try and ease the public transportation problem in Santiago de Cuba by allowing private trucks to carry passengers along selected routes. The trucks for private use (*camiones de uso particular*) take in about 1,000 pesos ($45.00) a day, a city worker told me, adding that his bureaucrat's salary is fourteen pesos a day, or a little more than fifty U.S. cents. The trucks are always manned by two individuals, the driver and *el machacante*, the crusher, the guy at the rear of the truck who waits at the top of the two steps welded on the back bumper and collects the fares from people as they step aboard. He then packs them in and puts a chain across the back when he judges that he cannot squeeze in another soul. He makes 10 percent of the take. "I have a friend who was a sociology professor at the university, and he quit to take a job as a *machacante*," the city employee tells me. "I asked him if he was doing research. 'No,' he said, '*hay que resolver.*'"

The trucks have narrow benches welded onto their beds and a frame mounted over them, which is covered with an awning to shade the fifty or so people who can be crammed aboard, sitting and standing, elbow to elbow, back to back, and front to front. In these situations, one is particularly glad for the notorious Cuban obsession with personal hygiene. Cubans would rather go hungry than smell bad, and many of them had to prove it during the Special Period when they had money only for groceries or soap. Still, being packed into the back of a truck among four dozen other bodies in the heat of a summer day in Santiago de Cuba is not a luxurious way to get from one place to another. The trucks run fixed routes and cost seventy-five centavos (four cents) to ride. It is a private business, and big old Chevy and Ford half- and quarter-ton trucks are the most popular, judging from the numbers at the stop close to the Plaza de Marte where I tend to catch the truck that drops me near the Universidad de Oriente, the university where I often go to use the library. In all likelihood, many of the trucks are surplus from the province's big sugar mills, which are rapidly being closed down. Those mills were serious customers of truck manufacturers in Detroit, and they renovated their truck and tractor fleets regularly, right up to the Revolution. The trucks running Santiago routes have their original bodies, but the only other thing that has not been changed, so the joke goes, is the serial number. The engines and transmissions have all been swapped out for more modern diesel models (Ivecos or Pegasos from Europe, Gaz or Kamaz from the Soviet Union).

EN LOS CENTRALES AZUCAREROS PREFIEREN
CAMIONES FORD
PARA EL TIRO DE CAÑA

TAMBIEN RINDEN MAS
DURANTE EL TIEMPO MUERTO

Por su rendimiento, los camiones Ford son impres-
cindibles en el campo. Su utilidad se extiende a mil
labores de transporte agrícola. Y por su economía
tradicional, tanto en zafra como en tiempo muerto,
siguen produciendo utilidades.

En el tiro de caña, puede Ud. cargar directamente
sobre los camiones Ford, o puede utilizar equipos
de remolque. Como los motores Ford trabajan siempre descansados, se puede aumentar el tonelaje
adicionándole un 3er. eje.

Solicite información de su Concesionario Ford sobre
las distintas aplicaciones de los camiones Ford. Hay
más de 150 modelos, con motores V-8 o de 6 cilindros, hasta 145 H. P. Los camiones Ford son los úni-
cos que tienen motores de 8 cilindros. Hay dos nuevos tipos para trabajos extra - pesados.

SIEMPRE HAY UN CONCESIONARIO FORD CERCA DE USTED

PARA VENTAS, SERVICIO Y FACILIDADES DE PAGO,
VEA HOY MISMO A SU CONCESIONARIO FORD.

There is no truck stop right in front of the university; the nearest is a couple of blocks away, and the first time I travel by *camión particular* the *machacante* squeezes me in near the back, where I keep a weather eye out for the stop. As we roll by the university's front gate, a young guy standing beside me, with a notebook held under his arm, ducks under the *machacante*'s chain and nimbly hops down the two steps at the back of the slowly moving truck to the street. He lands effortlessly, jogging a few paces and striding off. I decide to follow suit, duck under the chain and launch off the bottom step, intending to touch down lightly on the road. But instead of leaning forward so that I hit the ground running, I try to stand still when I come down, and in an eyeblink I am on my fifty-five-year-old back in the middle of the Avenida de las Americas, wondering if anything is broken. Fortunately, there is not another vehicle behind us. I get to my feet with nothing more than a bruised tailbone and scraped elbows, and wave, embarrassed, that I am all right as the astonished faces regarding me from the rear of the truck grow increasingly distant.

Every Cuban city and town has evolved its own response to the chronic nationwide crisis in public transportation. In Santiago de Cuba they use the trucks; in Baracoa, at the eastern tip of the island, they mount a two-seat platform on the back of bicycles; and in Banes, they also use bikes, but with one seat behind. In Cienfuegos, the public transport of choice is an eight-seat *carretona*, a horse-drawn wagon with a cloth roof and a bench on either side that holds four passengers, which costs a peso to ride. Stories abound of engineers and academics who have given up their jobs and turned to cutting grass to sell to the *carretona* drivers. *Hay que resolver.* A good horse in Cienfuegos will sell for 3,500 pesos, the price of a Lada in good condition.

In Havana, there have been numerous attempts to deal with the ever-present public transportation crisis. One of the most infamous and most effective is the *camello*, first used in 1995. *Camellos* are long trailers with some seats and windows and lots of standing room, each of which can hold 300 passengers. The trailers dip in the middle, creating a pair of camel humps at either end, hence the name. They are hauled behind a big truck tractor, and passage on one costs ten centavos, less than a penny. *Camellos* are slow, hot, and packed, but a lot of standing people can be squeezed onto them. A more unpleasant way to go from one place to another is difficult to imagine. Habaneros joke that every *camello* has a staff of four: a driver, a conductor, a *jamonero* (the ham-man, who constantly is putting his hands on the female hams around him), and a pickpocket. Wallets aboard *camellos* are easy pickings for the light-fingered and fleet. Another joke says that a *camello* is like an X-rated movie: filled with obscene language and a high content of sex and violence.

Most recently in Havana, it has been old Detroit-built passenger cars serving as *ruteros* that have filled the role of escape valve for an overburdened transport system. The old gringo cars serve as the trucks do in Santiago de Cuba and follow the same system, running fixed routes. It is scandalously expensive to take a *rutero*—they charge ten pesos (almost half a dollar) per passenger, while a person pays only forty centavos, not even five cents, to ride a bus in Havana, when one finally appears to be ridden. Those ten pesos are a significant part of monthly income for most Habaneros, but if it means not having to wait for a bus, or worse yet a *camello*, many people are willing to pay the price if they can.

The law regarding whether a *rutero* is allowed to carry a foreigner is a little unclear. It actually seems only to require that the fare be paid in pesos, not dollars, but many drivers interpret it to mean that only Cubans can use these taxis. Foreigners are subject to being refused passage. At any rate, anyone who looks remotely Cuban, knows enough Spanish to name a destination, and has ten pesos will be allowed to ride in a *rutero*. And what a ride. For me, ten pesos is a cheap way to get from old Havana to Vedado and enjoy a ride in some car that I never anticipated riding in again for the rest of my life: a 1953 Dodge, four of us crammed in the back seat and two in front with the driver; or a 1954

Ford station wagon with two back seats, the extra welded into the carryall space, and rear windows that slide back and forth instead of rolling up and down.

The cars have all been modified, many drastically, but they have not lost their souls. Most still have their big steering wheels and their gear shifts on the post, sticking out at a right angle to the steering column. The drivers prefer not to use first gear. After slowing down for a light or a stop sign, if they have any forward motion left at all, they go directly to second gear, arm pushing the gear shift out and up by the steering wheel. To ride in a car where the driver is making that motion is another thing I had not expected to do again. A small fan is most likely mounted on the dashboard in front of the driver, powered by a plug to the cigarette lighter, and music is provided by a cassette player installed in the glove box. The *ruteros* gather in front of El Capitolio to wait until they fill up with enough passengers to make the trip worthwhile, each with a shill who stands there calling out its route, the names of destinations sung out constantly into the air all day—*Vientitrés* or *Linea* or *Playa*—and when each is filled to capacity, off it goes on its route, leaving behind those still filling. The waiting beasts of burden sink ever lower on their springs and shock absorbers and patched tires as each new passenger piles in, but still they keep starting, keep running, keep ferrying Cubans—*compañeros* and *compañeras*—from one place to another.

chapter two

TUDORES & FORDORES

Havana's Vedado has to be one of the world's most amazing urban neighborhoods. Built during the last part of the nineteenth century and the first part of the twentieth, to the west of the central city's narrow streets, it occupies a huge expanse of land that for centuries had been reserved as a woodland, a vast area that was forbidden to be cut. Even before the war with Spain in the 1890s, it was being bought up by Havana's upper class and cleared to serve as a residential neighborhood, a wealthy suburb. It was upscale Havana in a big way, eventually spreading over hundreds of square blocks, reproducing with eerie similarity the astonishing early 1900s art deco marvels of Miami Beach, large homes built in a profusion of forms curving around open space, in a variety of elegant styles, many with broad porches and rooms with eighteen-foot ceilings. Like the cars from Detroit that are parked along the curb outside many of these residences, the houses once provided a high level of comfort for the well-to-do and privileged, but in 2002 they belong to the Cuban people. Now, they have been subdivided, of course, and the subdivisions subdivided, so there is at least a scrap of living space for everyone. A walk along Vedado's sidewalks is always visually rewarding, people living their lives against this elegant tropical backdrop. There are numerous parks with benches beneath spreading *flamboyán* (royal poinciana) trees, with their flaming blossoms, where a pedestrian can sit and rest, watch the old cars roll by and check out the laundry strung across the balconies of some extraordinary houses, of which there seems to be no end.

It is a great pleasure to sit on a bench, in a Vedado park, along the wide, shaded avenue called Paseo for instance, when the kids get out of class in the afternoon. They flood through the park like schools of darting fish, perch on the benches like flocks of talking birds before heading home. All dressed alike in their pressed Pioneer uniforms, red until seventh grade, then beige through high school. Pants or skirt, always with a white shirt and red or beige kerchief around their necks, they sit on the benches clutching their notebooks and chatter like schoolkids anywhere in the world about tests and grades, teachers and haircuts, and who is doing what with or to whom. Not a single working child is in sight, not one little girl selling Chiclets with snot dried around her nostrils or eyes crusty or shorts raggedy or undershirt torn; not a single boy importuning you to let him shine your shoes, small fingernails bitten to the quick, grimy with shoe polish, lips dry and cracked, an open sore on his leg, unable to read or write his own name, already accepting that the life of school is going to be denied to him, that he will be forever at the mercy of those born to better fortune. It cleaves the heart with sorrow to see how children live in the streets of many Latin American countries—Colombia, Nicaragua, Guatemala, Honduras, El Salvador, Haiti, the Dominican Republic, Mexico—children working or hanging around, unlettered and unskilled, abandoned to their narrow fates. There are over 17 million kids between the ages of five and fifteen who have to work in Latin America to help keep themselves and their families alive, according to figures collected by the International Labour Organization. They do not live in Cuba.

It was while the original clearing and construction in Vedado was taking place, according to a 1948 article by Guillermo de Zendegui in *Bohemia*, that one of Cuba's most distinctive transport words was coined: *guagua*. It is the word Cubans use for bus, and it is pronounced just the way English speakers convey the sound of a baby crying: wah-wah. While the land was being cleared for Vedado, the workers walked out every day from central Havana where they lived, a mile or two distant. After months, they threatened a work stoppage if they did not get a ride to work and back. The chief engineer, who had come to Havana from Peru

The first guagua to run between the market towns of San Antonio de los Baños and Guïra de Melena, southwest of Havana. The photograph is from 1907, according to El Automóvil de Cuba, *which also reports that the guagua had two horizontal cylinders under the chassis with a belt drive. (Biblioteca Nacional José Martí, Havana)*

· · ·

OPPOSITE

An upper-class Havana family and their 1940 Packard parked beneath the porte cochere of their Vedado home. (Biblioteca Nacional José Martí, Havana) to oversee the work, ordered that they be transported for free. In his hometown of Lima, kids were called *guaguas* and were allowed to ride free on public transport. He told the developers: "From now on, you must provide a ride to the workers in plan *guagua*." For free, like the kids in Lima. After that, wrote de Zendegui, public transport was called a *guagua*, even when it was not free.

By the end of the nineteenth century, horse-drawn streetcars—the first *guaguas*—were carrying the public out as far as Vedado before coming back to Havana. After the 1898 war, it took Cuba the better part of a decade to begin to recover. A great deal of the country had been devastated by the war with Spain. The country was being ruled by the authoritative hand of the occupying U.S. military, which would stay until 1905. In 1901, the Platt Amendment was accepted by a weakened Cuba. The amendment guaranteed that the United States could defend its interests in Cuba in the manner it saw fit—forever. The large U.S. presence was highly disagreeable to many Cubans, but it meant development of Vedado would continue at war's end. Many North Americans bought and built there, when even rich Cubans were too busy trying to recover a peacetime routine to think about investing in land or building new houses.

"Americans have bought much ground and are building many beautiful houses, houses of much better quality and more graceful architecture than is to be found in the average Cuban dwelling," wrote the U.S. ambassador and early automotive enthusiast, Herbert Squiers, in a 1906 letter to John Hay, as quoted in Louis A. Pérez Jr.'s *On Becoming Cuban: Identity, Nationality and Culture*. The neighborhood was populated by Americans and well-to-do, nonblack Cubans.

It was not until after the First World War, however, that construction in Vedado took off on a grand scale. By then, Cuba had turned entirely away from Europe and was sharing in the prosperity of the United States in its postwar, Roaring Twenties economy. Nowhere more so than in Vedado, and cars were an integral part of the picture. Not only did the neighborhood's residents have the disposable income necessary to purchase a car, a motor vehicle was of prime utility to them when they wanted to go to and come back from central Havana or out to a ranch in the country.

The growing consumer potential in Vedado was appreciated by more than just house builders and car dealers. The neighborhood not only contained a remarkable stock of residential housing, but also became a center of commerce, drawing people from all over the city. Gradually its main streets filled with consulates and elegant hotels, nightclubs and casinos, stores selling the newest and most modern domestic appliances from the States. So many new car dealerships and car-related businesses opened in one area of Vedado that the neighborhood was eventually nicknamed Detroit.

The heart of commercial Vedado was, and is, the five-block-long stretch of Twenty-third Street called La Rampa. At the top is the Coppelia ice cream park at Twenty-third and L, kitty-corner from the Havana Libre Hotel, originally built as the Havana Hilton. From here, La Rampa descends toward the sea. Either end of La Rampa has been prime car-watching territory since before the First World War. The intersection by the Coppelia is one of the busiest in Havana, with a steady stream of traffic. At the other end of La Rampa, Twenty-third runs into the Malecón by the sea. The Malecón is the broad, seaside avenue that traces Havana's perimeter along the curving seafront from one end to the other. It is bordered on one side by some of the city's finest colonial architecture and on the other by a seawall nearly five miles long, built by the gringos and finished in 1901, just in time for that first-ever procession of cars along the Malecón, convoked by *El Fígaro* magazine. It is still one of the world's great city drives, and a seat on top of the seawall along any stretch of the Malecón still provides, as it has since that first parade of cars in 1901, one of the better automotive observation points in the length and breadth of the Americas.

Along these genteel streets, the postwar residents of Vedado drove their cars, many taking pleasure in being seen in the most elegant of vehicles. An increasing number of families moving to Vedado were prosperous, nonblack Cubans, and, like their North American neighbors, they bought cars. By the 1920s, the country had recovered from the dev-

A crowd turned out along the eastern end of the Malecón for the arrival of the Spanish warship Almirante Cervera *(Biblioteca Nacional José Martí, Havana)*

• • •

astation left at the turn of the century by thirty years of fighting for independence. Business was good, and money proved a common denominator for the neighborhood's residents.

The daughters of Vedado's well-to-do Cubans grew up in a languid country club atmosphere, which nonetheless offered fertile ground for the women's suffragist movement from the North. Many of these young Cuban ladies had spent some of their formative years going to school in the States, and they knew that the notion of female inequality was being challenged there on many fronts. Many of them also learned to drive while living up North, and when they returned to Cuba they continued to drive, giving them a degree of independence unknown to their mothers.

"I think the woman who drives an auto has made a step forward in this century, given that in these times it's really necessary to know how to drive," Tina Sarrá, a young Habanera who drove a Bugatti convertible, told Simonne Ramet in an April 1930 interview published in the *A.C.C.*, the monthly magazine of the Automobile Club of Cuba, distributed without charge to club members between 1925 and 1960. "At the same time," she continued, "it's the most agreeable of sports. I think this sport has an influence that's partly moral and partly physical . . . moral because it is a means to add to a woman's independence, and it creates certain responsibilities that were completely unknown before."

The automobile was a shining adornment of the life of a young debutante from Vedado. What that life consisted of is hinted at in another one of Simonne Ramet's monthly interviews with women who drove, this one from August 1930. Ramet writes in her introduction, "In Vedado, here in Vedado, which is the birthplace of nearly all the young beauties who compose today's finest social nucleus, is where Carmita Andreu lives. Her home, like all those in the neighborhood, is surrounded with gardens, and as a compliment and primary necessity, today there is a garage with more cars than will fit inside."

Ramet opened the interview by thanking the interviewee for her time and making a little joke about how difficult it had been for Carmita to spare a moment. The young woman from Vedado answered, "It's not my fault, believe me; during these days swimming in the sea, a little laziness due to the heat, and the telephone always ringing have been the reasons you couldn't come to see me." Then she told Ramet that knowing how to drive had become a part of Vedado life. "Before, the piano, singing, foreign languages, and other details of social life were enough, but today it's also necessary to drive a car and if things keep going as they are, soon we'll have to fly."

The truth is, neither driver's licenses, nor voting rights, nor pilot's licenses, nor any of the other signs of equality acquired by Cuban women over the years seem to have made much of a dent in the island's machismo. It is still common for Cuban men to abuse their wives physically, and many of the women accept it as their lot. Male infidelity is the norm. The Revolution has put women into the workplace, but it has not relieved them of any of their domestic duties. Most men still expect their mates to have the kids in order, the clothes washed, and supper on the table after working an eight-hour day and waiting two hours for the crowded bus home.

The first driver's license issued to a woman in Havana did not go to one of Vedado's blue-blooded youths, but to a woman of ill repute, María Calvo y Nodarse, who ran a brothel and was infamous as La Macorina. A well-known song, a *danzón* of the time, was called, "Put Your Hand on Me Here, Macorina" (*Ponme La Mano Aquí, Macorina*). To obtain a license in those days, applicants had to pass a driving test, as well as provide a fingerprint and a photo. La Macorina's license is dated 1917, and the headshot shows a determined, attractive young woman with a ghost of a smile on her face.

She may have received the first driver's license issued to a woman, but La Macorina was not the first Cuban woman to drive, according to Eduardo Mesejo Maestre, director of Havana's Museo del Automóvil. "Women always accompanied men when they drove, and I suspect some of them must have tried driving for themselves. La Macorina was a whore, pure and simple, and everyone in Cuba knew her for her work as a high-class prostitute. Not everyone could pay her prices, and, since she charged a lot, she could buy herself a new car. The thing is, some journalists of our day got hold of the fact that La Macorina drove and decided she had to be the first woman to do so in Cuba and published it, even though it was incorrect."

The museum's collection holds thirty cars from before 1940 and some notable later models, including two that belonged to revolutionary heroes, Che Guevara and Camilo Cienfuegos. The oldest car in the collection is a sixteen-cylinder 1905 Cadillac that originally belonged to

*As time passed, the sight of animal-powered delivery transport grew rarer,
as commercial deliveries were increasingly made in motorized vehicles. This mule driver
seems to be looking back to see if a trolley is coming along the tracks.
(Biblioteca Nacional José Martí, Havana)*

• • •

the pharmacist Ernesto Sarrá. About 30,000 people a year pay a dollar
apiece to walk through the shadowy two-room shed that houses the cars
and which used to hold a ship repair business. Mesejo, whose own car is
the 1953 Dodge in which his father taught him to drive, is a handsome
man, with a square jaw and brown hair brushed back, but he has a certain introverted, weary air from years of protecting the cars, of waiting

for them to be recognized as the national treasures he believes they are. Resources are perpetually scarce.

"There are anecdotes that La Macorina had problems with the police after she got her license because she didn't drive very well," Mesejo told me. "It's possible someone did her a favor in exchange for something sexual, in evaluating her driving and giving her a license. Under the first traffic regulations, a driver's license could even be denied if the applicant was judged to be of immoral character. In order to give a well-known prostitute a driver's license, something of the sort had to occur. In those days, these sorts of things happened."

In 1917, according to Fernando López Ortiz's history, there were 4,426 privately owned motorized vehicles in Cuba, and another 5,000 or so publicly owned. Sales grew. More and more middle-class Habaneros and Santiagueros considered buying a car. By 1919, car finance companies like the Cuban Credit Automobile Company were making cars more accessible. That year, *El Automóvil de Cuba* pronounced the island the number one automotive market in Latin America. In population Cuba was the ninth largest country in Latin America but, per capita, the largest automobile market. With over $10 million in sales between 1916 and 1919, Cubans were buying more cars than people in Argentina, Brazil, or Mexico.

Between July 1921 and June 1922, 5,117 cars were imported into Cuba, of which 4,722 were American, according to a British government report cited in Pérez's *On Becoming Cuban*. A serious market existed where none had before. It was not just in Vedado that cars were selling well. The streets of the older parts of the capital, built for horse traffic, were packed with the relentlessly noisy, smoky, dusty, internal-combustion machines. Automobile travel had ceased to be the province of the rich. By the early 1920s, a Ford runabout, a standard *fotingo*, cost only about $300, and Ford offered a liberal credit plan to anyone with a steady job.

Automobiles were useful for getting around town, and fun to drive. Their utility was limited, however, by the condition of the roads, particularly those connecting cities and towns. Even urban streets left much to be desired. The first paved street through Havana was not completed until 1921. "Our Havana, a popular city, rich, happy, sunny and smiling, is very lovely. . . . How are the streets? Undriveable. There is not a single decent pavement. Places like Central Park and that of Martí, the streets of Obispo, Bolivar, Galino, San Rafael are a shameful collection of horrible potholes," editorialized the *Heraldo del Chauffeur* in May 1924. The *Heraldo* was a small, left-wingish newsprint magazine published monthly for "professional drivers in the tourist industry," which began publishing in 1921 and disappeared during the Second World War.

The following year, things had not improved. "Drivers guide their cars through the hundred thousand potholes of Havana," complained the *Heraldo* in March 1925. "The individuals who have to use a car for their occupations know what it is to drive in Havana. The humble, plebeian, democratic fotingo falls into potholes, bounces into them, sinks into their depths, occasionally to founder."

As bad as Havana's streets may have been, roads through the countryside were worse. The first dirt street was laid down in Cuba in 1517. The first five kilometers of dirt road were not built until 1796. By 1898, before a single car was in the country, there were 2,562 kilometers of roads. They were basically for agriculture and were built to accommodate ox carts. If people wanted to travel from Havana to another part of the island, they bought sea passage. After the First World War, as cars began to appear around the country, it was clear that improvements had to be undertaken. Construction of new roads was done with asphalt on a bed of concrete, designed to support automotive traffic. As early as 1919, the government of Mario G. Menocal had approved the Central Highway Law, pledging $12 million to construct a highway across the country, following the route of what was formerly known as the Royal Road, which was used for carriage travel. By the mid-1920s, however, nothing had been done, despite repeated pledges by officials at the Ministry of Public Works that something would be. It was still an adventure to cross the country. Fernando López Ortiz wrote on the editorial page of *El Automóvil de Cuba* in October 1952: "We still remember those times in the early 1920s when a trip by automobile from Havana to Oriente

Cubans closely followed racing, both cross-country and on urban tracks. Antonio Jané was a favorite among race fans. He won, among others, an important race in Havana in 1925 sponsored by the newspaper La Noche. *He worked in a garage that repaired Dodges and De Sotos and always raced a Dodge. (Biblioteca Nacional José Martí, Havana)*

or vice versa was an epic of many days going cross-country, a trip that merited the honor of a big article on the first page of the newspapers. It was a brave feat by valiant explorers."

In 1925, a record speed was established in driving the 856 kilometers between Santiago de Cuba and Havana in just over nine days. Five drivers, all members of the driver's guild of Santiago, did it in a car belonging to one of them, referred to only as *La Estrella* (The Star) in an account of the trip reported in the March 1925 issue of the *Heraldo del Chauffeur*. The *Heraldo* called the drivers "heroes." They left Santiago on February 14, 1925, under a torrential rain. "The trip was extremely difficult," the article said. "Various times they had to use a pick and shovel, and if they had brought oars, they could have used those too when they crossed rivers with the car nearly afloat, almost carried away by the current. Eight times it was stuck in the mud."

The record did not last long. A year later, a quartet of drivers set out from Banes, a small city in northeastern Holguín Province, to break the speed record. The men, each of whom was a professional driver, left

Banes on March 29 and made it to Havana, about 750 kilometers of driving, in sixty-nine hours and ten minutes, less than three days. They drove a Ford, a *fotingo* with its three pedals on the floor, in rotating shifts. One of the four, Santiago Zalvídar, told *Bohemia* years later that the roads were so uncertain he occasionally steered by the stars, feeling like a ship at sea.

In addition to a lack of passable highways, the countryside was marked by a general lawlessness. Ángel Quintana Bermúdez, who wrote the piece for *Bohemia*, went back to the newspapers of the days in March 1926 when the four were driving and did an inventory of headlines. In Camagüey alone, while the four made their journey, there had been newspaper reports of armed robbings, shootings, kidnappings, lynchings, a panther escaping from a circus, a train coming under rifle fire, and a government agent shot dead. To drive across Cuba in those years was a feat that excited the public's imagination.

───────────────

Cars have long been a feature of popular culture in Cuba. Many of the paintings and prints for sale in Havana's tourist markets feature the same iconic automotive themes: a 1958 Oldsmobile parked outside the bar/ restaurant El Bodeguito or a 1954 Cadillac Fleetwood placed beside the bar La Floridita (both famous with tourists as Hemingway hangouts), for example, or a 1956 Chevrolet Bel Air parked outside the Cathedral. The general idea is a Detroit dream model parked next to a Havana landmark. In Santiago de Cuba, representations of old cars made out of discarded tin *Tu Cola* cans sell well to tourists. At a more artistic level than the tourist traffic, cars often figure in contemporary Cuban painting. In Santiago de Cuba's Galería Oriente, one of the city's best exhibition spaces, old cars often turn up on the canvases of local artists like a painter I'll call Pablo. He is thirty-one but does not look it, with a young boyish face, brown hair, and brown eyes. His oils are characterized by bold, broad strokes—reds, blues, and whites—evoking postindustrial settings. Detroit's chargers regularly play a supporting role in his work. An entire car is never seen, but figures may be lounging against the finned rear fender of a Plymouth Belvedere or leaning against the wide chrome grille of a 1957 Chevrolet.

Pablo, unmarried, shares a house with his mother and younger brother. Well-read and intelligent, he speaks about his work as part of an intellectual process. He explains to me why he often includes gringo cars in his paintings: "I began with a statement by Leo Castelli about a piece of Robert Rauschenberg's—that gas pumps would be appreciated as art as much as the columns of the Parthenon in a thousand years. I believe the rhythm of contemporary life is so speeded up that it's already true. The American cars have graceful lines with a greater richness of form, more than the architectural aesthetic of the 1950s in the United States. The cars do a better job of translating this aesthetic in Cuba.

"In Havana, there's an unfortunate tendency to use the cars as an empty icon, without meaning. In the tourist market you see the same paintings over and over of old cars on Havana streets. In my work, I always avoid showing the whole car. I prefer that it's not the central object in the painting; I want to use it as a means of communicating something else."

He tells me about a mechanic he visited once with a friend. He does not remember the mechanic's name but recalls how the man had impressed him with his knowledge of cars and his approach to his work. It was like meeting another artist, in Pablo's description. He suggests that it would be worth my while to meet the man for a car conversation. A few days later, good as his word, he appears at the house where I am staying, and off we go to look for the mechanic, although Pablo is not sure he can find the man's house or, if he manages to locate the address, whether there will be anyone home. It is a long walk to the right neighborhood, but he has nothing better to do and is kind enough to do it with me.

It is a good hour's walk across Santiago on a burning afternoon to a neighborhood of mostly small cement houses. Even Pablo—half my age and twice my speed—is sweating and has slowed down by the time we close in on the right street. He rambles a bit, circles, backtracks, changes direction, and suddenly we are there. It is not Santiago's poorest neighborhood by any means, but one with a certain edge. Pablo introduces me to a mechanic I'll call José Rivera, thirty-seven, dark-skinned, balding, a fringe of black hair curled tightly around his head, with a bristly black mustache and lively, interested eyes, who seems perfectly glad and unsurprised to see us, inviting us into his house. His companion, a large blond woman, serves us coffee and beams at the mechanic. José offers to show me his own car. "I've got my Buick parked outside. It's a fine car. The engine is not made from aluminum or plastic. Four people couldn't lift that engine out."

It is a 1956 Buick Century with a 1958 engine and a 1952 carburetor, modified with parts from a Mercedes-Benz to reduce the flow of gasoline—a specialty of José Rivera's in GM cars. His gas tank is a five-liter plastic jug, holding a little more than a gallon, tucked down between the front of the radiator and the back of the grille with a plastic tube leading to the carburetor. "I can go sixty kilometers (thirty-six miles) on that jug," he tells me, "and come back with some left in it. And that's packing people in on Saturday or Sunday and driving to French Beach. Sometimes, coming back, I'll even open the trunk and put a couple of people in there, everyone drinking rum. We have a good time; the police aren't usually out on that stretch of road, and the car runs fine."

Buicks are his absolute favorites, then come the 1950s' Cadillacs, and then anything else built in the United States or Europe. His mechanic's skills are genetic, he insists. "My grandfather had a Buick, he was a driver, a chauffeur, and my father was a mechanic and ever since I was small I watched my father and started doing a little here, a little there. To be a real mechanic, a good mechanic, you have to be born with it and I was. They come to me with cars from as far away as Pinar del Río, more than a thousand kilometers to the west. There are people who know my work all over Cuba, and if they can wait to have something done to their cars until they're in Santiago, they wait."

Subsequently, I met three people in Santiago who took particularly good care of their Detroit-built cars, none of whom knew the others. Each of them used José as their mechanic. "These aren't things you learn how to do from a manual or a book, but by spending a lifetime of work on them," he says, as he shows me his small collection of repair manuals, including one for a 1926 Ford, all of which he keeps tucked away proudly in one of his few drawers.

Business is steady; cars are always arriving that need to be repaired. José works on them in the street in front of his little house. Not that he likes working in the street, but at the moment he cannot afford anything better. Parts, too, are a constant problem. "Anytime I hear that someone's had an accident or a car has stopped running, I go to try and buy parts. Buicks are my specialty and my favorites. I particularly like the way they're built, the drive shaft, the ease of access to the distributor—unlike Cadillacs—but I can work on any American car.

"All of these are original Buick parts," he says, as we contemplate the engine under his car's hood, "although they didn't all come from the same Buick or even the same year's models."

The engine is clean, cherry red, and without a drop of oil on it. "Of course there's no oil on it," he rears back from under the hood when I mention it, eyes flashing. "What kind of mechanic would I be if the car was losing oil?

"This is a strong car. Look, I hit a truck in this car last year and all it did was dent my front fender here," he gestures at some Bond-o work above the left headlight, "but the truck got pushed all the way across the intersection and had some serious damage."

A few days later, I walk over the hill to José's house on a scorching hot morning. The door is open, and he is lying just inside it, stretched out on the cool cement floor, asleep. Cubans regularly stretch out for naps on the floor: it is the coolest place to lie and just right for a brief rest. Even the Argentine, Che Guevara, got used to stretching out on the floor of his Havana office in the Ministry of Industry, according to Jon Lee Anderson's biography, *Che Guevara: A Revolutionary Life*. I do not wake José up, instead walking back to my rented room, where I stretch out myself for a good long rest, on the bed beneath the fan. The heat of the day in Santiago de Cuba is sometimes best borne in a rocking chair, making a little breeze moving back and forth, or fully horizontal.

I go around to see José another morning, and he has the Buick up on some short jacks and thick pieces of wood out next to the sidewalk. He is lying under it on ragged pieces of cardboard, his thirteen-year-old stepson, Jesús, under there with him. I do not ask the boy why he is not in school, even though it is a school day. A brutal sun beats down, so I take off my shirt and scrunch in under there, too. José is replacing the clutch plate with one from a Ford of the same year. The middle post may have to be ground down, he says, but there is someone in the neighborhood who has a grinder and will do it cheaply if need be; he is not sure if it will be necessary—first he has to pull the transmission, a slow process. At least he has a socket wrench, I see once I have squirmed under the car.

He stops his work regularly for a little pull on a labelless pint bottle of clear, homemade rum that looks fairly lethal. The stepson handles the bottle gingerly when José asks him to pass it, and this reminds me of my first taste of moonshine, experienced at about the boy's age, thanks to some older guys for whom I felt blind admiration. As soon as I swallowed it, I vomited it back up, into my hand and onto my sleeve, much to their amusement. "You've got to drink some in this heat," José says, offering me the bottle. I decline, pleading the early hour.

While working steadily with the socket wrench, he explains how he is saving money, trying to get 5,000 pesos ($227) together so he can buy a little parcel of land nearby that someone he knows wants to sell. Then he could put up some posts and a tin roof, and work in the shade. *¡Qué bien sería!*—how good that would be! He is saving, but it is a lot of money in a country where lots of people don't make more than 250 pesos, $12.00, a month. Maybe by next year, he says, if the same cancer doesn't get him that got his father, eleven years ago when the old man was just fifty-nine. "He was diagnosed with prostate cancer and was dead in forty-five days."

Once the transmission is out, lying in the street next to the car with the cover off exposing the gears, I can see it is flawlessly clean. It is the original, he tells me proudly. "I should have everything back in by the end of the week," he says. I offer to pay for some gas if he will take me along on a weekend test run out to French Beach.

Taking away the concrete molds from kilometer 27 of the Central Highway on May 7, 1927 (Biblioteca Nacional José Martí, Havana)

· · ·

The virtually roadless wilderness that was rural Cuba outside of its cities was tamed and opened up by highways under the administration of Gerardo Machado, elected in 1924 as the fifth president of the young Cuban Republic. Until then, streets and roads petered out not far past the city limits. From early on in the Machado administration, a lot of attention was paid to connecting the entire country by a network of roads. Machado took office in the midst of a booming sugar-based economy and for the first couple of years of his administration was generally viewed as an honest, pro-Cuban leader; but he became increasingly ruthless and corrupt as time passed. He appointed Carlos Miguel

Céspedes, a lawyer, as his minister of public works. By the time Céspedes left office in 1933, a highway, called the Carretera Central, or Central Highway, stretched across 672 miles of the island, from Pinar del Río, west of Havana, to Guantánamo, east of Santiago de Cuba.

"In the four years of President Machado's government, it was our desire to bring to reality the execution of this plan, using intensive methods," wrote Céspedes, in the February 1930 issue of the *A.C.C.* "We wanted to do and do quickly what could not be done, or it wasn't known how to do in twenty-five years of the Republic . . . and we have done it with a speed equivalent to the construction of a kilometer per day."

Machado was forced to resign in 1933, accused with good reason of everything from corruption to murdering members of the opposition over the course of his nine years in office. Céspedes's political life did not burn out with Machado's, however, and following his boss's departure in August 1933, he served as interim president of Cuba. Machado left a certain legacy, much of it engineered by Céspedes, including the construction of El Capitolio in the center of Havana, which was completed in 1930, and the 1,119 kilometers of Central Highway. The completion of the highway, at a cost of some 110 million pesos, much of it borrowed from New York's Chase National Bank, coincided with the shock wave of the Great Depression reaching Cuba, but after 1934, when the economy began to recover, the highway provided a tremendous stimulus for growth.

An ever-increasing reliance on automobile transport was growing among almost all sectors of government. For conducting citywide or provincewide business, a car was indispensable. Public service often came with a car. A car often came with public service. Typical are the minutes of a March 1930 meeting of the Santiago de Cuba Provincial Council at which councillors voted unanimously to authorize the expenditure of 6,000 pesos on a new car for the provincial governor. The appropriation specified that the money would be spent on a seven-passenger Packard Sedan Model 6-40 with the D'Luxe equipment package. Included in the package were two grooved mud flaps, two extra tires with two extra inner tubes, lights mounted on the bumpers, two drawers for extra parts, upholstery of Spanish leather, and a trunk lined with leather, which would hold three suitcases. The Provincial Council approved the purchase and further stipulated the sale at public auction of the governor's old car, originally purchased in 1926 and described, four years later, as being in an "unusable state."

In 1931, two years after Wall Street crashed, Cuba had 22,695 registered cars, according to the U.S. Department of Commerce. This placed it sixth in all of Central and South America, behind Argentina (345,000 cars), Brazil (165,200), Mexico (72,000), Chile (42,547), and Uruguay (42,300). In 1929, a record 6,013 cars were imported, according to *El Automóvil de Cuba*, but by 1931 the number dropped to only 824.

Things got worse. In 1932, when just 595 cars and 385 trucks were imported, Fernando López Ortiz opined in the pages of his magazine that the end of the Cuban automobile economy might be approaching. The numbers bottomed out in 1934, and by 1935 business was picking up again. The registration of privately owned cars in Cuba more than doubled between 1933 and 1938, according to figures from Cuba's National Registry. Ford's *tudores* and *fordores*, as two-door and four-door models were called in Cuba, were selling briskly in cities and towns across the island. The prevailing optimism about the Cuban car market was summed up in a December 1936 interview in *El Automóvil de Cuba* with Higinio Carsi, manager of the Ford dealership, Auto Universal de Cuba, in Havana.

"What worker or employee can't afford a Ford?" he asked. "The new car sales on the installment plan, and the service that Ford agents provide the cars' owners, do not call for any additional expense. On the contrary, people can save money on daily transport and live better."

When the Depression let up, the Central Highway was in place, unifying the country as never before, opening it up for trade and commerce. Even as early as December 1932, an ad was running daily in the Santiago newspaper *Diario de Cuba*, showing a long, gleaming Packard touring car, with a banner reading, THE CHEAPEST TRIP TO HAVANA. The ad beneath read:

You must measure the cost of a trip by its security, by the irritations you avoid and by the secondary expenses you save by arriving sooner. Time also is money.

Traveling without risks at a moderate speed but without unforeseen or unnecessary stops, our cars arrive in Havana at a reasonable time without having to be overnight on the road. For your own safety, observe the condition of the tires and of the vehicle before making such a trip. Departure at 5:50 A.M. One way, $11.70.

———————

In 2003, there are two different bus lines running along the Central Highway between Havana and Santiago de Cuba, and they are both owned by the state. The Astro buses sell tickets in pesos to Cubans for the equivalent of a few dollars. The buses are old, problematic, and frequently hours late. Vía Azul buses run much closer to schedule, charge $50.00 in greenbacks, and take fifteen hours to make the trip. Since passengers have paid in dollars, Vía Azul apparently feels obligated to provide them with as much air-conditioning as possible—the journey is invariably passed in polar temperatures—which cannot be lowered or shut down. The seats are not particularly comfortable either.

After seventy years, the Carretera Central, like many of the vehicles that use it, is somewhat the worse for wear, but otherwise not a lot different from how it was when those sleek, long black Packard touring cars plied it, not so different from the way it was the day it opened. It is still almost all two lanes without a shoulder. The lack of easy access for pulling off the road does not really matter, because there are virtually no cars on it. Someone sitting on a stone by the Central Highway to watch the traffic go by will spend most of his or her time watching an empty road. What little traffic does pass by is usually of the two-wheeled variety, such as bicycles, or horses pulling carts, or oxcarts loaded with sugar cane. A well-worn motor scooter may putt by going between farms, but more common are stretches of five or ten minutes when nothing at all will come down the road. Occasionally a truck will pass by, packed to the gills with standing people. The trucks can be heard for a long time before

A stretch of the newly finished Central Highway between Artemisa and Candelaria,
August 15, 1929. Note the distinctive trunk of the royal palm on the right.
(Biblioteca Nacional José Martí, Havana)

• • •

OPPOSITE
The Depression hit the auto industry hard, but it was beginning to be a bad memory and
prospects were looking up by the time this Ford ad ran in El Automóvil de Cuba
in January 1937. (Biblioteca Nacional José Martí, Havana)

they actually appear on the horizon of the empty highway, but they do not pass often.

Teams of oxen plow the fields alongside the Central Highway. Tractors are seen rarely: anything that runs on combustible fuel is simply too expensive to operate. The highway runs for mile after mile by vast fields of sugarcane, banana plantations, and stands of royal palms soaring well over a hundred feet into the air. There are tremendously lush green landscapes, wide skies, coast and hills, endless stretches of flat sugarcane land. Signs of population are few, the occasional figure in a field, or the humble, thatch-roofed wooden cottage called a *bohío*, or an ovenlike pair of cement rooms, tin-roofed, a patch of beaten dirt outside the front door. Occasionally, someone will appear standing off to the side of the highway, a regional specialty hoisted up, offered for sale: avocados, pineapples, *tamales* of corn mush wrapped in corn husks, different kinds of mangos (depending on the local variety), and papayas.

The place to see large crowds of people out in the countryside along the Central Highway is at every crossroads. Where roads meet, multitudes seem to be always gathered, waiting for a bus or truck ride toward wherever they are going. Sometimes small concrete booths are thrown up to shelter the would-be passengers, but sometimes they wait on the open ground. The most common sort of automotive traffic on the Central Highway is a rental car with tourist license plates, those that have a number preceded by a "T." Some tourists would never consider giving a ride to a Cuban, while others consider the hitchhikers they meet the highlights of their trips. When the rare car passes, rental or not, the ride-seekers draw close to the side of the highway and crook their thumbs into hitchhiking position (*haciendo botella*, making the bottle, as Cubans call it) or gesture desperately, waving pesos that they'll gladly exchange for a ride. Or they simply wait patiently—seated in a patch of shade if they have any luck at all—for some conveyance to come along with room for them, waiting hours to get down the Central Highway in a bus or open-backed truck. In the countryside, as much as in the cities, public transport, or the lack thereof, is a ruling factor in people's lives.

Initially, the Central Highway generated a growing network of con-

The Vía Mulata was the only road connecting Cuba's easternmost town, Baracoa, with the rest of the island in May 1954. (Biblioteca Nacional José Martí, Havana)

• • •

necting roads throughout the country to accommodate the increasing numbers of cars and trucks. Nevertheless, the vast majority of Cubans were as dependent on daily public transport then as they are today. Cars were prohibitively expensive for most people, whether they lived in a town or not. At least in the countryside, people often had a cart pulled by an animal when they needed to travel some distance. For the average

Tudores *and* Fordores : 77

resident of Havana or Santiago who needed to get from one side of the city to the other, buses, or street cars, or taxis were the options.

Both of Cuba's largest cities began to add bus routes to their existing trolley services early on. By 1928, some 1,600 buses were circulating in Havana, according to the magazine *Automovilista*. That year, the city enacted new laws regulating bus service, a move that had long been advocated by bus drivers and owners. To show their support for the new regulations, over a thousand of them drove along the Malecón in single file. The citizens of Havana were astonished by the immense line of buses stretching along the city's edge, according to the magazine. People had not suspected there were so many operative buses.

In April 1928, *Automovilista* editorialized:

> Here, the bus, like everything new, is in fashion; and this, combined with the huge extension of the city, means that these vehicles will be indispensable, in that there is no other means of traveling more comfortable and more in tune with our times.
>
> To make a trip in a trolley from one end of the capital to the other means to have to submit oneself to a truly distressing torture.

Public transport was an important and ever-present issue, and it played a significant political role in Havana's life. By 1930, some people were calling for the city to eliminate trolley service entirely and replace it with buses. Havana's independent bus operators mostly consisted of small-time entrepreneurs, people who had saved up some money and bought a secondhand bus and took a chance on an underserved route; typically such an operator might save enough to buy another bus and put it on a second route, and he might well drive one of his own buses with a brother driving the other. As an article in the General Motors internal publication, *General Motors World*, explained, "Buses in Havana are operated on the 'collectivo' system. Usually the operator owns his own bus; sometimes more than one. On his recent trip to Cuba, L. E. Nickerson, Transportation Engineer in New York, made the interesting discovery that a waiter in one of the popular cocktail lounges is the owner of seven buses."

Spoked automobile wheel, trolley, and horse dung on cobblestones, Havana
(Biblioteca Nacional José Martí, Havana)

• • •

A paddy wagon in front of the Havana courthouse in 1933, a year of great unrest in the streets, culminating in President Machado's resignation on August 9. (Biblioteca Nacional José Martí, Havana)

• • •

In early 1933, the bus owners formed the Cooperativa de Ómnibus Aliados (COA) to represent their interests. There was tremendous political unrest in Cuba in 1933, with groups as diverse as students, the middle class, and workers expressing their displeasure with the Machado government. Corruption was out of control, violence by the police and death squads was at alarming levels, strikes and aborted coups were frequent, and the opposition's numbers were growing rapidly. When Machado's government decided to impose a route tax on bus operators in the summer of 1933, COA's members went on strike. Bus service virtually stopped in August, the hottest month of the year, and the strike spread rapidly to other sectors, bringing the city to a halt and sealing the fate of the government. Machado resigned as president on August 9.

Following Machado's resignation, his former minister of public works, Carlos Miguel Céspedes, was named president. The most important qualification he seems to have possessed was not that he had overseen the completion of the Central Highway, but that he was deemed acceptable by Sumner Welles, the U.S. ambassador in residence, who maintained a pretense of complete neutrality while imposing Washington's will. But even goodwill from the North was not enough to keep Céspedes's government together for long.

In early September, a movement consisting of a range of disaffected people from university professors to noncommissioned officers in the army forced Céspedes from office and on September 10 installed Ramón Grau San Martín, dean of the University of Havana's Medical School, as president. Among the soldiers supporting this revolution was a sergeant named Fulgencio Batista y Saldívar. Grau San Martín immediately, and unilaterally, abrogated the Platt Amendment and began to move Cuba toward his idea of a socially just society with compulsory education, minimum wages, and agrarian reform. It was a platform that pleased neither the United States nor the reactionary elements among the military who had helped bring him to office. After only four months, Batista and his supporters forced Grau San Martín's resignation at the start of 1934. Batista's official position after the removal of Grau San Martín was chief of the armed services, but he was always the person who held the reins of power behind the scenes, as Robert Whitney records in *State and Revolution in Cuba*. Batista was elected president in 1940. When his party lost in the 1944 elections, he went into exile in Florida. By 1949 he was back in Cuba, serving as a senator, and in 1952 he announced as a candidate for president. When it became clear that he was going to lose, he led a bloodless coup, three months before the scheduled elections. He would remain in office until ousted by the Revolution in 1959.

Fulgencio Batista (seated just inside the open car door), chief of the armed services, arrives in Camagüey, February 24, 1939. (Biblioteca Nacional José Martí, Havana)

• • •

Batista's coups met with general approval in Washington. Like any long-term couple, Cuba and the United States had their spats over the years; but no one doubted that Batista would always bend his knee to North America. He had visited Detroit's automakers, and he was regarded as a loyal friend to their Cuban interests in the broader scheme, even if he was not quite so cooperative on a personal level. Batista always showed an eye for a nice car. In 1939, for instance, he ordered a Lincoln limousine from the Havana dealer, Auto Mundial, which in turn ordered it from Dearborn. For unknown reasons, he changed his mind

Fulgencio Batista (right) visits Benson Ford in Dearborn, Michigan, in the 1940s. (Benson Ford Research Center at Henry Ford Museum and Greenfield Village, Dearborn, Mich.)

• • •

and canceled the order, leaving the local dealership with a virtually un-sellable car, too expensive for any but the highest-ranking officers or politicians. A request from Havana was sent to Dearborn, asking that payment of the balance due be extended as long as the limousine re-mained unsold. "It was ordered on the basis of a firm order for the Chief of the Cuban Army, Col. F. Batista, who changed his mind with respect to it," C. A. Martínez from Ford's auto financing company in Havana explained. "They have tried to sell it in the past months without success."

It was not easy to move a Cadillac or a Lincoln off the showroom floor in 1939. Only 20 out of almost 2,000 cars exported from the States

A Lincoln garage in Havana in 1933 (Biblioteca Nacional José Martí, Havana)

• • •

to Cuba that year were Cadillacs, and just 51 were Lincolns, according to U.S. Department of Commerce figures. Most people who decided to buy a car generally bought a more affordable Ford or General Motors product. The same competitive battle being waged in the United States between the two Detroit giants was also being fought in Cuba during the Batista years. In 1936, for instance, General Motors exported 1,076 Chevrolets to the island. In the same year Ford shipped 1,069 cars to Cuba, only seven fewer. Between them, Chevrolet and Ford sold almost a third of the 3,749 U.S.-manufactured cars imported into Cuba that year. The corporate battle was not restricted to private auto sales. Competition for sales to public agencies was also fierce. The Havana police department ordered Fords, Oldsmobiles, and Chevrolets during different periods, depending on the deals available.

In addition, the Detroit giants battled for both truck and bus sales. Truck business in the countryside was substantial, and dealerships competed to see which trucks would be used most in the sugarcane field and mills. In the cities, the battle was over buses. In 1933, there were 1,585 passenger buses in Cuba, and by 1941 that number had more than doubled, to 3,422. Many of these were for long-distance provincial and interprovincial routes, but urban fleets had also grown, with virtually all of Havana's urban buses affiliated with the COA.

Ford and General Motors were, effectively, the only North American companies selling buses in Cuba in 1940. In October, Ford's Havana branch manager, Paul Heilman, found himself writing to R. I. Roberge in Ford's Dearborn office. In fierce competition with General Motors, and in negotiations with the COA, Heilman was trying to close a sale of some 200 Ford buses. He asked the head office for permission to offer special credit terms to the cooperative. "The bus business in Havana is an institution because Cooperativa de Omnibus Aliados, S.A. is an institution," he explained to the Dearborn office. "It is as much a part of the everyday life of the city as the telephone and electric light service, and regardless of economic conditions, bus service continues."

A couple of years later, Paul Heilman may have felt less kindly toward the cooperative. In June 1942, some COA members pressed for a moratorium on outstanding car, truck, and bus payments. To voice their position, the cooperative's president, Menelao Mora—a lawyer who served two terms as a congressman from the Ortodoxo Party of Eduardo Chibás Jr. and who would, in 1957, die a revolutionary hero's death at the age of fifty-two, storming the Presidential Palace occupied by Batista—met with C. A. Martínez, longtime employee at Créditos y Descuentos Mercantiles, the Havana automobile credit company that financed Fords.

In a memorandum to Dearborn executives, written on October 29, 1942, Martínez recalled that on July 31 Mora contacted him to complain that all the other U.S. companies, which essentially meant General

Motors, were willing to grant special credit terms because of the trying economic times and impending war. "[I] explained to Dr. Mora that the Ford Motor Co. did not sell on time and had nothing to do with time sales. That the Credit Company . . . was the one handling the financing of Ford dealers in Cuba."

Martínez seems to have thought that Mora and the COA would take no for an answer. He was wrong. On September 10 of that same year, H. L. Sugg, the manager of the credit company, wrote to Roberge: "A commission composed of three members of the Board of Directors of Omnibus Aliados, approached the writer to request that before proceeding to make repossessions in cases of Omnibus Aliados we should let them know so that they could take action on the matter to avoid such repossessions."

On September 29, a bill was introduced in the Cuban Senate by Juan Cabrera Hernández proposing a moratorium on payment for vehicles bought on credit. The bill read, in part

> The scarcity of gasoline and gas-oil is greatly noted in the Republic. All automotive vehicles using these products have been either removed from circulation or have been forced to greatly reduce their itineraries. Bus lines that are forced to retire from circulation a considerable number of units, transportation companies that also reduce the number of vehicles in operation, taxi drivers who are not in a position to work steadily as previously, private owners who cannot use their cars for their business and professions . . . in fact all automobile, bus and truck owners in general are not obtaining from these vehicles but a very small revenue compared to what they expected to receive when they purchased the units.

A week after the bill's introduction, as Martínez wrote to the Dearborn office, he attended a meeting with Senator Cabrera, several automobile dealers, and a number of bankers. Sugg reported that Cabrera was surprised by the amplitude of the bill's repercussions. "The Senator frankly admitted that he had no idea his proposition of law would have

A COA bus packed to overflowing in September 1950 (Courtesy of the photographic archives, Bohemia, *Havana)*

such far-reaching effects and that to save his face he could not withdraw it but that indirectly he would discourage the passage of it."

An agreement was eventually reached with Menelao Mora and all other parties whereby the moratorium bill would die a quiet death in committee, while Créditos y Descuentos would adopt a more lenient attitude toward debtors, at least until the end of global hostilities. As Martínez summed it up, "The Ford Motor Co. as well as the Credit Company would act in behalf of the bus owners by recommending an [sic] special consideration in accordance with the abnormal conditions due to the war."

From an initial position of self-assertion, Cuban politicians ultimately crafted an agreement with U.S. business leaders in which the interests of the people who elected them were less than optimally served. It was a pattern that got repeated time and again. During the Batista years, Detroit's automakers were assured of an attentive hearing, and the Cuban market was consistently a good one.

José Rivera's Buick originally touched rubber to Cuban roads while Batista was still in office. Unlike the dictator, it is still alive and running. A Saturday trip is on to French Beach, some fifteen or twenty miles west of Santiago de Cuba, to test-drive the car's new clutch plate. As we approach the police checkpoint on the outskirts of Santiago, José and I are in the front seat, both silently, fervidly hoping that the cop occupying the guard post will be content to stay in the shade of his shack rather than come out and give us a good going-over in the heat of the morning sun. I have brown skin and look pretty much as mulato as the next guy. We are hoping that, if the cop does come out, José's well-ordered documents and my Cuban aspect will mean José can do all the talking. If I do not speak, the law will not discover that I am a foreigner. But if I am discovered, there will be hell to pay. Private Cuban citizens are not permitted to give rides to foreigners, and any such arrangement is automatically assumed by the authorities to involve an illegal exchange of money. I will have to get out and wait for a taxi to take me back to town, and José will be fined heavily. We're in luck—the cop in his gray uniform peers out the door as the Buick rolls slowly past, raises a hand halfway in greeting, and ducks back in the shack.

José is driving, I am riding shotgun, and his stepson, Jesús, is in the front between us. In the back seat are José's friend, call him Eduardo, who looks vaguely like Hunter S. Thompson, dissolute, fleshy, and pale, and Eduardo's younger, round, and attractive wife—who is introduced to me only as such and whose name I never hear—and teenage daughter. Once we have passed the control point, the atmosphere in the car lightens noticeably. Eduardo opens a bottle of rum, unlabelled, and passes it to José, who takes a drink and kicks off his scuffed leather shoes. "I like to be barefoot," he sighs in relief. "That's how I always drive."

Eduardo had begun the morning by finding twelve liters of gas for $3.00 to provide fuel for the expedition. He kept the change from the $10 bill I gave him, and it will buy us all lunch later in the day. Already it has also bought rum, the other necessary fuel, and it is about to do so again. Ten dollars being two weeks' salary, my presence is acknowledged to be the trip's raison d'être. We stop at a roadside bar long enough to buy another unmarked bottle. José cuts off the engine to save gas while we wait for Eduardo. When Eduardo comes back with the bottle, we all have to get out and push so that José can jump-start the car, as he is having some starter-motor trouble. The clutch plate is functioning perfectly.

The scarcity and cost of gas are the most important factors in determining how José drives. On open stretches of downhill or even level road, he gets up to speed, say thirty-five or forty miles per hour, and then cuts the engine off, coasting as the Buick gradually slows down to nearly a standstill; then, at the last possible moment, he pushes the ignition button and pops the clutch to start the engine until he's going fast enough to kill the motor again. His clutch-popping is amazingly smooth—the car restarts with barely a buck or a bounce—and we go rolling along in the shadow of the Sierra Maestra, trying to avoid the *baches*, potholes, with Jesús super-attentively watching the road as José tosses back his head to take a swig from the bottle. Some of the *baches* look deep enough to swallow a Lada or a Moskvich. The air above the road is full of both white and yellow butterflies. We go through a long stretch shaded like a tunnel beneath big tamarind trees on either side of the road. Eduardo's wife passes around a handful of wax paper–wrapped tamarind jelly sticks, a local specialty in Santiago de Cuba. The sticks are loaded with sugar, but it still does not cut the tart acidity of the tamarind—I have one, and that is plenty.

French Beach is a typical sand-and-dirt-mix Cuban beach. We sit down on the sand, under a pair of low, scruffy tamarind trees. Eduardo's wife pulls out a big towel for her family. José takes off his T-shirt, as do I. The sea is tepidly warm and not overly attractive, more gray than blue, with sizable waves churning up the bottom and making the water opaque. People are having a good time, sitting under trees, drinking, taking the occasional dip in the unappealing surf. During the few hours we are there, two ribby horses pass by, pulling carts, one with a pile of mangos, the other with avocados and plantains. Each is driven by a skinny old man singing out his product. We also see two sows, mottled gray and black, dugs dangling, rooting among the trash people have left behind. The hogs have it good. The people on the beach seem not to bother looking for a trash can; when they are done with something, they drop it where they stand or sit. Plenty of mango skins and chicken bones with a little meat left on them dot the sand. Some Cubans blame socialism for the national habit of littering, saying that since there is always a government-employed street cleaner to come along and clean up, no one looks for a trash can. Others say that a complete disregard for Swiss-style neatness of living was a national trait long before the Revolution. These days, of course, there is not a lot to throw away in Cuba.

Just enough room separates us from the next group of people on the beach that José feels free to expand on how profoundly and bitterly anti-government he is. Especially galling to him are the travel restrictions and the lack of any free press. He does not want any help from the state, he says, only the right to have a small business of his own in which his fortunes will depend on personal effort and not government whim. What bothers him most of all is the disparity between those who have dollars and those who do not, and the disappearance of the revolutionary idea that everyone is equal. These days, without dollars, it is bone breaking just to get by. "Except for those with pull," chimes in Eduardo, gesturing behind us, where, across the road from the beach parking lot, built up on a hillside overlooking the water, is a big resort hotel. It is, he tells me, exclusively for the use of the military.

By 3:00 P.M., we have finished two liters of rum, and we have each eaten a quarter of a chicken and *tostones*—plantain chips—out of a greasy cardboard box, the only lunch available at the beach's little cafeteria. Fortunately for me, Eduardo's well-fed young wife brought along some succulent local *bizcocho* mangos and *zapotes* (the sapodilla plum, a regional fruit that looks like a brown-skinned avocado and has a meaty, deliciously sweet, red flesh inside). I, in true dumb gringo fashion, have forgotten to bring anything to drink and am too paranoid about my gastrointestinal well-being to drink her ice water, so sips of rum and the juice from the mangos and *zapotes* are the only hydration I get.

On the return ride, we are caught behind an old bus, also heading back to Santiago, full of people who have come out to spend a day at one of the string of beaches, similar in composition to French Beach, strung out west of Santiago. The road twists and curves, and on the straight stretches it seems always that something is coming toward us in the other lane—usually a horse and cart. The bus is already full when we get trapped behind it. Without room for even one more standing person, its driver passes by the large knots of people at various points along the roadside who frantically gesture at him to stop. Without the luxury of a private car, beachgoers are likely to spend as much time waiting for transport to and from the beach as they will by the sea.

José immediately focuses on one of the old bus's back tires. "That tire's not going to make it back to Santiago," he declares. "You can tell by the way it's turning. It's going to blow out." Sure enough, as we round a curve we come upon the bus stopped in the middle of the road, dejected passengers dismounting. The rear tire is well and truly flat. It is likely to be a long time before anything else comes by with room to accommodate the suddenly stranded passengers. We can now leave the bus in our dust, but the ten minutes we spent trapped behind it ruin José's careful gas/distance/speed calculations. We make it back to Santiago de Cuba, but not to his house, before running out of gas. There is nothing to do but pull over, get the other five-liter jerry can of gasoline with a length of clear plastic tubing out of the trunk, and feed gas into the tank, a process that begins with a person sucking it up into the tube and sticking the tube into the gas tank. The trick is to transfer the tube from mouth to tank just before tasting the gas, but what usually happens is that the taste of gas is the unwelcome signal to stick the tube in the tank. The face a person makes when tasting gas, the distasteful squint and wrinkled nose, is encountered frequently in Havana or Santiago, where men bent to hoses running into gas tanks are a common sight.

———————

Keep it running. Use it. Make it last. Hold its costs down. Use as little gasoline as possible and do what is needed to keep it on the road. As it is in Cuba now, so it was in the early years of mass-produced automobiles. Those early models were built to keep running. My grandfather, Reuben Mills, had a Rolls Razor, which was a stainless steel safety razor in an oval nickel-plated box that fit in one hand. The box lids were lined with a leather strop and a stone hone, so one could sharpen the blade daily before taking it out to fit on its handle. Box and blade were designed to provide their owner with a sharp razor, every morning, for a lifetime. This was the kind of industrial design that appealed to both my grandfather and to Henry Ford, whether for razors or cars. Others who subscribed to this doctrine of utility were among the founders of various automobile companies, including Ransom E. Olds, the founder of Oldsmobile; the Dodge brothers; David Dunbar Buick; and William C. Durant, who built the first Chevrolet. What appealed to the market up until about 1925 was something built so well it would never need to be replaced.

The years between the Depression and the Second World War saw a sea change in attitude among Detroit's carmakers, moving from Ford's production concept of standardization and durability to the marketing concept of "planned obsolescence," of designing and building a car that was expected to last only a minimum amount of time before being deemed aesthetically old-fashioned and outdated and the mechanics of which were also programmed to self-destruct. Things began to be built so they would need to be replaced. By 1934, according to Vance Packard's *The Waste Makers*, speakers at the Society of Automotive Engineers' annual meeting proposed limiting the life of automobiles.

Alfred Sloan of General Motors and Walter P. Chrysler were a couple of the early and most influential proponents of planned-obsolescence marketing. Sloan lured a car customizer and designer named Harley Earl away from Hollywood, where he was designing cars for movie stars. His initial designs were for the 1927 Lasalle and the 1928 Cadillac. Sloan then named Earl as head of General Motors' styling, a position he occupied until he retired in 1959. His flamboyant designs, sleek, exuberant lines, exaggerated fins, and aeronautical flourishes resonated with both Cubans and North Americans, and they still do.

Other companies followed Earl's lead. The proponents of styling and planned obsolescence carried the day, and the century for that matter. In the United States, figures for 1924 showed that Ford accounted for just over 50 percent of new car sales, according to Richard Wright's *West of Laramie: A Brief History of the Auto Industry*. In second place was General Motors, with about 19 percent of new car sales. By 1926, the ratio was 35 percent Ford and 28 percent GM. In 1931, General Motors passed Ford in sales, and it remained ahead thereafter. Henry Ford resisted Sloan's marketing techniques for a time, but when his son, Edsel, took over, he decided Ford had to compete on General Motors's terms or lose the automobile market.

The industry turned from utility to style, with exterior designs changing each year, built around an unchanging, lead-burning gasoline combustion, and each year's model costing more, not less, than the previous year's. In this new market, an automobile represented more than transport in the life of its owner. It was an indication of status, success, of a driver's identity. The new approach was the beginning of a profit-driven shift by manufacturers that would grow only more intense as the years passed, until things reached the state that Jonathan Raban described in his 1974 book, *Soft City*: "Cars have had to carry an excessive burden of symbolism; they have been decked out with every sort of frippery, used as promiscuously as tailor's dummies to promote a style. The car is a special simulacrum of the self; it goes where its owner goes; it forms his outer suit, his most visible and ubiquitous expression of choice and taste; it is most often seen briefly, on the move—like the citizen himself, it has to make its message plain in an instant."

Cubans have always responded favorably to GM's concept of styling, every bit as much as people in the United States, and they have made these cars their own. Cuba was one of the largest markets for Detroit-manufactured vehicles in the Americas. An island—albeit 750 miles long, the Caribbean's longest—with no more than a few million residents: not much of a market on the face of it, but the volume of cars purchased in Cuba was prodigious. The island was among the half-dozen

Taxis in front of Havana's Hotel Inglaterra, ca. 1929. By the eve of the Great Depression, cars packed the city, but the car market ground to a halt as the effects of Wall Street's crash were felt. (Biblioteca Nacional José Martí, Havana)

· · ·

best markets in the hemisphere, year after year. Every year consumer excitement was whipped up by newspaper ads for new models, and Cubans fell prey to planned obsolescence in the same way North Americans did.

In January 1932, as the Cuban car market disappeared beneath waves from the Depression in full force to the North, an editorial in *A.C.C.* called for a tax break for older cars, pointing to France, where it was policy to exempt from taxation cars over nine years old: "In Cuba there must be very few cars or trucks that are more than nine years old, because of the practice adopted from the Americans of changing an old vehicle for a new one every two or three years. It's highly probable that with the crisis whipping us more automobile and truck owners will have to make do with what they have for as long as they can."

Maybe even now Cubans would buy a new car every couple of years, like North Americans, if they could. Maybe they would, and maybe they will get the chance to do so again, but the fact is right now they cannot. So they have cared for and maintained the same models that North Americans bought and threw away in great numbers, so many of them scrapped that the remaining few have become collector's items. The mechanics in Havana and Santiago de Cuba who have kept these cars running all these years belong to a genre of Cuban genius. They have done these cars much prouder than the manufacturers who built them to throw away. Cubans have turned dishwashing detergent into brake fluid, enema bag hoses into fuel lines, and gasoline-burning engines into diesels in order to keep Detroit's dream cars on the road. They have accorded respect to these cars, taken them into their families, treated them as well as they could, provided the level of care that befits an elder, fed them and kept them moving, not tossed them away.

chapter three
BUSES & TROLLEYS

Call him Jorge, a guitarist in one of the licensed groups that play on a circuit of three or four clubs in Santiago de Cuba, *casas de la trova* (houses of the ballad), where every night people come to dance and listen to the infectious rhythms of that purely Cuban music called *son* and discreetly hustle tourists. He is thin, in his early thirties, angular and intense, with his hair in dreadlocks. The young, attractive, raven-haired, olive-skinned Israeli girl who rents the room next to mine on a rooftop patio brings him back every night after the clubs close. Through the thin walls I hear them making love should I happen to awake at two, three, or four in the morning. Sometimes I go back to sleep and wake up again, and the cries of passion—hers—are still coming through the walls above my head.

Occasionally our schedules coincide at early evening and we drink a beer on the patio. Jorge has been to Spain, touring with a *son* sextet. Between endearments in broken English to the Israeli, he complains to me, in Spanish, that the nightlife in Santiago is not healthy and fun as it is in Spain. There, everyone likes to go out and meet their friends for a drink in the evenings, but here, he tells me, people go out to get drunk and pick up foreigners. It gets old after a while, he grouses, leg stretched out and sandal off, his bare brown foot resting on the chair between the pale thighs of the Israeli sitting opposite him.

Midway through a month's stay in Santiago de Cuba, I spend the morning of September 11, 2001, in the Elvira Capé Library, Santiago's main public library. As on most days, the reading room is full of a wide variety of citizens thumbing through the card catalogue or sitting at long tables on uncomfortable metal chairs to read, not a computer terminal in the place. From the street outside, occasional snatches of *son* drift in the open windows, the music intended to attract the attention of the handful of tourists strolling along Calle Heredia. It is 90°, and inside Elvira Capé there are neither fans nor air-conditioners. Still, it is crowded. Sitting around me are students, a middle-aged man wearing a *guayabera* and thick lenses, and an older woman wearing glasses with tape around the green plastic rims who is taking notes from a hefty volume lying open on the table beside her. Two young girls in their school uniforms of pressed white blouses and beige skirts are hunched over a slim volume titled *Pregnancy and Adolescents*. A young guy sleeps, head down on his folded arms, with an open notebook beside his elbow on the table. "Without culture, liberty is not possible," says the Fidel Castro quote on a placard by the circulation desk. It is a variation on José Martí's "Be cultured to be free."

At midday, I leave the library to go back to the house where I am renting my rooftop room. Nancy, the homeowner—a rotund, always slightly harried woman with bottle-blond hair and a chronically ill husband—is sitting in the living room with her son, Dani. He is a handsome thirty-two-year-old who works in public health programs in Santiago. His is the third room on the roof. The television is on, and the midday newscaster is talking about the antimosquito campaign that has been successfully carried out in Camagüey. It is not an unusual configuration—various family members can usually be found sitting in rocking chairs in front of the television at any given time of day. Dani still lives at home, as does his older sister, along with her husband and their daughter. Two other grown children have places of their own, but the whole family gathers here for the evening meal each night.

Nancy asks if I have heard what is happening, and I say no. The Israeli girl got a call from her parents in Tel Aviv this morning, she tells me, just after the World Trade Center towers collapsed, and the TV has been on ever since. I still have no idea what she is talking about. "They've destroyed the World Trade Center and the Pentagon with passenger jets," Dani says. "Thousands dead."

I wonder silently how two people could get a news report so wrong, thinking they must have it wrong, when Cuban TV newscasters on the screen are replaced by images being broadcast directly from CNN. The CNN reporters are talking about the collapse of the two towers, and showing the footage. After a few minutes, CNN disappears and the local newscasters return to the top story of the day, Fidel Castro preparing to reopen the Salvador Allende High School in Havana after extensive reforms, the latest example of the nationwide campaign to improve schools and reduce class sizes.

This, in turn, is soon replaced by more CNN footage of the first tower collapsing. I run up to the Plaza de Marte and flag a Lada cab over to the Hotel Meliá Santiago. The best tourist hotels are all allowed to have direct satellite feeds, unlike the rest of Cuba, which must make do with two channels of standard state television, plus an educational channel. Foreigners in luxury hotels always have channels like CNN and ESPN on the televisions in their rooms, pulled down with a satellite dish, but having a dish is strictly illegal for Cubans. Hotel employees frequently videotape sports events and films and sell bootlegged versions.

A kind young woman at the front desk gives me her heartfelt condolences on behalf of the Cuban people and takes me to a gym/exercise room, where a TV on the wall has CNN direct from a satellite. From the nearby hotel swimming pool, the sounds of children's laughter and shouts of pleasure drift into the gym. I spend the afternoon watching people die as the towers fall in endless replay, listening to CNN report President George W. Bush's seemingly panicked flight westward.

Back at Nancy's that evening, we eat supper—a zesty garbanzo soup, followed by red snapper breaded in a tasty batter, eggplant stuffed with cheese, a plate of black beans and rice (*moros y cristianos*, Moors and Christians, as the Cubans call them), and another plate piled with avocado, cucumber, and sliced tomatoes. Nancy explained to me once that it was not just her prodigious skills in the kitchen that brought her children and their families to eat at her house every night. Her children all had jobs that paid them in pesos, while she was paid in dollars for her rooms, and thus she could shop at the dollar stores for the ingredients of the toothsome meals she laid before her family and her guests.

We eat, and afterward we sit in rocking chairs half-circled around the television. Fidel Castro addresses an overflow crowd in the renovated auditorium of the Salvador Allende High School, lauding the tremendous efforts Cuba is making to reduce the numbers of students per class to twenty, in renovated classrooms all across Cuba. The new classrooms are there, he says, thanks to the heroic sacrifice of the Cuban people, determined to consolidate the Revolution's tremendous gains. However, it seems that the *comandante*, like I, cannot quite clear his mind of the horrific image of that jumbo jet entering the office windows at the World Trade Center. He veers off the topic of education and repeats the statement that the government gave that afternoon to the foreign press in Havana, words of condolence for the families of the thousands killed. Then, he begins enumerating the terrorist attempts on his own life, the efforts of the CIA to bring him down with everything from exploding cigars to contract assassination. At one point, Castro stops speaking in mid-sentence and looks up and off to his right, pointing with that long slender index finger that every Cuban has seen him extend straight out thousands of times to emphasize something, or bring to his temple as he is wont to do when searching his mind for statistics or for the just-right phrase. He aims that well-known forefinger with its perfectly clean crescent nail toward the upper reaches of the high school auditorium and says reproachfully: "You're making too much noise up there. Stop talking and listen." Then he returns to the theme of *yanqui* terrorism where he left off. The father of the Revolution treats the *compañeros* and *compañeras* as if they were children, dictating with that elegant index finger what they can and cannot do, what they can and cannot read, where they may and may not go. All for their own good.

I rise, excuse myself to the family—*con permiso*—and go out to walk. Along the shadowy backstreets, Castro's voice comes out of each successive open window, inside each room old women in rocking chairs in the middle of their evenings, watching TV under high ceilings. There is a strong preference among Cubans for rocking chairs; from one end of the island to the other entire living rooms are furnished with them. They are often made from hardwoods, solid and beautiful, with broad arms and high backs, supremely comfortable and elegant. Many of them are oriented toward a television, which may be black-and-white or color but is situated in a clear sightline from the chair. The same arrangement is repeated in house after house as I pass by on the sidewalk, stealing glimpses through tall jalousied windows open to the fresh night air, through which Castro's voice drifts out to meet me. He has returned to the campaign to rebuild schools and reduce class size. Through a window I see the index finger swoop down from shoulder level, stabbing the air above the podium.

In truth, Santiago de Cuba seems well away from any terrorist attacks. Most of the news analysis on Cuban television in the days and weeks that follow September 11 is of the Yankee-chickens-come-home-to-roost variety, and life for Santiagueros goes on as always. It is a relaxed city, despite its traffic. The lumbering old products of Detroit and the diesel burners that the Soviets left behind belch exhaust fumes as they climb the steep hill from the Plaza Dolores up to the Plaza de Marte, sidewalks chockablock with people making the same climb and sucking the diesel smoke, a slow constant flow of folks up- and downhill. The *camiones de uso particular* trucks packed with bodies come and go, as the long lines of patiently waiting souls congregate at bus stops. For all the hustle and bustle of the daily scuffle to keep body and soul together, Santiago de Cuba is a laid-back, tropical city where nothing moves too fast and the world's geopolitical eruptions can seem remote, no matter how awful they may be.

––––––––

Sometimes, however, the waves of the wider world do reach Santiago, as they did in the Second World War, for instance. The war's requirements for personnel and materiel halted the U.S. automobile industry—and its exports to Cuba—in its tracks. In 1941, 29,762 cars were registered in Cuba, according to figures from the Cuban Ministry of Transport compiled by the U.S. Department of Commerce. By 1945, that number was down to 22,583. Only a handful of new cars or trucks arrived in Cuba in 1942. None at all are on record as having arrived in 1943 or 1944. All raw materials were going to the war effort. There was not enough steel to build cars. For Cubans who wanted one, only the used car market remained, and even this was limited. Fuel was in short supply also and new tires were virtually nonexistent. Rubber and gasoline were needed elsewhere.

Despite the absence of new products, automakers did not disappear from the Cuban scene entirely. For example, Ford's records show that the company spent $2,053 on daily newspaper ads in Havana for the first six months of 1944. A typical ad advised Habaneros: "Now that new cars and trucks are no longer available, you need ALL the extra service your car or truck was built to deliver. Get in the good habit of giving your car the constant care that adds years to its life. Take it to your Ford dealer regularly."

Once the war ended, the industry came roaring back to fill the renewed demand generated by postwar prosperity. Gas was cheap, and a surplus of rubber and steel existed. In Cuba, employment increased, particularly in the cities, and more people than ever could afford to purchase a car on credit. On the island, as in the States, a car was often the second greatest expense in a family's life, after their home; but with credit easily available, a car became an accessible dream for middle-class Cubans.

In "The Great Tragedy of Buying a Jalopy," in an October 1950 *Bohemia*, Fausto Miranda wrote about a secondhand car market filled with unscrupulous hucksters, and he described the situation of their prey:

When a small business, or good job, liberates an individual from worry and doubt, when a person arrives at that happy moment of economic independence in which there is a guaranteed three or four hundred dollars in the bank each month after filling the refrigerator, that is when one begins to get interested in buying a car. The bus, full

Photograph that accompanied an article in Bohemia *on October 1, 1950, warning of the dangers of buying a* cacharro, *a jalopy (Courtesy of the photographic archives,* Bohemia, *Havana)*

to bursting, a torture, it makes a person desperate. The friend who lives at the corner does not have the problem: he bought a car. Why not do the same? . . . The alleged victim, the future car owner, has been bitten by this cruel microbe.

While the majority of Cubans lived in poverty during the 1950s, the island still boasted, proportionally, one of the largest middle-class populations in the Western Hemisphere. Out of a total population of approximately 5.9 million in 1953, more than half a million could be categorized as middle class, or belonging to the bourgoisie, according to Hugh Thomas's *Cuba.* In that same year, some 53,000 people held a university degree, about 70 percent of them men. There were 140,000 office workers and 120,000 sales people, as well as 185,000 public employees.

The number of privately owned cars grew at an impressive rate. In 1946 only 16,258 cars were registered to private owners in the whole country, but by 1952 that number had increased to 77,017, according to National Vehicle Census figures quoted in *El Automóvil de Cuba* in May 1953. The 14,725 autos imported to the island in 1952, some 95 percent of which were made in the United States, were worth more than $25 million at wholesale prices. In addition, 7,852 trucks, worth more than $13 million, were exported from the States to Cuba, as were 236 buses, costing more than $4 million. Along with the cars came replacement parts valued at $5.8 million. These included everything from spark plugs to mufflers, brakes to batteries, hubcaps to seatcovers.

"Most of our dealers have been making a lot of money," wrote the general manager of Ford's Havana branch, C. M. Doolittle, as soon after the war as September 22, 1947, in a letter to his boss, R. I. Roberge, the export sales manager in Dearborn. "We have realized that there was a possibility of a dealer resigning here and there, firstly on account of the accumulation of large profits now available in the form of cash and secondly on account of not wanting to face the hard work which will be required when real competition begins again."

Of course, postwar prosperity did not reach all parts of Cuban society, and even for those who had work and a place to live, life was not easy. A *Bohemia* magazine poll of Havana voters in 1948, just after the elections that swept Carlos Prío Socarrás into office as president, listed their top priorities for the new government in the following order: do away with the black market; do something about *pistoleros* and the routine gun violence; govern without corruption; and do something about improving public transportation. The number of shootings and stabbings and drug arrests and armed robberies that filled the front pages was astonishing. Still, unsafe as the streets might have been, people had to make their way through them. While private transport was becoming an increasingly popular means of doing so, it was, as always, public transport that preoccupied most Habaneros, and most Santiagueros as well.

In both Havana and Santiago, the trolley systems were being treated like faithful old dogs that had outlived their day and were now nothing but unwelcome burdens that dribbled on the carpets and smelled bad. Trolley tracks were being torn up and streetcars sold for scrap. The trolleys were being replaced by buses with combustible fuel engines, and there was fierce competition to sell buses to Cuban municipalities. Early on, in 1947, General Electric was pushing hard for Havana and Santiago

de Cuba to adopt electric buses, with full-page ads touting the idea in popular weekly magazines like *Carteles*. They came close—Havana Electric Railway actually put in an order for forty-four of them but never took delivery. The money ran out, and in the end, both cities opted for gasoline-powered buses.

In Santiago, the last streetcar ran up the hill on Enramada Street on January 27, 1952, and the next day the daily newspaper, *El Oriente*, editorialized:

> Now we shall hear no more that screeching along the parallels of Enramada, nor suffer the interminable waits for broken cables or low current. It's gone, taking with it a piece of Santiago's old-time, traditional soul. . . . Progress has swept it away to make the way clear for the luxurious "omnibus," which comes bearing perspectives of the future and promises of comfort for the people of Santiago.
>
> In spite of the speed of the "*guaguas*" in relation to the obligatory limitations of mobility of the streetcar, people continued preferring the tram until its use became impossible because the company that had the concession did very little to renovate its material, and a moment arrived when they fell completely from the public's favor. . . . Now, at forty-four years old, when its incessant to-and-froing is no longer felt in the old Santiago streets, it leaves behind a certain sadness, as naturally occurs at any burial.

In Havana, the government of Carlos Prío Socarrás decided to phase out the streetcars and began doing so in July 1950, but the pace of work was too slow to suit *El Automóvil de Cuba*. An editorial in the July 1951 issue was titled "We Insist on the Suppression of the Methuselah-like Trolleys," and in it Fernando López Ortiz wrote:

It's no longer a question of a phobic antipathy, not even for these noisy hulks and their electric cables with their attack on the aesthetic, a depressing and pejorative note for the prestige of the Republic's capital in front of the tourists who visit.

The streetcars are, every day more so, a grave urban problem. . . . In certain important zones they constitute a latent danger of accidents that threaten the other vehicles and pedestrians. While the streetcars exist, it is not possible to improve traffic, and much less to resolve problems of circulation in some very busy areas.

The Second World War provided a brief resurgence in streetcar ridership, because the rubber and fuel needed for buses were severely rationed, but people abandoned them once buses were running again. Havana had a record streetcar ridership of 146 million passengers in 1945, according to Allen Morrison in "The Tramways of Havana." By 1950, however, people were back on the buses. The Havana Electric Railway Company was deep in debt and without sufficient cash flow to renovate its stocks. The bus system was still in the hands of Cooperativa Ómnibus Aliado, which was also having grave cash flow problems. In fact, in December 1948, the government froze credit for the COA at the same time it announced that it would buy hundreds more buses to pick up the transit slack that would be caused by the elimination of streetcars. Menelao Mora was president of the COA at the time and lobbied hard to win the contract to operate the city's new buses so the COA could put more vehicles on the streets. He was popular with the COA's bus owners, but he did not win the contract. It went instead to an American businessman and diplomat named William Pawley, who had, in the 1920s, founded Cubana Airlines (which, though now state-owned, is still flying). Pawley offered to assume Havana Electric Railway's debts if he was given a license to mount a private bus company to compete with the COA and trolleys were completely eliminated.

Prío's government, through José Bosch at the Ministry of Revenue and Sergio Clark at the Ministry of Communications, negotiated a remarkably lenient contract, which included numerous tax breaks, deferred payment plans, and guaranteed that the government would buy the bus company should Pawley ever wish to sell. The COA claimed that $1.5 million involved in the deal was never accounted for, with the implication that everyone except the public treasury made money.

Pawley was a shrewd operator who served as U.S. ambassador to Brazil and Peru under Truman and as a troubleshooter for Eisenhower. His name would later turn up as a player in a number of Kennedy assassination conspiracy theories, and in interviews he acknowledged his participation in a CIA-blessed, convoluted plot to bring the United States into a war with Cuba in 1963. He has been described by historian Hugh Thomas as "a veteran anti-Communist" and by others, such as Warren Hinckle and William Turner in *The Fish Is Red*, as a CIA conduit, involved in numerous covert operations. When the CIA wanted to send someone to convince Batista to resign the presidency in 1958, they picked Pawley, although he was unsuccessful.

By the time he began eyeing Havana's bus system, in 1949, Pawley had plenty of contacts in the highest echelons of Cuban government, made over the course of his many years doing business in the country. His installation of a new bus company over the dead body of an urban streetcar system in the Cuban capital was a repeat of his performance elsewhere. In 1941, a year after the city of Miami had eliminated streetcars, Pawley bought a local bus company, and by 1948 he controlled the city's buses. In 1962, Dade County bought his bus companies from him for more than $8 million.

Pawley's company in Havana, Autobuses Modernos, S.A., was founded in 1950 with an initial fleet of 400 buses purchased from England's Leyland Motors. The purchase of English vehicles gained Pawley enemies right away. Bus sales were extremely important to General Motors' man in Havana, Amadeo Barletta, whose dealership sold Cadillac, Oldsmobile, and Chevrolet cars, along with Chevrolet trucks and GM buses.

Barletta, born in the Calabria region of Italy in 1894, went to Puerto Rico in his youth, joining an uncle and two brothers who owned several businesses there. He later moved on to the Dominican Republic, where, in 1920, he founded the Santo Domingo Motor Company, the country's first Chevrolet dealership. Roads were scarce at the time, and in the first year the company was open, it sold only three cars. Business picked up rapidly, however, and one of the people who bought stock in the company was the dictator Rafael Leónidas Trujillo Molina. Later, Trujillo had a falling-out with Barletta, jailing him briefly, until the Italian consul, and Benito Mussolini himself, intervened.

In 1939, Mussolini named Barletta as the Italian ambassador to Cuba, and Barletta stayed in Havana until he was expelled in 1942, when Cuba sided against the Axis powers. He went to Argentina to bide his time, according to Enrique Cirules's book *El Imperio de La Habana*. He returned to Cuba at the end of 1945 and began selling Chevrolets, Oldsmobiles, and Cadillacs, as General Motors resumed production and shipment. His Havana dealership was called Ambar Motors.

Ambar, and Barletta, prospered. By January 1949, Ambar had more than thirty agencies and subagencies in Cuba, including ten in Havana alone. The company moved its headquarters and sales floor into a streamlined building at the foot of La Rampa, with huge plate glass windows at the front of the showroom wrapped around two converging blocks, at Twenty-third and Infanta. Ambar employed more than 200 people in Cuba and in 1951 sold more than 7,000 units.

When the COA's members bought new buses, they traditionally bought from General Motors, and by 1952, 65.5 percent of the buses on Havana's streets were GM products, according to *El Automóvil de Cuba*. This was a feather in Amadeo Barletta's cap, and it was accompanied by a hefty commission in his pocket. When the Prío government froze the COA's credit in late 1948, Barletta—already one of Havana's most powerful men (he had acquired a Havana daily newspaper, in addition to Ambar Motors)—eventually signed a guarantee of more than $3 million to return solvency to the cooperative, allowing it to continue operating and buying buses. In March 1950, the COA bought 300 new GM buses. William Pawley's decision to spend almost $1 million on Leyland buses from Britain was not well received.

LA AMBAR MOTORS CORPORATION

Ambar Motors, from the Libro de Cuba, *published in 1954*
(Biblioteca Nacional José Martí, Havana)

. . .

Regular columns about Havana's auto-related businesses appeared in a number of the half-dozen dailies published in the city during the years after the Second World War. One of the most widely read was "Con El Tanque Lleno" (With a Full Tank), by Octavio Jordan. An artist's sketch of Jordan's face running at the top of the column showed a moonish visage with a pencil-thin mustache and a shrewd expression, a slightly dandyish but knowing sort of fellow. The column began appearing in Amadeo Barletta's daily, *El Crisol*, on Mondays; and in 1949, when Barletta bought a bigger paper, *El Mundo*, he took Octavio Jordan with him. *El Mundo* ran Jordan's column three times a week, and on Sundays the sports section featured a full page called *Automovilismo*, edited and written by Jordan. Not surprisingly, Jordan did not have kind words for William

Pawley's fleet of Leylands. In November 1951, he wrote: "More than 100 Autobuses Modernos are out of service awaiting repairs. It was not advisable, at least from how things appear, to have begun this operation with English buses, particularly with the Americans—of much better quality at first glance—just around the corner, as they say, with accredited representatives and agencies in Cuba, and a service that replaces spare parts in less than 24 hours."

Others beyond Amadeo Barletta and his minions took a disliking to Pawley. Juan Gómez, sympathetic to the COA, wrote a small book, *Ultraje a la Constitución* (Outrage against the Constitution), tracing what he saw as the collusion of the government with Pawley against the best interests of the Cuban people. In it he asks:

> Is it just luck that this foreigner [Pawley] is one of those fortunate people we have whose encyclopedic ignorance and lack of scruples are protected by immunity, the exemptions and privileges that are strictly prohibited in our Constitution? Did he fight, as did some North Americans in some Cuban sea or battle, for our independence? Perhaps he has made the kind, generous, and exalted gesture of other North American philanthropists to establish scholarships, create beneficent institutions or fund scientific research in our country? Has he done anything that would incline the Cuban people and government toward him, in spite of his turbulent and not very clean history? He has only these privileges that it seems now will convert him into the sole master and arbiter of the destiny of Cuban transport.

Pawley—who reputedly found Cuban labor law and unions more irksome than he had anticipated—did not last long at the head of Autobuses Modernos, but he did not suffer for the company's failure to thrive under his direction. For whatever reason, in 1953 the Cuban government was obligated by the terms of its contract with Pawley to buy back Autobuses Modernos. The buy-back, as Enrique Moreno noted in *Bohemia*, marked the first time in the island's history that the government had to nationalize a private service.

The space that was gained in Havana's streets by eliminating streetcars was instantly lost to the increase in bus traffic. Most of the streets of old Havana were not made for a bus and a car to drive down abreast. After the relative calm of the war years, dust and noise and traffic jams had become a part of daily life all over the city by the start of the 1950s. Gabriel Miguez Deus wrote in mid-1951: "Our beautiful city, Havana, is an immense garage, where the parking and driving of each automobile means resigned patience, and finely honed skills, now that our principal streets and avenues are congested with automobiles, buses, and trucks without, so far, the least effort being made to remedy the situation."

Streets in the countryside were no better, according to Rafael Tejada, who wrote an automotive column called "Cuentamillas" (odometer) for *El Crisol*, replacing Octavio Jordan's column when he left with Amadeo Barletta for greener pastures at *El Mundo*. In August 1952, Tejada wrote: "The Central Highway is a shame and a danger. . . . There are no stretches where the driver doesn't encounter problems with some huge pothole at a speed of 55 miles per hour."

Deteriorating traffic conditions did not, however, discourage car sales. In 1952, *El Automóvil de Cuba* noted that the year's sales placed Cuba fifth in all of Latin America—behind only the much more populous countries of Argentina, Brazil, Mexico, and Venezuela—in the number of registered vehicles. Auto revenues were substantial and created numerous ancillary jobs, which in their turn generated more revenue and more auto sales. In postwar Cuban cities and towns, trucks and cars were becoming as common as once-unchallenged four-legged beasts of burden. The ripples generated by the industry reached far down the socioeconomic ladder and touched the lives of people like a Havana mechanic I met in the summer of 2002, a tall, dark-skinned, clean-shaven man, then sixty-eight years old, his hair short and whitening in tight curls. Juan Carlos, as I'll call him, was twelve years old when, in 1946, he walked to Havana, seventy-two miles from the tiny country town of San Antonio de Blanco, to become a mechanic.

"I was born in 1934," Juan Carlos told me. "I was a love child. My father was a mechanic working in a garage in Havana, and he used to pass by the house where my mother lived, and he saw her and he fell for her. She returned his love, and after a while I was born. My father and his two brothers bought a bus and started a route, and they did well with it. He and my mother moved in together.

"When I was six months old, my uncles and my father acquired a second bus to put on their route. To celebrate, they decided to throw a Sunday party out in the country on a little piece of public land under a bridge out in Guayanaba. There was a patch of quicksand there that no one knew about. They said the last time they saw my father he was standing in it with his shoes off and the sand up to his ankles, and the next time they looked for him he was gone."

When his father died, Juan Carlos's mother sent her infant son to live with her father in San Antonio de Blanco. "He was a hard man, my grandfather, whose principal occupation was raising his fighting cocks. I had to wheel a cart through San Antonio and around its outskirts, selling vegetables. My grandfather drank, and if I didn't bring back enough money when I got home, he'd beat me. Sometimes he'd make me kneel for long periods on upturned bottle caps.

"I decided to leave there and took off walking. I caught a couple of rides, but they didn't amount to much. Mostly I walked and slept by the side of the road. My mother was living in Havana in one room with her new husband and two sons. My uncles were working at El Relámpago, and they found me work there. From the beginning, I had it in my head to be a mechanic."

El Relámpago was a General Motors agency, primarily selling Buicks, as well as used cars, and behind the showroom was the largest junkyard and parts supply house in Cuba. The company was begun in 1927 by Carlos Alonso with an initial investment of $300. By 1952, it had forty-two employees and paid over $100,000 in salaries, according to *El Libro de Cuba*. When the agency switched over to selling Fords in 1956, Juan Carlos stayed right with them, despite offers to leave and work for competitors. He eventually became a senior mechanic at the agency. His first years, though, were less glamorous.

"When I got the job, they paid me seven pesos a week. The cars came assembled, and also unassembled in crates. For every assembled car that we drove off the boat and back to the Relámpago agency, we got an extra peso. Son, let me tell you, we drove like hell through the city to get back to Relámpago and come down to the port for another one. We checked the oil and poured in some gas and put in a battery and we lined them up, twenty or thirty, everything full of grease.

"That seven pesos a week didn't go too far in my mother's house. I was shining shoes after work at Relámpago, or wheeling people's groceries home from the market for them in a little cart I made—doing whatever I could to bring in a little more. Then, lots of nights, I'd get home at seven in the evening and my *vieja*, my mother, would say that the *caldera*, the pot, was empty. I'd take whatever I'd made that evening and go buy rice, beans, a little piece of meat in some sauce, for her and my brother. It wasn't easy, but we got by."

Despite these money problems, Juan Carlos had it a lot better than many around him. A mechanic, or even a mechanic's helper, was fairly high up on the automotive food chain—below a dealer, or garage owner, in the job hierarchy, certainly, but occupying an important, relatively well paid and secure position. People took many more humble jobs in the sector, and even they thrived, relative to many Cubans, after World War II. Salesmen traveled the length and breadth of the island, selling spare parts as the traveling representatives of stateside automobile accessories companies: Goodyear Tires, Champion Spark Plugs, Willard Batteries, Snap-On Tools, and many more. In the cities, the next rung down on the job ladder consisted of the numerous people who made their livings by parking cars. Even lower down were those who, once the cars were parked, offered their services to watch the car and make sure no harm befell it. Octavio Jordan reproduced in his "With a Full Tank" column in July 1953 a letter of complaint he received on the subject from an unnamed female reader:

Part of the Relámpago agency's junkyard, behind the dealership and garage
(Biblioteca Nacional José Martí, Havana)

· · ·

I work as a typist, and although I don't make much money, by sacri-
ficing I managed to possess a little secondhand "jalopy." I've solved
a lot of problems by having the car, which is economical and without
serious mechanical complications.

And here's my point: you can't imagine how it bothers me that each
time I go to the movies, or out for a drive, to the office or anywhere in
Havana, when I come back to get my car I run into one of these parasites of Havana falsely called "car parkers." I promise you, Mr. Jordan, these people have discovered how to make a living without lifting
a finger.

"Cheap spark plugs can prove costly," warns this ad for Champion, a brand people trusted, which ran in El Automóvil de Cuba during 1932 and 1933. (Biblioteca Nacional José Martí, Havana)

A cut below the *parqueador*, Jordan wrote in his April 23, 1955, column, was the *cuidador*, the guy who says that he'll keep an eye on your car while you leave it parked. "At least the car parker does something," wrote Jordan.

> The parker will park your car or bring it to the entrance to the theater or restaurant or nightclub and he, in general, only asks for something when you use him.
>
> But what does not make sense is the '*cuidador*.' Who told this man that his job is to watch our car? There's not a movie theater, a nightclub, a wedding, a baptism or any other act celebrated in Havana that doesn't attract a plague of *cuidadores* who appear there with no other reason than just because, with their dirty rags in their hands.

At the opposite end of the automotive income spectrum were the owners of dealerships and parts houses, tire factories and garages, law firms and customs houses. The industry provided a middle ground on which Cuban and North American businessmen could join forces, compete, forge economic and social ties. The doings and social notes of local players in the automotive industry were reported in the car columns of the newspapers, and in the half-dozen auto-related magazines published in Cuba in the early 1950s. The big fish in the industry lived in Vedado, belonged to all the right clubs, and schooled their children in the United States and Europe, traveling regularly to visit them there.

When the Confederación Nacional Automotriz (National Automotive Federation) and the Camara de Comercio de Automoviles (Automobile Chamber of Commerce) held an annual banquet, the tables filled up with the Cuban branch representatives of stateside businesses. Each table had a sign on it identifying the company whose agents were seated there. The banquet took place each year on November 18, El Día del Comercio de Automóvil (Day of the Automobile Business), and every December's issue of *El Automóvil de Cuba* devoted extensive coverage to the event. The magazine would run twenty pages of photographs, depicting two or three dining tables to a page, year after year, so readers could glimpse the goings-on in the elegant pillared salon of the Centro Gallego de la Habana, the Galician Center of Havana, one of the city's grand halls. Altogether, it was a huge, thriving crowd made up of oil company representatives, garage owners, car dealers, parts manufacturers, accessory manufacturers, accessory vendors, and tiremakers. People ate and drank and gabbed. The photographs show men at the tables, their hair slicked back, many wearing dark glasses although they are in a moderately lit room, tumblers of whiskey over ice cubes or cocktail glasses raised to the camera, a cigar between their fingers or smoldering in an ashtray on the tablecloth at their elbows. The women seated alongside them are coiffed and wear gowns that leave their shoulders bare. From the visual evidence these photos provide, white people and mulatos were welcome, the latter as long as they fell within an unwritten but well-known set of guidelines about racial gradation based on a complicated set of factors including thickness of lip, width of nose, and type of hair. Blacks, apparently, were not allowed: at all the tables, in all the

As Batista's 1952 coup gets underway, President Carlos Prío Socarrás abandons the Presidential Palace in what appears to be a Cadillac en route to the Mexican embassy and exile. (Courtesy of the photographic archives, Bohemia, Havana*)*

• • •

pages of photos from all the years when the banquet was held, not an Afro-Cuban is to be found.

"Ambiguity is what best defines the evolution of race relations in twentieth-century Cuba," writes Alejandro de la Fuente in *A Nation for All: Race, Inequality, and Politics in Twentieth-Century Cuba.* In the early 1950s, Cuba was as racially segregated in many ways as Florida, or Georgia, or Tennessee, but the question of race in Cuba incorporated subtle variations that were not recognized in the Jim Crow South. Fulgencio Batista—himself a mulato—led a coup in 1952, forcing the elected president, Carlos Prío Socarrás, into exile and installing himself as president, canceling scheduled elections. Early hopes that Batista's administration would support guaranteed civil rights for all the races, and social programs to assist the poor, soon evaporated.

Car sales may have been up, and the middle class expanding little by little, but life for most people remained precarious at best. A 1952 census showed that 45 percent of urban residents and 98 percent of rural residents were without running water. In Havana, almost half the children under fourteen did not attend school. Ninety thousand women in Cuba worked as domestics, as opposed to a meager thirteen who worked as scientists. Thirty percent of people under twenty-one years old had intestinal parasites. A quarter of the adult population could not read or write at all.

For foreigners, Havana at this time was a city of gambling and sex, Las Vegas and Tijuana combined, running wide open. Travelers viewed it as a destination of tropical breezes and friendly natives, where any kind of pleasure was for sale. In 1952, the Hungarian-French scholar Tibor Mende made a trip through Latin America. Of Havana he wrote:

> A beggar asleep on a bench in a garden; the dreadful poverty in the neighborhoods far from the center; the army of prostitutes that roams the streets; the innumerable street vendors and individuals of dubious profession who try to earn their livings; all of this forms part of the city with the same rights as the insensate luxury of the private beaches of the millionaire politicians, the ostentatious receptions of high Cuban society and the exclusive snobbism of the rich people's clubs. . . . Its climate, its rum, its roulette and its luxury make the city center the most frequented destination for North American tourists. When they leave their hotels, their Cadillacs and their taxis disappear into the Cuban night and, in exchange for dollars, Habaneros obligingly provide them all the illusions of the tropics.

Batista carefully maintained good relations with North American visitors, and with the commercial sector. He fully appreciated the give-and-take nature of doing business with U.S. automakers. He got along with them, had visited them, and was a known quantity to them. A letter from

A 1954 Cadillac Fleetwood waits outside Havana's Tropicana nightclub.
(Biblioteca Nacional José Martí, Havana)

• • •

J. M. Cerviño, controller at Ford's Havana branch, to P. M. Heilman at Ford headquarters in Dearborn, written as early as June 19, 1940, explained that fund-raisers for Raúl Menocal, a Batista-sponsored candidate running for mayor of Havana, were pressuring Ford to pony up a donation:

> This morning Sammy Tolón told me that Raúl Menocal was very *resentido* [resentful] about our attitude. Tolón says that the United Fruit Co., the Standard Oil Co. and other concerns are assisting Menocal with from $1,000 to $2,000 a piece [*sic*], and that we could very well give $1,000, charging it to propaganda, knowing for a fact that this investment will afford us substantial return in our dealings with the City Hall and Public Works. Incidentally, he says that the head of the Public Works Department will be named by Menocal, Sr.

There is a handwritten note on the letter's margins, dated July 3, that says, "Auth $500 verbally," and is signed with the initials RIR, which would likely be R. I. Roberge, the director of Ford's foreign sales. The Havana police force regularly purchased new Fords for its fleet. But Batista was not just a Ford man. The police force also bought Oldsmobiles and Chevrolets, and Batista was friendly with General Motors' Amadeo Barletta. Batista was a friend to North American business in general and car companies in particular. The call for a contribution and Ford's willingness to authorize it represented politics as usual in Cuba, which translated into a favorable ambiance for investing dollars. It was not surprising that car companies were expanding their inventories and dealerships on the island.

Take Pontiac, for instance. In the first year after the end of the Second World War, only seventy-nine Pontiacs were delivered to Cuban dealers. By 1952, the number had jumped to 588, according to figures in *El Automóvil de Cuba*. Luis Bassart, a popular man in the business community and longtime Havana sales director for General Motors, left his post in 1952 to become sales director of a refurbished and expanded Pontiac division. Rafael Tejada's "Cuentamillas" column for *El Crisol* on July 30,

Photograph by Adalberto Roque

Photograph by Adalberto Roque

Photograph by Adalberto Roque

Photograph by Adalberto Roque

Photograph by Adalberto Roque

Photograph by Adalberto Roque

Photograph by Adalberto Roque

Photograph by Adalberto Roque

The Malecón, July 1949 (Courtesy of the photographic archives, Bohemia, Havana*)*

• • •

1952, featured an interview in which Bassart said: "In reality, the Pontiac is the car with which I can best serve my clients, both those who want a luxurious car, as well as those who want a so-called economic model. Really, it's the car of my future."

Not everyone working for Pontiac in Havana at the time felt the same way. Abel Santamaría Cuadrado, who would become a revolutionary hero, was hired to work as an accountant in the office of the Pontiac garage in Vedado toward the end of 1951. Santamaría had come to Havana from his birthplace of Encrucijada, in the central province of Las Villas. It was sugarcane country, and at the age of nine Santamaría had begun working at the North American—owned Constancia Sugar Mill as a cleaning boy. School in Encrucijada went only to the sixth grade, so in 1947 Santamaría moved to Havana in order to continue his education and attend high school. His sister, Haydée, older than Abel by twenty-one months, went too, and they shared an apartment, eventually settling at 25th and O Streets in Vedado.

A picture of Abel Santamaría taken in the Pontiac office shows him sitting at his desk behind a typewriter, a pale, earnest young man, wearing thick, black-rimmed glasses and an expression of concentration, his back straight, his tie knotted tightly. A thinker, a reader, a great admirer of Lenin, and a competent, efficient bookkeeper, he worked at the office during the day and took classes at night. The classes were usually followed by hours of study and discussion with his friends in the small Vedado apartment.

Abel Santamaría formed a close friendship with another General Motors employee, Jesús Montané Oropesa, who was an accountant at GM's Havana headquarters. Montané and Santamaría favored the same café for lunch, located about equidistant between their two offices, and they got to know each other there, according to Robert Merle's book *Moncada*. Dismayed by Batista's usurpation of power and the cancellation of elections, they began collaborating on the publication of a clandestine, mimeographed newspaper called *Son los Mismos* (They Are the Same). One day in early 1952, Montané met Fidel Castro Ruz at work, writes Merle, when Castro came in to ask for a loan to buy a slightly less used car than the one he was driving. He did not end up buying a car, but he and Montané discovered that they had similar feelings about Batista's dictatorship. It was Jesús Montané who introduced Santamaría to Fidel Castro when, on May 1, 1952, they all attended a graveside remembrance for a worker fatally shot by police, a memorial service in Colón Cemetery, Havana's vast city of the dead in Vedado. Castro is said to have struck up an immediate friendship with Santamaría, whom he later called "the most generous, loved and brave of our youth."

Castro was anxious in those days to establish a clandestine radio station in Havana, and he wanted to visit a friend of his, a doctor in Matanzas Province, just east of Havana, who was an amateur radio expert. His own brown 1950 Chevrolet was not working, as was frequently the case, and he did not have the money to get it fixed. A few days after the meeting at the cemetery, he called Jesús Montané at his General Motors office, according to Robert Merle's account. Montané then talked to Abel Santamaría, and the following Saturday the three of them drove in Santamaría's old Buick to consult the radio expert.

Shortly thereafter, Castro convinced Montané and Santamaría to change their publication's name to *El Acusador* (The Accuser), and he began writing regularly for it. He stayed for a time with Abel and Haydée in Vedado, and it was in their apartment that the idea of an assault on the Moncada army barracks in Santiago de Cuba was conceived. It would be the first coordinated guerrilla assault on Batista's troops, and it was decided to attack simultaneously the Palace of Justice and the civil hospital behind the Moncada garrison. The assault was planned in Havana during the intense spring of 1953, a time of protests, arrests, and the recruitment of new members. The assault was intended as the first step in a series of actions that would quickly lead to a rout of Batista's forces from Santiago de Cuba. Despite having only about 150 combatants, compared to the thousand or so soldiers quartered at Moncada, Castro's followers were counting on the surprise factor to help them carry the day. Abel Santamaría was designated second-in-command. He sold his Buick, the only thing of value he owned, and brought the money to Castro. Jesús Montané cashed in his General Motors pension plan, his only savings.

Others close to Castro did similarly, and some $16,000 was raised to finance the action.

The first logistical difficulty to overcome, given the vigilance of Batista's security forces, was how to move the *fidelistas* to Santiago de Cuba inconspicuously. Abel Santamaría went ahead to make arrangements and rent places for them to stay. The rest of the combatants came to the Oriente in small groups from Havana. Some twenty cars made the trip, most of them rented. Castro's own car, the 1950 Chevy, which had served him tirelessly in the year's worth of work preparing the assault, did not live to see Moncada. "I covered some 50,000 kilometers in a little car I had, a Chevrolet 50-315," he recalled in his memoir, *Fidel: My Early Years.* "I had bought it on credit; they were always taking it away from me. It burned out two days before the Moncada attack. However, at that time we rented cars. We were working in a different way, as you would expect, fitting to the conditions."

For the Moncada assault, Castro came to Santiago in a rented blue 1952 Buick. At the wheel was a former truck driver named Teodulio Mitchell. Jesús Montané came in his own car—a 1949 Pontiac, which he had bought at the beginning of 1953, according to Merle. At one point on the trip, in the dead of night on the Central Highway, with five others in the car, Montané fell asleep behind the wheel and swerved off the road but managed to bring the car back up on the asphalt. Shortly thereafter, he pulled over to take a nap, and when he woke up, the car would not start. Montané grew desperate at the prospect of arriving late in Santiago.

"They opened up the hood," writes Merle in *Moncada*, "but solely out of habit: neither Montané nor any of his companions knew anything about mechanics. 'It's the battery,' said Montané, taking off his glasses.

'No it's not,' said Ernesto González. 'It's the points.'"

After an hour's wait, they got a push from a passing truck, the Pontiac started, and they made it to Santiago on time. Thirty more *fidelistas* came by bus and sixteen by train. Since their arrivals came right in the middle of the riotous celebrations of Carnival week, they went completely unnoticed. The attack was planned for July 26, Carnival Sunday, one of the most relaxed days of the year, a lot of time spent in the shade indoors, recovering from Saturday's excesses and preparing for more.

Everyone had made it from Havana by the Saturday night, and most of them were quartered in Siboney, a coastal community about ten miles southeast of Santiago. They spent the night there in a rented farmhouse. Some of the rebels were also sprinkled throughout Santiago in cheap hotels, lying low in the midst of all the revelry. Raúl Castro, Fidel's younger brother, who has always been at his side, arrived that day with fifteen others by train from Havana. Raúl wrote down his memories of the assault while in jail in 1954, and some of that material was published in *Bohemia* in July 1963. He recalled how it was for him in the *Hotel Perla de Cuba* (Pearl of Cuba Hotel), across the avenue from the train station. He would be getting up the next morning with little sleep to drive a 1951 Chevrolet to the Palace of Justice, which he and a handful of men would briefly capture. As he lay in bed waiting, he could hear the Carnival night unfolding outside his room:

> Because the walls that separated the rooms reached up only halfway to the ceiling, you could hear, with total intensity, the sound of the drums of the small conga bands that passed by in the street. . . . At times I heard the conversation going on in the room next to mine between a Spaniard and a prostitute who were making love, a final change of tone substituting words of love for the commercial tone the Spaniard initially adopted because of the high price he was being charged.
>
> For an instant I thought that it was not right, not just that while some danced and drank, or made love . . . that we were there waiting to be called to imminent action. . . . Of the eighteen that formed our group, I think only three escaped with their lives.
>
> As the first hours of the night passed, the Santiaguero Carnival developed with a growing frenzy and intensity.

Detroit's finest played a critical role in the next day's Moncada assault. A caravan of cars came in from the farmhouse in Siboney that served as the point of departure. There were 113 rebels in some 26 cars, according

The Moncada military barracks the day after the July 26, 1953, attack
(Biblioteca Nacional José Martí, Havana)

• • •

to Hugh Thomas. One car got a flat tire and left its occupants stranded. About half the others made wrong turns and got lost in the city. Abel Santamaría led three cars to the hospital, and Raúl Castro steered the Chevy toward the Palace of Justice. The rest headed for the military barracks. Fidel Castro was driving the blue Buick, second in line behind the car carrying Jesús Montané. By the time they got inside the gate at the barracks, guards had opened fire. When Castro saw two of them taking aim at his car, he jerked the wheel, hoping to surprise them by heading straight at them. He ran up on the sidewalk, and the Buick stalled. The surprise factor was quickly lost. The rebels were overwhelmed, forced to retreat after a brief combat, dooming the initially successful assaults on the Palace of Justice and the Saturnino Hospital.

Although wounded at Moncada, Jesús Montané survived. Abel Santamaría did not. When Castro's forces retreated, Santamaría and those with him were trapped inside the hospital, which they had occupied. The former Pontiac accountant was captured and tortured within earshot of the cell where his sister, Haydée, was being held. Also captured was Haydée's boyfriend, Boris Santa Coloma.

Haydée later testified about the interrogation following her arrest on July 26, and her testimony was quoted in a *Bohemia* article by Marta Rojas in July 1964:

> They asked me who Boris was, and I said he was my boyfriend. I asked where he was, and I was told he was in the room next door, and I asked what they had done to him, and what they told me is what I did not want to tell the tribunal out of shame. . . . They told me they had taken out his testicles . . . and all the rest of the tortures they had done to him to make him talk. One of them said to me: "We haven't killed him yet; you can save his life; tell us who else was involved in this." I answered him: "If he knew how to keep silent, I am not going to betray him now, you criminals. . . ."
>
> Regarding my brother Abel, they took out one of his eyes while he was still in the hospital. I went to him and they separated us, pushing me. "It's better to know how to die in order to live forever," Abel told me. "Then I want to die," I said, hugging him, and he answered me, "Yeye, you and Melba [another of the *fidelistas*] have to live; you have to tell everything that happened here."

Those who were captured but not killed at Moncada—including Montané, Melba Hernández, Haydée Santamaría, Fidel and Raúl Castro— were sentenced to prison. At his trial, held on the grounds of the Saturnino Hospital, Castro gave what may be his most memorable speech. He declaimed, "History will absolve me," and went on to outline the six problems his movement would address: land, housing, unemployment, education, industrialization, and health.

Moncada might have served as a wake-up call to Fulgencio Batista, but it did not. Santiago de Cuba was, after all, at the other end of the country, and as pitched battles go, the turning back of the assault had been brief and decisive. Batista maintained that things were fine in Cuba, except for a few malcontents who were now in prison. He insisted that there was no better place in the world than Cuba to do business and make money. For him, at least, that was true. By the time he was forced out of office at the end of 1958, he had amassed a personal fortune, often at the expense of social spending and public works.

But Batista constantly underestimated Fidel Castro. After Castro had served only three years of a fifteen-year sentence on the Isle of Pines, Batista felt confident enough to grant an amnesty to the Moncada assailants, providing they left the country. In July 1955, Castro and his followers went off to exile in Mexico, from where they returned on the boat *Granma* in December 1956 to begin the Revolution in earnest.

The 1950s were years of political strife, guerrilla actions in the cities and the countryside, torture and assassination, violent student protests, and clashes with police. Hunger and poverty were common across the country, but lives went on apace in Cuban cities, and much of Cubans' lives were spent in cars from the United States. At the end of 1954, Mario Parjón wrote in *El Mundo*:

> Twenty years ago, the car was a luxury, a species of liberating, elegant extra that the "good people" incorporated into their aura of riches. The first announcement of a family in financial difficulties was when you heard, "They've just taken their automobile!"
>
> Families had cars to pass the evening hours, at very little speed, enjoying the night air, and the spectacle of the front doors bathed in lights, the pallid light of the moon and the rustling of the palms. . . .
>
> That villagelike calm of those days already enjoys sainted peace in the graveyard of memories. Now, the city grows, it invades rural areas with unusual speed. The workplace is ever farther from the home. . . . The car has lost its liberating quality, its condition of a luxurious extra. Now it is an exigency, an imperative, a necessity.
>
> The century has created a new type of man: he who is in love with his car, who knows brands, types, classes, lines, models, how the parts

work, how to "make the car better" and ways of keeping it clean and lovely.

By the end of 1952, for the first time, more than 100,000 cars were registered on the island, and a year later the number was over 112,000, according to Cuban Ministry of Transport figures published in *El Automóvil de Cuba*. Business was good at dealerships and garages alike. The mechanics at El Relámpago, where Juan Carlos worked, were kept busy from the time they got to work until the time they left. After a long day in the garage, he recalled, they would wash up, change their clothes, and go up the street to a bar run by a man from Galicia who laid on a mean *pierna asada*, (a roasted leg of pork, which Juan Carlos described with a note of longing in his voice), where they would eat and drink a few beers. Or they might pile into someone's car and go to Vedado's "Detroit" district.

"That's what they used to call this part of Vedado, in the 1950s, these blocks down here," he told me, as he led me on a walking tour of what used to be the heart of Cuba's auto industry. All the big players were represented in those few square blocks in Vedado at the end of Twenty-third Street, where it runs into the Malecón. The district included some of the most upscale commercial real estate in the city, housing the most important car dealership showrooms, as well as garages and parts vendors. Oldsmobile, Chevrolet, Cadillac, Pontiac, Buick, Packard, and Ford all had showrooms in the Detroit neighborhood. Juan Carlos showed me where a vast garage called El Garaje de Mi Tío (My Uncle's Garage) had been located.

We stopped for a quick draft beer *a la Cubana*, in the open-air Bar Detroit, where the barmaid filled a cut-off plastic liter bottle with beer, which she then poured into glasses as people ordered them. The beer in these places has the advantage of costing less than a nickel a glass, but those unused to it should not trust it. When consumed in quantity, it virtually guarantees a lot of sitting on a toilet the next day. Well, in Cuba it will be squatting over a toilet, as no one's has a seat: commodes come without them. We drank a glass of beer, and then another.

SAN RAFAEL

The neighborhood changed its character after the car salesmen and parts house employees knocked off and went home for the night, Juan Carlos explained. Bars, nightclubs, and houses of ill repute opened their doors and kept them that way until the wee hours. He pointed out the building across the street, kitty-corner to the Bar Detroit, that used to be a bar and whorehouse. The property was owned in those days by the Sarrá family, the same pharmaceutical family that had brought the second car ever seen in Cuba. Now, the building has been subdivided into apartments. "Before the Revolution, this area down here was really something," he said, shaking his head at how wild it seemed in retrospect.

"During the day, it was really pretty glamorous, with all the showrooms and the new cars on display. At night, it became something else. For ten dollars, you could get something to eat and drink and then go upstairs with a woman."

Havana in the 1950s was wild and wheeled. Murder and mayhem filled the pages of the city's newspapers. A lot of the murder victims turned up in Fords or Chevys or Cadillacs, where they had been shot to death. A lot more fatalities were caused by speeding vehicles. There were more than enough deaths by automobile to run an account of one on the front page every day of the year. In 1952, according to *Bohemia*, 776 people died across Cuba in 3,597 recorded traffic accidents. Gruesome crash fatalities and bullet-riddled cars were the stuff of everyday news, as they still are in many Latin American countries. Death was a staple on the front page. Each day's papers had photos of corpses under headlines like, "Gunfight Leaves Two Dead" or "Head-on Collision Kills Four." There they would be, splayed out dead on the sidewalk. An enlarged inset photo of a dead man's head on the cement would be included in the larger photo, the cadaver's vacant stare drawing the reader's gaze to the death-mask eyes, as if by paying a nickel for a newspaper he or she could know what the dead see.

These days, the only daily newspapers in Cuba are the eight-page *Granma* and *Juventud Rebelde*, where neither crime nor traffic fatalities are ever mentioned, and where no close-up photos of dead faces ever appear. By reading the current Cuban press and watching the news on Cuban television, an observer would assume the country to be crime free. And, for many years, it virtually was. Break-ins were rare, and outbursts of violent crime seemed to be restricted to celebrations like Carnival, when personal grudges were settled and vengeance wreaked. People left their doors open when they went out right up until the Special Period, beginning in 1990, when Cuba's economy collapsed following the disintegration of the Soviet Union. They did not spend a second of their lives worrying that they might be victims of a crime, nor did they know anyone who had been. Since the Special Period, however, ironworkers have been in demand: many houses in Havana and Santiago de Cuba have bars on the ground-level windows and a serious gate protecting the front door. Leave a car parked for an hour in daylight with anything of minimum value inside, a pair of sunglasses on the shelf beneath the rear window or a plastic bag with anything in it on the back seat, and a window will be smashed and the object snatched. People did not need a newspaper to tell them that break-ins were reaching epidemic levels and that they needed to take security measures at home. All they did was tune in to their neighborhood news broadcast on *Radio Bemba*. If someone on your street gets robbed, your neighborhood has a crime problem, and people do not need CNN, or even a local newspaper, to tell them.

This reappearance of crime has led to the return of one branch of the prerevolutionary auto industry. The high-rolling car dealers, and the rest of the ancillary businesspeople, from traveling parts salesmen to accessories suppliers, are all gone. They have disappeared as completely as the annual exhibitions of new U.S. models in dealer showrooms, as completely, for that matter, as dealers' showrooms or the dealers themselves. The only automotive professionals that remain are *mecánicos* to fix the parts, *chapistas* to repair car bodies, and *cuidadores* to guard the vehicles. They have proven indispensable. People still watch cars, and they are licensed by the state. The rest of the world that peopled Octavio Jordan's "With a Full Tank" columns has disappeared without a trace, but those who Jordan held in greatest disdain ("with their dirty rags in their hands"), are still on the job.

Just a couple of blocks down from Havana's central bus station is the wide Avenida Salvador Allende, which was Avenida Carlos III before being renamed, one of the city's primary avenues connecting Vedado with old Havana. It runs all the way to the Parque de la Fraternidad (Brotherhood Park) in the center of the city, a street laid out in the early nineteenth century and extended to reach Vedado when it was cleared and settled. About midway along its route is the Plaza Carlos III shopping—a "shopping" being what Cubans call any store in which goods are paid for with dollars—which is actually a gathering of dollar shops under one roof, a Havana version of a mall. It has a food court, offering hamburgers and pizzas, a shoe store, a clothing store, and an auto parts store, where everything from tires to spark plugs is on sale. A chaotic flood of people swirls around the front doors to the shopping, families entering with children in tow, or people leaving with big boxes in their arms, or holding a half-dozen plastic bags. Their cars, many of them *cacharros*, overflow the available parking in front of the shopping and end up across the broad avenue, filling the parking spaces by the opposite curb.

Those cars are Luis's responsibility. Luis is a thin, seventy-eight-year-old retired long-haul truck driver who works as a *cuidador* across the avenue from the Carlos III shopping. He sits on a rickety folding chair, in a narrow patch of shade, up on the curb under a skinny acacia, and he watches parked cars. He charges a peso to watch a car, and he pays thirty pesos a day to the state, via a collector. This is ten pesos less than the forty a day that is collected from the *cuidadores* on the other side of Avenida Salvador Allende, in the preferred parking spaces right in front of the shopping. On a good day, Luis makes fifty or sixty pesos, so after he has paid his day's tax, he might go home with a dollar. He works 10:00 A.M. to 6:00 P.M. He shrugs his shoulders: "Twenty pesos is twenty pesos," he tells me.

He has stopped men breaking windows of cars to steal cassette players three times in the six years he has been a *cuidador*. In broad daylight. Once he beat a guy with a stick. "If people paid me to watch their car and I had done nothing, they could have put a *denuncia* against me."

He is leaning back with one shoe off, scratching his socked foot with a veined, liver-spotted hand. He is missing most of his hair and quite a few teeth, but he has some stringy muscles left, and I would not have wanted him beating on me with a stick. Two young women walk by in tight, shiny Lycra stretch pants. One pair is hot pink, the other an electric lime green. The girls cannot be even twenty years old, but they have the Cuban butt thing down pat. Paeans have been written to the backsides of Cuban women, and it is particularly difficult to ignore a rounded *culo* if it is wrapped for public presentation in skin-tight, brightly colored, shiny material.

"Look at that," Luis marvels, eyes shining, looking up at me. "Do you see anything like that where you live?"

chapter four

1957 CHEVYS

Each of the three main squares in Santiago de Cuba has a different feel. The knot of debating men around the benches and the goats pulling carts full of children are emblematic of the Plaza de Marte. This is a big, wide space with lots of benches and shade trees. It is a family park, where all the social niceties apply. People meet here and take great pleasure in greeting each other: the men shake hands all around, slapping palms effusively, and the women's eyes light up at seeing each other, even if it was only yesterday they last met. People bring great drama to everyday life, to knowing and being known, being accepted into a circle of friends. An elaborate sense of public courtesy also is apparent. When a Cuban moves between two people or across another person's line of sight, or when he gets up and leaves a group, he asks permission to do so—*con permiso*—and kids are taught to do this at an early age. In fact, good manners seem to be the rule here for young and old.

As Aguilera Street descends from the Plaza de Marte west toward the sea, it passes the other two squares, first running by the narrow two-block-long Plaza Dolores, located at the bottom of a long hill in front of the Church of Nuestra Señora de Los Dolores, Our Lady of Suffering. The plaza is shaded and comfortable, although its narrowness, squeezed in between a little strip of dollar restaurants on one side and a bank and a police precinct on the other, gives it a certain exposed feeling. There is lots of coming and going. People cross the park as a shortcut, and traffic passes not far from the backs of the benches. Horns honk and engines race as the vehicles rev up to climb the hill. Diesel fumes hang in the air. Among the city's squares, the Plaza Dolores is not the most relaxing or pleasing to the eye. But ¡wow!, at midnight on a Friday or Saturday, it is full of people drinking, gay men camping up and down the park's length, and lesbians sitting on the benches with their hands on each other's knees. Disco music is piped via loudspeakers from one of the restaurants, and everyone seems to have a bottle of snakebite sticking out of a pocket or waistband.

Cops stand at various points around the plaza's perimeter just looking on, unconcerned. Unless a fight breaks out, the police are not going to act. If a fight does break out, a police presence will be welcome, as far as I'm concerned. I have seen men drink and fight in Cuba, particularly during Carnival and other public celebrations, and when a fight breaks out, the only thing going on is to hurt someone else as badly as possible with fists or stones or machetes, whatever is to hand. These are mean, do-damage fights, and it is the kind of brush-fire violence that rapidly burns out of control, turning a reveling crowd into a brawling mob. Innocent bystanders are advised to take cover quickly, or they stand a chance of being hurt as well.

This is not likely to happen, however, on an average Saturday night in the Plaza Dolores. The police will not have much to do as the night wears on, and the park fills with homosexuals. This, in itself, is an astonishing scene for anyone who has read Reinaldo Arenas's *Before Night Falls*, or anything else about the persecution of gay Cubans during the first quarter-century of the Revolution. From the mid-1960s until the early 1980s, all "ideological divergence," which included homosexuality, resulted in a person's being virtually buried alive. Having no work was the best thing that could happen; the worst was being sent to rehabilitation camps in the country, as happened to the singer Pablo Milanés or the writer Virgilio Piñera.

The change came when Fidel Castro said for the first time publicly, in an interview published in 1992 by the Nicaraguan writer Tomás Borge, that there was no official policy against homosexuals in Cuba. "I, myself, don't have any phobia against homosexuals. I've never felt that phobia and I've never promoted or supported policies against homosexuals,'' he said in the interview. "I am absolutely opposed to any form of repression, contempt, scorn, or discrimination with regard to homosexuals.''

Even though nobody with a memory that stretched back more than a decade believed Castro's disclaimers, it was clear that many years of pressure from human rights groups around the world had finally brought results. From the moment Borge's book, *Un Grano de Maíz* (A Kernel of Corn) was published, things got much easier. Homosexuality was no longer considered a crime. That much was evident from just sitting in the Plaza Dolores after midnight.

The third square, three blocks further down Aguilera Street toward the sea, is the most famous of Santiago's plazas, the Parque Céspedes. With the Cathedral on one side and City Hall on the other, this has always been the heart and soul of the city. It was called the Plaza de Armas for centuries. The name change to Céspedes Park honored Santiago's first revolutionary son, Carlos Manuel de Céspedes, who issued Cuba's original freedom proclamation in 1868, sparking an unsuccessful war for independence from Spain. On the third side of the park is the Hotel Casa Grande, where well-to-do tourists sit in shaded comfort on the hotel's elevated terrace and look down on the doings below.

The park makes a great stage, with a cast of loungers and loafers and townsfolk and gringos crossing it. Almost every tourist in town will pass through it during the course of a day moving around Santiago. Where there are tourists, there are *jineteros* and *jineteras*, male and female "jockeys,'' as the young men and women who hustle foreigners or work in the sex tourism industry are called. Anyone betraying the slightest sign of being a foreigner, a "Pepe,'' as tourists are tagged in Santiago by the *jineteros* and *jineteras*, is sure to be approached. If a *jinetera* harbors some doubt about a person's origins, a simple question will suffice. A favorite is *Compañero—la hora?* (What time is it, comrade?), a question that anyone wearing a watch, be he Cuban or otherwise, can expect to be asked at least once a day regardless of neighborhood, because a lot of people do not own watches and depend for the time on those who do. However, in the locales known to be frequented by foreigners carrying money, a request for the time is often preliminary to a question about a person's origins. The experienced jockey can guess just by hearing the other tell the time of day where he or she is from, and a quick *jinetera* or *jinetero* responds, "English?" or "Español?" or "Français?"

From that point in the exchange, anything can happen, depending on what a Pepe's needs and wants are. Budgetary problems are rare. Anyone who can afford to get to Cuba is traveling with dollars, and it does not take many dollars to buy almost anything—from cigars to company. For balding, paunchy, florid-faced white men whose tastes run to sixteen-, seventeen-, or eighteen-year-old dark-skinned girls in short skirts and deep-cut tank tops, a meal, a drink, and maybe ten dollars will buy what they are after for a night; the young women will even hold their hands and laugh at their jokes. Muscular, attentive, twenty-one-year-old Afro-Cuban men will proudly shepherd unattractive, middle-aged European women around Santiago, filling their days, and especially their nights, with the romance they do not enjoy at home. These sorts of couples are a standard sight in the Parque Céspedes.

In addition to the Casa Grande Hotel, the plaza's perimeter features other tourist draws, including a shopping, a place to buy film, a bookstore, and a pair of car rental agencies. At the top of Céspedes Park, for foreigners with dollars, are a half-dozen of Detroit's dream cars available as taxis. These are not taxis that locals take—those are boxy little Ladas or Volgas. Unlike in Havana, where North American makes and models beat the streets for pesos, carrying Habaneros along their established routes, in Santiago de Cuba the old cars are at the pleasure of tourists. *Cacharros* are not among this fleet of cabs: these cars are cared for and polished. The fare is paid in dollars, so the drivers are not too worried if they have to spend a lot of time hanging around the taxi stand across from Céspedes Park. They do not need many fares and tips to make for a decent day. One will do it. The taxis, with their sharp lines and bright colors, provide a delightful visual backdrop for the loungers on the hotel's terrace. Chevrolets are usually among them. Frank Cabrera's 1953 Chevy can often be seen waiting here, along with a 1959 Chevrolet finned like a jet fighter and a red-upholstered 1957 Chevy Bel Air, which may have been Santiago de Cuba's favorite model of all, according to car aficionado Leonardo Rodríguez, a lifelong Santiaguero.

"We have always loved Chevrolets and none more than the 1956 and 1957 models," he tells me. "Those were really special. I remember, when I was growing up we had some neighbors who had a lot of money and their son got a new '57 Chevy. It was green. Man, it was something to see it pass by. Beautiful, really beautiful.

"The cars of 1955, '56, and '57 were terrific cars, the best. Then in 1958 they began to get worse, to go definitely downhill. For instance, I know from my own experience that in 1958 Chevy changed the stabilizer bar in such a way that the head would come off after being driven, jounced, and bounced for a while. It didn't take long for word to get around, and by the end of 1958, that year's models were selling for less than a 1957, or even a '56.''

I met Rodríguez at the old car rally in Santiago, and he invited me to come see him at his house in the center of the city. Like so many others built in the nineteenth century, it does not seem promising at first; from the outside the entrance is a thick, scarred and scraped, unattractive wooden door set into a rough-plastered wall. Through the doorway, however, is an ample and comfortable living space, airy with fifteen-foot ceilings and a wide, shadowy open-air patio, pleasant and comfortable.

White-haired, tanned, and fit at fifty-three, Rodríguez has worked at a number of jobs, including a long stretch at the city historian's office. He welcomes me to his house wearing jeans and a white T-shirt, with a string of white beads around his neck. His smiling and graceful wife, who appears to be considerably younger than he and is, he tells me, his second, serves coffee and then disappears. He opens the rum I have brought and pours a little onto the floor for the household saints, something that believers and nonbelievers alike do. We are sitting in his living room, identical to the living room of many Cubans, with an abundance of decorative novelties, little porcelain figurines and knickknacks covering every flat surface. It is midafternoon and terrifically hot; sitting there, sipping rum I am sweating like an open faucet. Mopping our faces, we talk rather formally for a while. As the amber level in the bottle of dark rum descends, we grow less formal, laugh a little louder and a little longer. Eventually, we move out to the breezy patio and its metal rocking chairs, and the sweat begins to dry on my brow.

"The American cars have a *técnica noble*," he tells me. "When I got out of the military, my father—who wanted me to manage our land, our *finca*—gave me a Willys, a horse, and a saddle. I sold the horse and saddle, and kept the Willys. That was my first car. I bet I've had twenty since then. I've bought and sold them for years."

His latest, which he has had for three years, is a black 1953 Cadillac Coupe de Ville, in impeccable condition, in a garage next to his house. "The car had always been in a friend of mine's family since it was bought from the dealer. I always liked that car. He took great care of it, he always had it under a roof and just took it out to go to the beach, things like that. I always told him if he wanted to sell it, I'd buy it, and one day he showed up here and said he had come to sell me the Cadillac.

"I had a car, and this one uses a lot of gas, and I put him off. Then he came back in a couple of weeks and said there were some other people who wanted to buy the car, but he wanted to sell it to me. He just about obliged me to buy it, so I sold my other car and borrowed some money and bought it. And, I'm glad I did. I've gotten used to it and just don't feel comfortable in any other car. You sit up so high in that Cadillac and it's so powerful you just feel like you're the master of the road. The same as in those '56 and '57 Chevrolets. As much as I like this Cadillac, I might still rather have one of those, if I found one that was available and in really nice shape. They have something really special."

He has a grown daughter who lives in Havana and a four-year-old son by his second wife whom he shamelessly indulges. The boy comes over and opens the sugar bowl on the coffee table where the bottle of rum and our glasses rest between us. He starts dipping handfuls of sugar to his mouth. Leonardo gets up and fetches a coffee cup, scoops a load of sugar into it, and gives it to the boy. "So your mother won't see," he says.

Roberto Pérez, director of Santiago de Cuba's automotive museum, concurs with Leonardo Rodríguez that Santiago was a Chevy city. Different Cuban cities had different preferences in cars, he says, and nobody is quite sure why. Maybe it had to do with which dealers did the best job where, or maybe with climate, or with terrain, but the various cities of Cuba each had their favorite models. In Camagüey, for instance, there were, and are, more Mercurys and Oldsmobiles than other brands, and in Holguín there's a preponderance of Dodges. Ciego de Ávila was a Ford town, and in Santiago de Cuba, the car of choice between 1954 and 1958 was a Chevrolet.

"In the first place, this is a hilly city, and the Chevrolet of those years was a strong vehicle," says Pérez. "It was well-designed for working, stronger than others in its class. What this means, in turn, is that now you have a lot of mechanics in Santiago who do particularly good work on Chevrolets. There's a guy here who has built wooden molds to make front windshields for 1956 and 1957 Chevrolets. He did it because there were so many here. People have concentrated on recycling these cars because there are more of them."

In Havana, too, Chevrolets dominated sales. In 1956, a record 2,412 new Chevrolets were sold in Havana Province, for a 27 percent share of the year's new car sales, according to registration numbers kept by the Fonda Especial de Obras Publicas; Ford occupied second place, with a 15 percent share, selling 1,245 new cars. A total of 11,379 new American cars were sold on the island that year, and about $25 million was estimated to have been spent on cars, according to the magazine *Carteles*.

The new-model fever and publicity blitz started well before the new year arrived. In Cuba, as in the United States, the coming year's models were previewed early and with much fanfare. Older Cubans invariably remember that the new models were tried out on Cuban sensibilities before being exhibited in the States. An article entitled "El Motorambar 1957" in the December 1956 issue of *El Automóvil de Cuba* described the excitement attendant on the unveiling of 1957's models. December 1956 was the same month in which Fidel Castro—along with his brother Raúl, Che Guevara, Camilo Cienfuegos, and seventy-eight

*The number of cars in Havana grew rapidly after the Second World War,
and thousands of them headed to the Malecón for an air show by the
U.S. Air Force in February 1954, causing an immense traffic jam.
(Courtesy of the photographic archives,* Bohemia, Havana)

• • •

others—clandestinely returned to Cuba from Mexico on the boat *Granma*. Once ashore in Cuba, the *fidelistas* soon fell afoul of Batista's troops, who killed twenty-four of them and scattered the rest into the Sierra Maestra in the Oriente. The press quoted government sources saying that Castro was among the fallen. At the other end of the island, in Havana, it was taken for granted that Castro's revolution had been nipped in the bud. Once again, *batistianos* had made the mistake of counting Castro out prematurely.

What caused more excitement in the capital than the arrival of the *Granma* was the arrival of the 1957 models from Detroit. Ambar Motors had to rent Tropical Stadium to hold the people who turned up to have a look at the new models, according to the article in *El Automóvil de Cuba*. "As in past years, last October 28, the Motorambar 1957 was held with more than 40,000 people present for the unveiling of the new 1957 models of Chevrolet and Opel. Once again, Ambar Motors Corporation was able to bring together a multitude that established a new record for this type of event. A magnificent artistic show was offered, and also the National Police motorcyclists put on a magnificent demonstration of skill. After the new models were presented, a drawing for two magnificent Chevrolets was held."

The article was accompanied by photos, one of which showed Amadeo Barletta giving an after-dinner speech to the annual convention of Ambar agents from all across Cuba, which always coincided with Motorambar so that the agents could leave their orders for the number of new models they thought they could sell in their hometowns and could perhaps even drive one back themselves (Ambar employees were expected to drive General Motors cars). In one photo, Barletta is standing behind a microphone with his hands in his pockets. He is a man of medium height, with slumped shoulders and a paunch, clean-shaven, with an aquiline nose and thinning silver hair, which is brushed down and slicked back. Seated next to him on the podium is Roy Larcher, GM's director of international sales at Michigan headquarters, leaner and taller than Barletta, smoking a cigarette in a short holder.

After each year's Motorambar, anyone passing by the vast showroom with its huge plate glass windows at the end of Twenty-third Street, across from the Malecón, could look in at the brightly lit platform on which the latest model would be slowly revolving. The 1957 Bel Air must have looked good up there under the lights. It was the year of the fin, with both Chevrolet and Ford abandoning any idea of rounded curves. Everything was sharp edges, reminiscent of sharks' tails or airplane wings. Slicing, aggressive, male lines defined the form of the cars. The idea seemed to appeal to Cuban buyers, because overall new American car sales rose in 1957 to 14,493, with 2,632 new Chevys and 1,667 new Fords being sold in Havana, according to figures published in the June 1958 *El Automóvil de Cuba*.

In the city of Santiago de Cuba and the rest of its province, 312 Chevrolets were sold, compared to 281 Fords in 1957, but Chevy did not outsell Ford all over the island. In Matanzas 110 Fords were sold, compared to 68 Chevrolets; and in Pinar del Río 129 Fords were bought, compared to 74 Chevrolets. Ford still had a reputation as the best working car, suitable for a taxi, inexpensive and reliable. It was the model of choice for those who needed a car for practical purposes and were uninterested in acquiring a status symbol. In a February 1950 interview with Octavio Jordan in *El Mundo*, Paco Andrés Rodríguez explained why, after thirty years spent working as a taxi driver in Havana, he preferred to drive a Ford: "It's economical and its parts are cheap and you can find them just about anywhere, even down at the corner store. This is important these days, when cars are very expensive. In the old days, with a thousand dollars and a little more, you could buy one of the really good cars and have something left over to put some extras on it."

Among them, Detroit's big three automakers held almost four-fifths of the 1957 new car market in Cuba—General Motors with 37.8 percent, Ford with 23.2, and Chrysler with 17.4—according to government figures given in *El Automóvil de Cuba*. That year the total number of cars and trucks on the island surpassed 200,000 for the first time, and more than 167,000 of the cars had been made in the United States.

Only about 10 percent of new cars sold in 1957 were European, but this, in itself, was a big jump over pre–World War II figures. After the

*Even as cars completely dominated Havana's roadways, older forms of transport
sometimes persisted: a living diorama of the history of Cuban transport crossing
streetcar tracks on Havana's Avenida del Puerto in June 1953.
(Courtesy of the photographic archives,* Bohemia, *Havana)*

• • •

war, the market for the more economical European cars grew slowly but
steadily around the world, and Cuba was no exception. As early as March
1951, Octavio Jordan had written in his "With A Full Tank" column,
"In Cuba, we are seeing a growing number of small-sized cars on the
road, and today it's happening not just in the capital but all over the

island. . . . Everything seems to point to English Ford's Prefect model as being the most responsible for this growth." The occasional Prefect can still be spotted cruising on Havana's streets. A small, trim model, not unlike the Soviet Lada in size and shape, it rapidly gained in popularity. In 1954, 93 of them were sold on the island, and by 1957, that had jumped to 522, according to the National Vehicle Census. Behind the Prefect, in this category, was the Volkswagen, which sold 48 in 1954 and 444 in 1957.

The Detroit-made cars experiencing the largest jumps in sales were not the most luxurious but those boasting utility and a lower price, those that appealed to the middle class. In a 1957 piece for the magazine *Carteles* called "Economical, Lilliputian Autos and Gigantic Dream Cars," Jorgé Vega wrote:

> The distance between models of North American cars that cost a lot and those that cost a little has been continually diminishing, at the same rate as the latter have been augmenting luxury, comfort and power. Currently, the traditional "small" North American cars are not so small as before. The body is bigger. Power has been fortified more and more, to the point that the more common models have as much power as the more elegant models of years past, luxury cars like Cadillac, Oldsmobile, Lincoln, Chrysler, and Packard.
>
> The increase in the size, the horsepower, and the compression ratio has been accompanied by more elegance of line and in what is built-in for the greater comfort of driver and passenger. . . . The average person can find practically no difference between a car that costs $10,000 and another that costs only $3,000.

It was the lower-priced models—the Chevrolets and the Fords and the Dodges, along with the occasional Buick or Oldsmobile or Pontiac—that carried the Cuban Revolution from its beginnings. Just as they carried Fidel and Raúl Castro and Jesús Montané and Abel Santamaría to Moncada on July 26, 1953, so in the mid-1950s they moved the members of the 26 July Movement through the streets of Havana and Santiago de Cuba. The cars brought them to and from actions against Batista's government, carried arms and fugitives. Much of the armed opposition was made up of students and professors, and these people were not likely to be driving Cadillacs or Lincolns.

A news photo taken on March 13, 1957, and published in *Bohemia* showed an empty 1956 Ford Fairlane in front of the entrance to the university, the door on the driver's side hanging open. Two bullet holes have shattered the wraparound windshield in front of the steering wheel. The body of twenty-four-year-old José Antonio Echevarría lay crumpled on the ground, not far away.

The photo showed part of the aftermath of a failed assault on the Presidential Palace by a group called the Directorio Revolucionario. The group was codirected by Echevarría, a charismatic student leader, and none other than fifty-two-year-old Menelao Mora, former congressman and president of the COA, the bus cooperative. The assault had comprised a frontal attack on the palace. A group of some hundred men planned to rush the building in two waves, outgun the presidential guard, and kill Batista. At the same time, *Radio Reloj*, or Clock Radio—the Cuban broadcasting institution that breaks into the news every minute to give the time—would be occupied. The thinking was that when news went out over the radio that Batista was dead and the palace occupied, the regime, decapitated, would collapse. Most of the participants were students. One of them, Faure Chaumón, wrote that between Echevarría and Mora there seemed to exist a great depth of understanding. "Those two men, so different in age, were very much alike in their form of speaking, clear and unequivocal."

Although Fidel Castro, in the mountains, did not lend his support to the plan, it commenced on schedule, as two waves of fifty rebels apiece started out for the palace. There were three vehicles in the initial assault group: a Buick sedan carrying four men, a Ford occupied by another four men, and a paneled delivery truck with forty-two armed rebels crammed inside. The truck was a Dodge Fargo, a solid, covered workhorse of a model, which also saw action resupplying Castro's lines in the Sierra Maestra. This one had last been used by a company called Fast Delivery, S.A., which is what was painted in big black-and-white letters

Red Cross workers pinned down behind their ambulance by fighting at the Presidential Palace, March 13, 1957. (Biblioteca Nacional José Martí, Havana)

• • •

on a red background on the truck's sides. The rebels left the signage on the truck after they bought it. A sympathetic garage owner went over it, tuned it up, and readied it for the run to the palace; but despite his care, it blew a tire under the weight of so many assailants. The Fargo had two back wheels on each side and was able to arrive at the palace with one of the back tires on a rim. A fierce gunfight broke out when the truck pulled up and its back doors were opened. The fight raged for the whole afternoon in the center of old Havana. Nine rebels, led by Menelao Mora, reached the second floor of the palace before being repulsed by heavy fire. Mora died on the palace's marble staircase. The second wave of attackers never arrived, as they were unable to get close to the palace once the pitched battle was under way. Thirty-five rebels and five members of the palace guard died, along with a thirty-eight-year-old North American tourist named Peter Korenda, who was killed by a stray bullet as he watched the fighting from his hotel room window.

Meanwhile, Echevarría and a colleague went to the radio station, which they took over at gunpoint, and broadcast a message saying the palace had fallen and Batista had been executed. The police were waiting for them when they came out, but they managed to reach the car and drive to the university. At the gates to the campus, Echevarría jumped out of the Ford and was cut down. The present-day whereabouts of the car are unknown, but the Fast Delivery, S.A., truck, the Dodge Fargo that delivered Menelao Mora to his death at the palace, stands in practically the same place today as it did on that March day in 1957. The Presidential Palace now serves as the Museum of the Revolution, and there, still pockmarked with over a score of unmended bullet holes, the truck takes its place in the museum's pantheon of revolutionary tanks, planes, and boats.

The Fast Delivery Fargo may be living out an honorable old age in a museum, but many of its contemporaries have not been so lucky. They survive because they work, and neither retirement nor lighter labor is likely to be in their immediate future. Nobody knows how many of Detroit's models are still working daily in Havana—certainly there are enough that while it never ceases to be a pleasure to spot them beating through the oven-hot streets or parked along the curb, it does cease to be a surprise. Daily work for many Habaneros means finding dollars, and numerous cars are employed in a wide variety of means to that end.

First are the standard ways to work a car, like renting it out as a *rutero*. Even this is frequently not so straightforward, as described in a scene from Pedro Juan Gutiérrez's novel, *Dirty Havana Trilogy*:

A hick from Guantánamo who lives in the building across the street rents out his car, and he has money. The car is a '54 Plymouth, a big, red beast with huge mudguards, extrawide. It's a monster, all red metal and little windows. In my opinion, it has a sinister look, but the tourists call it a "classic car" and they like to rent it and drive around Old Havana or pick up whores in it and take them to the beach. As I was admiring the condition of the old heap, he said, "Man, this car is a gold mine; it's a porn gold mine."

"What do you mean a porn gold mine? Are you crazy?"

"You have no idea, man. Lots of foreigners like to pose with whores inside there or on the roof or on the hood. . . . And all that costs extra! You don't know how much money I make out of this piece of junk."

Cars can be used to generate dollars in as many ways as people can imagine, and those prove to be numerous, indeed. I see it again when my allergy to bureaucracy causes me to wait until a Wednesday, the day before my visa expires, to go to the Ministry of the Interior and renew it. To overstay one's visa by even a day in Cuba is something that a traveler is strongly advised not to do. The visa renewal office is in a lovely, huge old stone house in the Miramar neighborhood. I arrive at five minutes before twelve to find that the office closes at noon on Wednesdays, and I will have to come back the next day, my last opportunity. "Don't forget to bring the $25.00 fee," the guard, a tall, young, dark-skinned fellow, stiff in his pressed military green ministry uniform, tells me as I pass through the gate.

The next morning, I wait in line an hour and a half, finally to be seen by a young, friendly Cuban woman, also in a pressed green uniform, who informs me that she cannot take the $25.00 I have brought because she does not take cash; she takes only government stamps, and the nearest place for me to buy government stamps is a bank some forty blocks away. I storm out, furious, to find a cab, stopping at the gate to berate the guard a bit for not having told me to bring stamps. "You could have saved me a trip," I say on my way out the gate. "I hope I won't have to wait in line on my way back in."

He steps up close to me, and I have a moment's chill in my gut thinking I may have spoken too harshly, crossed some boundary. I try hard to avoid conflict with Cubans in uniforms. "See that guy standing under the *flamboyán* at the end of the street?" he asks me in a casual, low voice. His eyes flick to the right.

I look. "Guy in the green T-shirt?"

"That's him. He'll sell you the stamps," and he turns away from me to close our conversation.

I go up the street. Parked under the *flamboyán* with its flaming blossoms, beside the man in the green T-shirt, is a black-and-white 1957 Chevrolet Bel Air, the paint looking as if it had been applied in the not-too-distant past. I approach the man, who is white, nondescript, in his mid-thirties. "Look," I say, stepping up beside him, "I need some stamps."

He glances up and down the block. No one. "Okay, get in the car."

I walk to the passenger's side. The door is a heavy, clunky, familiar weight at the end of my arm as I swing it open. Like many North Americans my age, I went through some formative experiences in 1957 Chevys. I get in. He walks to the front of the car and lifts up the hood. I watch from the front seat, under the upraised hood, as he unscrews the top of the air filter and takes a tiny metal box out of it, puts the hood down gently, and comes around to sit behind the steering wheel. When he is settled he asks how many I need. He sells me $25.00 worth of government stamps for $25.00 and tells me, "If they ask for the receipt from the bank, tell them you bought the stamps in a *consultorio jurídico*, because they don't give receipts."

I go back down the block to the visa office, repeating *consultorio jurídico* under my breath so I will remember it, but it is not necessary. The attractive young woman in the olive green uniform does not ask how I got to the bank and back so fast; she simply affixes the stamps to my documents and renews my visa.

I tell this story to someone I know, a university professor who chose, in 1961, to stay and work for the Revolution while many of his family fled to prosperity in Florida, and who says he has never regretted it. Still, in the privacy of his home he laments the cult of the personality built around Fidel Castro and the authoritarian restrictions on freedom of movement and freedom of access to information. When I recount the tale of the black-market stamps, I tell it to him as a humorous incident, laughing. Out of courtesy, he returns me a tight-lipped smile, but it is evident that the story pains him, especially coming from the lips of a non-Cuban. It particularly smarts that it should be the dollar that has created once again a vast income differential in his country. The real market in Cuba is the black market. There is practically nothing un-available if the price is paid in dollars. After almost forty years of being absent, the greenback is once again trading on the street, undermining Cuban society. In the wake of the Special Period, with the dollar legal-ized, a waiter or car parker at a hotel can make in dollar tips ten times the monthly salary of a doctor, dentist, lawyer, university professor, or any other worker being paid in pesos.

"For me," says the professor, "to have lived through what we've lived through, with both its sacrifices and triumphs, and then see sixteen- and seventeen-year-old girls selling themselves for dollars, well, it's some-thing I never thought I'd see again. The younger generation knows only the Revolution and what they see on television of the rest of the world: they don't have any idea how it was here before 1959, and they don't care. They didn't live it. They just want Walkmans."

Since it became legal in 1993 to use dollars in certain stores and busi-nesses, and in 1996 for anyone to have and spend them, just about every-one has come up with a way to obtain some, particularly if his regular job pays in Cuban pesos. Most wages paid in pesos are worth between $15.00 and $30.00 a month, depending on salary level, and everything except the most basic staples is now for sale only in dollars. Without dol-lars, life is lived close to the bone. Very close. With a few pesos and a ration book, a person can get six kilos of rice a month, as well as some beans, eggs, bananas, okra, potatoes, cucumbers, and cooking oil, plus a handful of coffee. Not enough of each item to last a month, perhaps, but close. So, everyone has a *búsqueda*, an extra hustle, a way to come up with greenbacks. People who have family in the States are lucky, and the total number of dollars estimated to flow south annually to Cuba reached 1 billion in 2002, according to an article by Christopher Marquis in the *New York Times*. After all, the $50.00 that a Cuban American family of four in the States would spend going out to see a movie could put a month's worth of decent food on the table for their relatives in Cuba. People without someone to send them money from *el norte* have to find some way to participate in Cuba's dollar economy. Dollars are necessary in order to have anything more than the most day-to-day items, which are themselves precarious within the confines of the national currency. For Cubans dependent on the peso, some days there is not enough of one thing, some days not enough of another. People queue up for hours to buy a fish or a piece of meat when it is for sale in pesos.

To satisfy one's hunger on the street-food sold for pesos in cities like Santiago de Cuba is no easier. Occasionally, little roast pork sandwiches, with thin slices of cucumber on top, are sold for two pesos (about ten cents) from downtown pushcarts, and for one peso a person can buy a sandwich made of mayonnaise on bread. A slice of "peso pizza," dough with a thin veneer of catsup and plastic-tasting cheese, is usually available. In the mornings, skinny men walk through the neighborhood streets, ragged jute sacks full of ripe avocadoes over their shoulders, calling out *aguacates maduros*, and people come out to part with pesos for the day's ration of ripe avocados, or zucchinis, or mangos.

Every other Saturday, there's a "fair" on Santiago's Avenida Garzon, closing it to vehicular traffic. The *guajiros*, the country people, come into Santiago and sell whatever fruit, vegetables, and poultry are left over after their state-mandated production quotas have been filled. Prices are in pesos. A live hen might cost 20 pesos, about one dollar. It seems cheap until you remember it is more than a day's wage. Numerous people are buying two or three at a time, and they will resell a couple of them later in their neighborhoods, making a peso profit on each, maybe. A motorcycle rickshaw goes by with a seat rigged for two people behind the driver. Two thin, middle-aged men wearing beat baseball caps are the passengers. At their feet is a huge hog, so corpulent it hangs down off both sides, snout almost brushing the pavement on one, foot-long tail on the other. A pair of uniformed policemen stand chatting under the awning of a store, each holding a hen by its feet, chicken heads hanging down, eyes blinking resignedly.

"It's the economy that needs fixing in Cuba," says an older woman, the mother of a doctor I know in Santiago de Cuba whom I'll call Olga. We are sitting around Olga's kitchen table, sipping good black-market coffee, and her mother is explaining the hardships involved in simply keeping a household functioning in light of the uncertainties about what basic staples will be available on a given day, where they can be bought, and how many people will line up to buy them. Olga's coffee is always a treat—not a hint of the chicory frequently mixed with coffee to make it go farther. In this house, they know someone who knows someone who works in the state-owned coffee plantations up in the Sierra Maestra, someone who comes down to the city occasionally and shows up at the door with beans for sale at a reasonable price in dollars.

Olga's mother is in her late fifties. She has high blood pressure. Many Cubans do, according to Olga, who says that as many as sixty people turn up over the course of a weekend at each neighborhood clinic scattered around Santiago de Cuba to have their blood pressures checked. Her mother holds the economy to blame. "The fact that you don't know from one day to the next what there will be to buy, or whether you'll have money to buy it. It's no wonder so many Cubans suffer from high blood pressure. Who wouldn't if they had to live every day like that? Too much time spent worrying about not having enough, and then having to stand in line for what little there is.

"Nobody wants to go back to the days when not everyone could go to school and there wasn't any health care for poor people. But, the economy makes it too hard to get through each day. If that could just be fixed, it would be paradise here. Don't get me wrong. Things are improving. It's a lot better now than during the Special Period."

When she says "special period," there is the same ring of distaste and disbelief in her voice, a persistent undertone of shock, that is almost always present when people talk about those years. There was no money and nothing to buy even if there had been a little money. People took rags and boiled them and put them in a mass and flattened them and ate them. Banana peels were mashed and pounded into fake beefsteak. Soap was made from maguey ashes.

Olga, a short, energetic woman of thirty-five, is the mother of two girls. She puts in long hours at work, and she keeps her household running when she's not seeing patients. The great strides Cuba has made in universal health care have not been achieved without a lot of hard work on the part of doctors. Infant mortality rates are lower than in the States, organ transplants are common and free, and life expectancy is as long as it is in North America. More than 67,000 doctors practice in Cuba. Medicine is a popular and demanding profession, and a doctor's work is always subject to rigorous examination. Family medicine is the most stressful, says Olga. If an infant or child under your care dies, your smallest decision in the care of that patient is reviewed and scrutinized. "I used to lie awake worrying much more about the sick children who were my patients than about my own children when they were sick."

The Special Period came just when Olga was busiest trying to balance her domestic and professional life. "I had two little girls, one just a baby and no soap to wash her diapers," she tells me. "My grandmother was still alive then, and wouldn't let me go through her things, even though we were selling everything. One day I was desperate for something to sell and went through her wardrobe when she was out of the room and found a box of soap bars she had saved from before the Revolution. She had bought them and put them aside, and I had enough to wash diapers with for a long time. That was a great day."

People came from Havana with money or food, buying heirlooms and antiques dirt cheap. Olga sold her great-grandfather's pocket watch "covered with gems" for $200. All of her family's old jewelry and furniture went. Her mother shakes her head sadly, listening to Olga tell it.

Everything went. Anything of value. And, sometimes, even when there was money there was nothing to buy. What Cuba did not produce was simply not available, and Cuba did not produce enough to go around.

"Everyone was thin like this," Olga says, holding up her little finger. "I went on a house call once, and they were getting ready to have lunch. Six people around the table with one egg between them.

"Everyone had lice and scabies. The Germans sent over some medicine, but people used it for soap. My husband would take ragged old clothes out to the country to trade for food. In the countryside they had some vegetables, but no clothes, and in the city it was the reverse.

"Things are better now, but there's a new, worrisome kind of thing you're beginning to see, and that's young people with fast, new cars or cell phones. You see a Cuban . . . renting a cell phone, that person is doing something illegal to be able to afford that. Or driving a fancy car. That person is not playing by the rules, because you can't live your life legally and have enough money to rent a cell phone or get a new car. Cubans have always liked to look sharp, wear nice clothes, drive nice cars. Some people will still do anything for that."

For people who like being noticed for their clothes or their cars, perhaps no automobiles ever made were as satisfying as those made in 1957. Detroit's finned marvels that year were the most *llamativo*, most attention-getting, ever to roll off the assembly line. They were the extreme of Harley Earl's expansive aerodynamic style. In 1958, the first compact cars would appear on the streets, and lines would begin to be tucked and tapered, but in 1957 it was all flaring edges and lots of brightwork. Already by January of that year, people must have been catching occasional glimpses of those big, sleek beasts gliding through traffic in old Havana, or parked beside a long stretch of Vedado sidewalk. They must have turned to each other on the street and asked, wow, did you see that? as a new elongated, angular, winged Plymouth Belvedere drove by, or a shiny Chevrolet Bel Air, its fins slicing the air behind, its huge rictus grin of a chrome grille in front.

The biggest automotive event of early 1957 in Havana was, without a doubt, the first Cuban Grand Prix, the nation's inaugural Formula One race. It was run on February 25, accompanied by much propaganda from the Batista government in the international press. The world's best race drivers were competing, including the great English driver Stirling Moss and the Argentine Juan Manuel Fangio, who, in 1957, became the first driver to win five world championships. Driving a Maserati, he won the Havana race, his second win of the year. Fangio, nicknamed *El Chueco*, meaning bowlegged, was forty-six years old and had been racing since he was twenty-three. Quiet and soft-spoken, he is regarded by most people—from the current king of the sport, Michael Schumacher, on down—as the greatest race driver ever. Fangio's mere presence signaled that the Grand Prix de Cuba was a world-class event.

The race wound along the Malecón, and more than 100,000 people turned out to watch. Havana's tourist commission spent some $150,000 promoting it, and the sporting press from around the globe was represented. In the six weeks preceding the race, some twenty-two bombs were placed around the city by anti-Batista rebels, according to Rosalie Schwartz's book *Pleasure Island*. Unsuccessful attempts were made to bomb the Ambar Motors offices and showroom, as well as the Telemundo television tower, both belonging to Amadeo Barletta. Batista had imposed a strict press censorship during those six weeks, and the explosions were virtually absent from the news.

The main race of that first Cuban Grand Prix, which Fangio won in dramatic, last-minute fashion, was preceded by a number of warm-up races, which were of no importance to the international racing crowd but mattered a great deal when it came to local prestige. A Ford in one of the races was maintained by the mechanics at Relámpago, and mechanic Juan Carlos remembered that many hours had been spent preparing the car. "It did not run in the big, international race, but one in which various small, more inexpensive models competed, like Fords, Chevrolets and Dodges," he said. "And, we won. The winner's banquet was held at the Sans Souci casino. They told us we couldn't go because we were black and they wouldn't let us in. But, due to the intervention of Carlos

*Fulgencio Batista (right) congratulates Juan Manuel Fangio (wreathed in flowers)
on winning the first Grand Prix of Cuba, February 25, 1957.
(Biblioteca Nacional José Martí, Havana)*

• • •

Alonso [owner of Relámpago], and some Americans who were there with Ford, they let us attend. We each received a gold medal on a chain, which I still have, and a diploma.''

The entire event was a triumph for Batista, putting Havana on the map with other Formula One cities around the globe and bringing the international press to town to extol the virtues of its vibrant nightlife and good times waiting to be had. It was one of Batista's few public triumphs that year. The assault on the Presidential Palace took place on March 13, less than three weeks after the race. It was followed by a series of rebel actions both in the cities and up in the Sierra Maestra, where Fidel Castro was ensconced.

In February 1958, as the date for the second Cuban Grand Prix approached, Batista assured the world, time and again, that Cuba was entirely safe and peaceful. The rebels had been completely neutralized in both the mountains and the cities, and his government was in firm control. The night before the race, on February 24, as Fangio and his entourage stepped out of the elevator into the lobby of the Hotel Lincoln, on their way to a restaurant for dinner, a thin, dark young man with nervously darting eyes came up swiftly to Fangio's side, showed him a .45-calibre pistol, and told him he was being kidnapped by the 26 July Movement. In his autobiography, Fangio wrote that he went without question because the rebel was shaking so violently he was worried the pistol would discharge accidentally. "Four machine guns outside are aimed at you," the kidnapper told the group around Fangio in a voice that trembled slightly. "Don't try to leave the hotel for another five minutes or people will die."

Outside, the young man put a hand on Fangio's elbow and led him down the block to a nearly new green 1957 Plymouth parked at the curb. He put Fangio in the back seat, next to a man already waiting there. The driver pulled away from the curb, and a second man in the front seat turned around to apologize: "We are great admirers of yours, Fangio, but the 26 July Movement has decided to show the world that Cuba is living through a tragic time of blood and death, and that it is not a time for parties and celebrations. As soon as the race is over you'll be set free."

Fangio missed the evening's meal at the restaurant, dining instead with his captors in a house in the neighborhood of New Vedado where they had brought him. He was hungry and supped well. They told him about their cause. The next day he stayed in a bedroom, listening to the race on the radio. His kidnapping was front-page news all over the world. Many years later, Fangio recalled that day in an interview with Miguel Masjuan in an October 1981 issue of *Bohemia*: "[One of the kidnappers] brought me the newspapers in the morning when I woke up, and I saw that the thing was really serious. When I saw the headlines, I said, 'Look, I see you are well-organized and all I ask is that you let my family know I'm fine, that I'm with you and that nothing's going to happen to me.' And that's what he did. That same day."

Batista held out hope right up to the start of the race that Fangio would be there, liberated at the last second by his police, who were frantically combing the city. Fangio's Maserati was even brought to the starting line.

A huge crowd of spectators, estimated at 250,000, lined the Malecón, many certain that Fangio would appear. It was not to be, however, and the race was run without him, tragically marked by more than Fangio's absence. A Cuban, driving a Ferrari, hit an oil slick and skidded into the crowd, killing six and injuring forty-eight. The Grand Prix was suspended. Fangio heard it all on the radio.

Great concern arose among the 26 July members about how to return Fangio to freedom. The rebels were afraid that if they simply turned him loose, Batista's police might kill him and say the Movement had done it, according to Arnold Rodríguez, a Movement member who was assigned to the task. They decided that the best way was to return him directly to the custody of the Argentine ambassador.

By the time Rodríguez had completed telephone negotiations for Fangio's return, it was about 10:00 P.M. Rodríguez accompanied the race car driver to a waiting car, a gray 1957 Rambler, which belonged to Emma Montenegra. She rode in the front seat and her boyfriend drove. Rodríguez got in back with Fangio. Montenegra had nicknamed her new Rambler *la gorriona* (the sparrow) for its unassuming appearance. While the body was gray, the chunky car could have been thought of as modest only in an era full of design excesses. It had fins, and white sidewall tires and was hardly unassuming. The *gorriona* delivered Fangio to the ambassador.

"A strong feeling of friendship grew up between Fangio and us; it was a curious thing," said Arnold Rodríguez, who was seventy-one when I spoke to him on the screened porch of his large, shadowy Vedado house. Bright, broad oil paintings hung on the walls, and a caged parrot let out screeches that punctuated our interview. Rodríguez was a man of medium height with his remaining gray hair brushed back, bushy gray eyebrows, and brown eyes that lit up when he talked about Fangio, who died in 1995 at the age of eighty-four.

"He told us he would like to return after the Revolution triumphed, and he came back to Cuba in 1981 to fulfill his promise. I went to Argentina to visit him in 1992. We went to Balcarce, the place where he was born, some 400 kilometers from Buenos Aires. He was eighty-one years old, and he drove me from Buenos Aires to Balcarce in his Mercedes-Benz at what he assured me was the 'very moderate' rate of 85 or 90 miles an hour. The Mercedes had an automatic transmission so he never had to shift gears. He used to make the drive every couple of weeks to see his relatives in Balcarce. He was a very controlled and austere man, but he also had a great deal of warmth."

When I asked Rodríguez if Fangio's kidnapping had served its purpose, he said he would rather answer me with something he had written. He went to the back of his house and brought me a copy of a 1988 article about the action in *Juventud Rebelde*, which concluded:

> No more was Havana seen only as a center for gambling and prostitution. It began to be perceived as it was at its core. The Havana of student struggles and of dozens of martyrs; the Havana of the assault on the Presidential Palace; of the night of a hundred bombs; the Havana with its political prisoners in rebellion and on a hunger strike; the Havana with its workers conscious and organized; the Havana with its revolutionary militias that would not allow the tyranny to have its pantomime on the twenty-fourth of February.

As the rebels in the mountains continued to strike and frequently rout army units, people began to believe that Castro would not be easily eliminated, and by the time Fangio was kidnapped, many had begun to rally to his cause. Hugh Thomas wrote: "Castro had now been in the Sierra for over twelve months. Instead of being a hunted fugitive, he commanded a guerrilla army which could roam at will over nearly all the territory south and west of the *carretera central* in Oriente—almost 2,000 square miles."

Up in the Sierra Maestra, Detroit-made vehicles were getting plenty of use. But, rather than passenger cars, most of them were Dodge Fargo trucks and Willys Jeeps. All during the 1950s, army surplus jeeps were cheap and plentiful on the market. Of all the vehicles imported into Cuba from the United States during 1957, Willys ranked fourth in number, behind only Chevrolet, Ford, and Dodge. In fact, some rebels learned to drive when they were fighting in the Oriente, including

Ernesto "Che" Guevara, who spent much of his youth traveling through Central and South America on a motorcycle, but who had never sat behind the wheel of a car. The closest he seems to have come, judging from what he wrote in his diary, was holding hands as a teenager in Argentina with his girlfriend Chichina "in the enormous womb of a Buick."

Jon Lee Anderson tells the story of Che Guevara's first time behind the wheel:

> Che went to visit some farmers in the mountains close to where they were fighting Batista's army and when they were ready to go back to camp he told his companion, Oscarito (Oscar Fernández Mell), that he would drive. Later, Oscarito said Che drove their Jeep back to camp at breakneck speed along a narrow dirt road that skirted steep precipices. Noticing Oscarito's nervousness, Che told him not to worry, and added, "When we get where we're going I want to tell you something." When they arrived Che informed Oscarito that it was the first time he had ever driven—which was true.

Rebel fighting was nearly constant in both the mountain vastness and the city streets. Batista and his police were feeling the pinch of strengthening rebel offensives, but life for Havana's well-to-do was not greatly affected by the back-and-forth; neither the assault on the Presidential Palace, nor the kidnapping of Fangio in the city, nor the skirmishes in the countryside put the brakes on business.

In rural Cuba, the seasons of the sugar economy came and went. The sugar economy, like the cotton economy in the southern United States, guaranteed an ample, prosperous class of landowners and managers and a workforce that lived in brutal poverty. Working in cane fields is something a person will do only when there is no other way to bring in even the smallest daily wage. Sugarcane mills supported a small group of wealthy people, a small managerial class, and a large underclass. Banana plantations did the same. Towns like Holguín, Banes, and Matanzas all had their new car dealerships selling to owners and managers. In addition to private car sales, they did a brisk trade in trucks and tractors.

In Havana, disturbances like the kidnapping of Fangio or the occasional bomb were disconcerting but hardly a threat to the general well-being of the populace. Tourist and casino revenues were rising, and North American Mafia money was financing more hotels and casinos. Plans were afoot to seed the Malecón with these cash cows from one end to the other. The presence of organized crime in Havana went back to the days of the Volstead Act, which initiated Prohibition in the United States in 1919, when the mob set up in Havana to move crates of Cuban rum across the Florida Strait. The post-Prohibition Mafia arrived in the person of Meyer Lansky, a Jew from Manhattan's Lower East Side who acted as a representative for both Charles "Lucky" Luciano and Santos Trafficante. Between 1937 and 1940, nine casinos and six hotels were built, most often collaborations between Mafia money and expertise, on the one hand, and politically connected Cubans with money to invest, on the other. From the time the first shovel of dirt was dug, the government was skimming money. A Batista bagman visited each casino every night.

When the anti-Batista Auténtico Party candidate, Ramón Grau San Martín, was elected president in 1944, Lansky left for New York and Batista went to Daytona Beach, Florida. While business as usual continued under Trafficante's watchful eye in Havana, expansion plans were put on hold, and some of the casinos closed. Others made sure, by the use of everything from rigged slot machines to crooked dice games, that the possibility of gamblers winning was virtually nil. When Batista returned to grab power in 1952, his admiration for Lansky and company was undimmed. Lansky came back and set to work cleaning up Havana's casinos, reestablishing "honest" games, making money for himself, his underworld associates, and Batista. Cuban hospitality, combined with the U.S. Senate hearings on organized crime held under Senator Estes Kefauver in 1951, which had shone a light on organized crime for the first time, induced many of "the boys" to head south.

Then, in 1955, Lansky's friendship with Batista bore rich fruit. The Cuban government passed a law providing that anyone who invested at least $200,000 in a nightclub, or $1 million in a hotel, automatically qualified for a gaming license. Such an investor was also spared background checks, granted tax exemptions for ten years, and allowed to enjoy duty-free importation of equipment and furnishings. In addition, his dealers and croupiers could have two-year work permits, which had the effect of reducing the jobs available for locally hired Cubans to mostly menial ones.

An ever-increasing number of people involved in organized crime in the United States heard that Havana was a great place to be. They were still smarting from Kefauver's dogged inquiries and were happy to find friendlier shores only 90 miles from Miami. People like Lansky, Trafficante, and Amadeo Barletta had paved the way and were there waiting to make new arrivals feel comfortable. Sales of new Cadillacs in Havana increased by 50 percent between 1956 and 1957, from 211 to 310, according to figures in *El Automóvil de Cuba*. Amadeo Barletta counted many of his customers among his friends.

When the mobster Joe "Bananas" Bonano surprised everyone by living long enough to die in his bed at the age of ninety-seven, his son Salvatore eulogized him by saying, "His values and his principles would have been the same if he had been running the Mafia or General Motors." It is a comment that brings to mind Amadeo Barletta, who seems, in Cuba, to have come close to doing both at the same time. The official revolutionary history holds that he was much more than the man who sold the Italian mafiosi their Cadillacs: an article in *Granma* called him a Cosa Nostra member and an "infamous mobster." Others who knew him do not believe he was personally "mobbed up," but no one denies he had close ties to the gangsters. Whatever else Barletta was, he was powerful, and he seems to have gotten along well with fascists of many stripes, from Benito Mussolini in Italy, to Rafael Leónidas Trujillo in the Dominican Republic. As the owner of one of Havana's two television stations, a popular daily newspaper, the biggest car agency in town, and some forty other businesses, Barletta was a big player in the local economy during the 1950s.

A lot of money was waiting to be made in Havana. Meyer Lansky's Riviera hotel and casino, for instance, which opened at the end of 1957, turned a $1.5 million profit in the three months of April, May, and

Meyer Lansky leaving his Riviera Hotel in Havana on the way to the States to answer questions about the October 25, 1957, murder of mob boss Albert Anastasia. In the Bohemia *story that ran with the photo, the woman was unidentified and the satchel in Lansky's hand was said to hold $200,000 from the Riviera's casino.*
(Courtesy of the photographic archives, Bohemia, Havana*)*

• • •

June 1958, according to Rosalie Schwartz's *Pleasure Island*. At least a dozen casinos were running full bore every night, without any signs that a saturation point had been reached. Some twenty new hotels had been built since 1950, and still the rooms kept filling.

Not all of the money pouring into casino coffers came from the 3.5 million tourists who visited Havana each year. Much of it was local. Many Cubans enjoyed gambling. The lottery was traditionally an important source of government revenues in prerevolutionary Cuba, and by 1958, according to one report, $266,150 was being gambled daily in Havana on lotteries, of which $32,115 went to the Batista government. Betting on cock fights was as common as playing dominos.

"We are not a drunken people although we make good rum and like to drink. Neither are we, as some tourists with bad intentions would have it, a people of sexual perversions and excesses. In these fields—alcoholism and offenses against modesty—other countries are way ahead of us. Gambling, however, is something we could qualify as a 'national vice,'" wrote Andrés Valdespino, who was to serve as undersecretary of the treasury in the first year of the Revolution.

His February 1958 article for *Bohemia* continued, "The Spanish organized gambling on the island and made a lot of money from it. The Count of Lucena, with bald-faced cynicism, even got to the point of saying that 'with a rooster and a playing card, peace is assured in these lands.' . . . Every time the Republic has had governments of a 'colonial' structure, a marked emphasis has been placed on the promotion of gambling by those in charge of the public sector."

The Batista government had released a plan of "economic and social growth" financed by the conversion of much of the Malecón into casinos, hotels, nightclubs, and restaurants, all conveniently located next to the beautiful seaside promenade. This was to be undertaken with government backing and private investors, which meant organized crime interests and well-connected Cubans. In early 1958, it was still possible to imagine Havana becoming the next Las Vegas, the reigning jewel in the mob's economic crown for years to come, each casino a highly profitable enterprise. Barletta's media, *El Mundo* and Telemundo, supported the plan, representing it as an important expansion of the tourist industry. Valdespino, on the other hand, scoffed at the government's projections of how this would help the Cuban economy:

Are we going to ingenuously think that these experienced promoters of such a lucrative enterprise, a majority of whom are foreign gangsters, are going to dedicate their fabulous earnings to build schools, open highways or raise the standard of living in the countryside?

They want to convert the Malecón, one of the most beautiful avenues in the world, into a vast hotel zone to exploit gambling run by foreign gangsters. . . . But, in a country of beat-up schools, starving peasants, widespread poverty, and chronic unemployment, it's striking that all this is financed through public bodies, the investments of undesirable emigrants who will not even leave behind their thanks for this country that has sheltered them.

With the hotels and casinos turning such handsome profits and so many more people buying ever-bigger cars, parking was becoming a problem in Havana, according to Hank Messick's book *Lansky*, a biography of the gangster. Batista installed parking meters, which infuriated the working people, who could barely afford to keep their Chevys and Fords on the road as it was. They understood the meters were there to guarantee parking spots for the rich, because no one else could afford to use them. What was worse, the dictator's detested brother-in-law, Roberto Fernández y Miranda, was in charge of the parking meter revenues. He was also the person who collected each day's take from the slot machines in the casinos. A percentage of each was known to stay in his pocket. The high price of gasoline was bad enough, but to have to pay Batista's family for parking was too much. Messick writes: "Enough people lacked the coins needed, to leave ample room for the elite. Came the Revolution, and the first things smashed were the parking meters. After them went the slot machines."

Sex and drugs accompanied the casinos in a "sin city" aura around Havana in the minds of North Americans. Opium parlors and traffic in marijuana, heroin, and cocaine were widespread. Every day's newspapers contained reports of arrests for narcotics possession and sales. This was not a new phenomena. As early as 1916, newspapers had decried the presence of opium dens. In the 1920s, when the drug of choice for many was liquor, which could not be legally obtained in the United

Fulgencio Batista (left) and son posed at the Havana airport on a sunny day in August 1957, in the younger Batista's 1956 Corvette. Behind them is a plane belonging to Air Cubana, the company founded by William Pawley.
(Biblioteca Nacional José Martí, Havana)

• • •

States, Cuba offered a haven close by. In Havana, New Year's could be toasted in legal champagne, and all year round any number of bars and nightclubs served perfectly above-board drinks. More than 7,000 bars operated in Havana during the years of stateside Prohibition. In the 1930s, Lucky Luciano had elaborate plans to use Cuba as the transshipment point for his narcotics business, a project interrupted by his deportation to Italy.

Havana, for most of the twentieth century, has been represented as a place where any sort of sexual experience is available to a traveler. As early as the 1920s, guidebooks were giving explicit directions to brothels, and the image of Cuba as the tropical paradise where anything pleasurable was allowed had taken firm root in the minds of millions of North Americans. By the late 1950s, clubs where well-heeled gringos could pay to see live sex thrived in Havana, and more than 11,000 women in the city were estimated to be making their livings as prostitutes.

Sex shows and conspicuous drug consumption have disappeared from the roster of available entertainments in Cuba, but visitors and residents can still avail themselves of theater, music, art exhibitions, readings, and a variety of cultural offerings, often of a high quality. One of my weeks in Santiago de Cuba is marked by the fourteenth annual International Bolero Festival, held each late afternoon and early evening for five days on the patio behind the National Writers and Artists Union offices. A bar is open at the back of the patio, and a small stage is set up. The festival's international aspect is limited to a couple of singers from Venezuela, and it seems more than anything to be a chance for people to get together and listen to the best of the local balladeers and guitar players. I am there every day. There are more unpleasant ways to pass a late tropical afternoon than sitting in a chair with a cold Bucanero beer listening to boleros.

Many of the performers are people I have heard before on the back patio of the Casa de las Tradiciones, a small club on Rabi Street in the south end of Santiago de Cuba. The House of Traditions is one of a handful of clubs scattered around Santiago where a *son* group plays for foreigners who pay a dollar at the door and fill the club each night. Cubans are there, too, not so much to listen to the traditional *son* rhythms as to make sure the foreigners get up and dance, to see that they have the carefree, pleasant Cuban holiday they have been dreaming about in their gray cities and workaday routines, and for which they have paid. The Cubans are encouraged to come to the club with the offer of a free drink or two and the chance to meet foreigners. A half-dozen groups of Santiaguero musicians make the rounds of these places, full-time musicians paid by the state and expected to rehearse regularly and play every evening on time. In exchange, they receive upward of 300 pesos ($13.50) a month, a decent wage in the peso economy. The young, dreadlocked guitarist Jorge, for instance, plays with a group on this circuit, and to make a few dollars extra he gets into adventures with young foreign women, like the Israeli renting the room next to mine.

In these clubs, the people venturing onto the dance floor are of various, generally predictable, types. Usually, there will be a pair of older Cuban couples who dance like they have spent the last twenty-five years dancing with each other, moving like flowing water in an effortless synchrony. Then, there is often a pair of younger Cuban couples, sensuous and exciting to watch dance, the men's muscles tight and bulging under clean white T-shirts, sweat gleaming on dark skin, the women moving in total rhythm, skirts looking like they were sprayed on. A tourist couple or two will likely be moving clunkily around the floor. And, usually, there will be a few mixed couples of the same sort observed in the Parque Céspedes: paunchy middle-aged foreign men, trying to move their hips in front of the tightly Lycra encased bodies of the eighteen-year-old mulatas who are theirs for the night, or gawky European women giggling self-consciously at their efforts to follow the moves of the beautiful young dark-skinned men who attend them. All underpinned by the infectious sound of *son*.

At the House of Traditions, however, something else is also going on. Those who walk through the dancers in the front room and out the screen door at the back find a patio where people sit some nights on chairs and benches in the open air, taking turns playing guitar and singing. They are not young, for the most part, or sleek, and nothing about them would have attracted the attention of a European looking for company. But management encourages their presence with a judicious glass of rum or bottle of beer, and listening to them, it is easy to appreciate why. People who come back to the patio to listen are not there for the rhythmic explosion of sound required to get a European dancing, and they ignore the raucous strains of *son* coming from the front room. Sung and played on the back patio are the soulful renderings of much-loved ballads, the pairings of voice and guitar in highly evocative duets.

Over the course of the week, most of those back-patio denizens appear onstage at the bolero festival. The audience members seem to have a high proportion of gray hairs, but some younger people turn up each afternoon, and everyone mouths the words to most of the songs. Union members, which means virtually every writer and artist in Santiago, can enter the festival for free from the offices in front of the patio, but the paying public has to enter by way of a side street off Calle Heredia. I go up the pair of steps to a desk set in a doorway, where foreigners pay $1.00 and Cubans part with five pesos before stepping around the desk and passing into the patio. One afternoon, an unnaturally thin, dark-skinned young woman, with stringy black hair, is leaning against the building at the bottom of the steps, and she asks me in a low voice as I pass her, *De donde eres*, where are you from?

Spain, I half lie for no good reason, and turn away from her to the young guy behind the desk who has not glanced up from the *Granma* he has spread out flat before him. I wait patiently for him to do so, bracing myself with a hand on the doorway. She steps up close to the wall and runs her tongue over my fingers where they rest on the jamb, gently licking the backs of my knuckles, sealing a promise of unspeakable delights. I do not look at her, ashamed that my groin tingles. Finally, the guy at the desk looks up, takes my dollar, and lets me in while the young girl returns to her wait by the bottom step. I walk into the patio, where a large, dark-skinned older woman wearing an electric blue dress is singing *Bésame Mucho*, in a voice that comes ringing out from somewhere deep inside her chest, accompanied by a pale, thin guitarist wearing a white shirt and shiny black pants, seated behind her with his skinny legs crossed, bony white shins visible between cuff and sock, scuffed black loafer tapping time.

chapter five

CHE'S CHEVY & FIDEL'S OLDS

I wake up every morning in Havana by seven, with no need for an alarm clock. This may be the capital city and the most cosmopolitan place on the island, but it is not an urban sparrow's chirping or pigeon's cooing that greets the dawn. It is a rooster crowing upstairs in full throat that wakes light sleepers every day. Habaneros tend to think of themselves as worldly-wise and sophisticated and of the rest of the island as lush green countryside peopled with *guajiros* and *guajiras*, hardworking but gullible country people with no style. Nevertheless, the Habanero who lives on the second floor of the house where I rent a comfortable room in the ground-floor flat, has a sow living on his patio, in addition to hens, a rooster, rabbits, and pigeons. All that livestock smells bad and brings bugs, my landlady tells me, but it is worth it to him in exchange for the assurance that there will always be some meat and eggs around. Oftentimes, I encounter the rooster, a lean, stringy, high-combed cock, pecking away at the narrow verge of grass between sidewalk and curb in front of the house. The bird has a mean look in his eye when he glances up at me, and I am always careful to give him a respectful berth.

Once awake, I take a while to heave myself out of bed to face the morning, and another while to have my breakfast coffee—leavened with chicory—along with bread, butter, and a plate of fresh mango, papaya, and watermelon. By the time I leave the house, it is nine, and the day is already hot enough so that it envelops me in a big, wraparound hug as soon as I step outside. I break a sweat within the first sixty seconds of my fifteen-minute walk out along Paseo to the Plaza de la Revolución and the José Martí National Library.

Not only does the walk have a series of interesting way stations, but during the course of it, as during the course of any walk through Havana, a high possibility exists of seeing on the street a car that most North Americans think is extinct. I have heard of folks who maintain a life-list of cars in much the same way that other people have a life-list of birds, keeping track of every model they have ever seen. A trip to Havana is, for an automologist, the equivalent of an ornithologist's trip to the highlands of Guatemala in search of the quetzal or to southern Spain to scan the azure sky for a glimpse of an imperial eagle. Each day in Havana holds the possibility of becoming luminous and rare with a Detroit sighting that makes the heart beat faster. One day it may be a 1957 Edsel convertible struggling to fit its broad, long self into a narrow parking space along the curb, or a 1939 black, four-door, elegant Packard touring car coming down the street, or a flawless 1956 Studebaker Golden Hawk with what looks like the original dusky gold paint, purring along Paseo. The next day might bring a 1954 Ford woodie station wagon parked in front of the Capitolio, or a red 1957 Chevrolet Bel Air convertible with white, pleated seatcovers, waiting for a light to change on La Rampa.

My route to the library takes me by a big ceiba tree out on the sidewalk along Paseo. Ceibas, closely related to the African baobab tree, have oddly segmented, almost wavy trunks, can grow up to 150 feet tall, and have been venerated in Cuba for a long time. The tree is sacred in both the Santería and Palo Mayombe religions brought from West Africa, and it has been reported that in some parts of the island newborn babies are taken and presented to a ceiba tree. The buoyant kapok fibers from the ceiba tree's fruits were once used as stuffing in things like automobile seats and life jackets, although they have now been replaced by synthetic fibers. At the bottom of the trunk of this ceiba on Paseo, tucked in among one of the folds of its base, offerings are frequently left—a pile of rice, a handful of bananas, a mango, a half-smoked cigar. These are not tossed there as garbage, but left as tribute, as succor. This is a stately, elegant tree that has stood at the edge of Vedado for a long time.

A bit further beyond the ceiba is a block of little rundown houses behind a stone wall, on a section of which is painted the word "*plomero.*" The plumber in question is Juan, who is selling a 1951 Studebaker Champion, gleaming black with a big polished chrome, jet-fighter nose cone gleaming in front of the radiator. "It's all original parts," he says, when I stop to cast an eye over it. "Runs fine. I'm selling it for $2,400 and it has a *traspaso.*"

Juan has sparse white hair under a Florida Marlins baseball cap, a seamed face, skin the color of *café con leche*, with small, lively blue eyes and a handful of snaggly teeth. If there is no plumbing work, which is the case most days, he parks the Studebaker just outside the stone wall next to a big round boulder, tapes an *en venta* (for sale) sign to the door, and sits beside it on the boulder. A pint bottle holding a clear liquid leans discreetly against the base of the rock. "People can't afford plumbers. They have problems, but they can't pay to get them fixed."

He tells me that the car has a trim, six-cylinder engine and runs like a top. "I bought it a few years ago from the man whose father bought it new. He was having a tough time financially, and he held out for as long as he could. Imagine, it was his father's car and his father had died, but finally he had to sell it. I didn't like the fact that happened to him, but I had the money and it's a great car, so I bought it."

He has only now decided to part with it, and the first day I stop to talk to him is only the second time he has taped the sign on and brought the car out to the sidewalk. He is confident that a buyer will turn up quickly. This car will do just fine as a *rutero*, he says; it won't take a buyer long to make back the purchase price. Nevertheless, the days and weeks go by, and I see him sitting out there every day with the car, and each time I stop to say hello his confidence in an imminent sale is undimmed. When I leave, six weeks later, the car still has not sold.

A couple of blocks on toward the library is a baseball diamond with a half-dozen rows of bleachers. It is reserved for army use according to a posted sign, but in fact is used by everyone from little kids playing hardball with what must be one of the raggediest, most threadbare, tattered baseballs in the hemisphere, to big guys in their early twenties in uniforms, hitting a ball as hard as I have ever seen one hit. In the afternoons, the kids' teams practice, and the players all have real gloves, and most are wearing at least half a uniform. Some even have baseball shoes. Coaches hit them flies and grounders: clink go the aluminum bats in the hot afternoon air. It is a far cry from the many times I have watched kids play baseball in other Caribbean countries, when pieces of cardboard served to catch a ragged, bumpy piece of wound-tight fabric hit with a stick. On a morning when a couple of good teams take the field, before it gets too hot, the siren call of the library becomes faint indeed, and it is well worth the time to take a bleacher seat and watch a few innings of a close game.

Whoever is using the diamond, it is a good bet that the game in progress will have to be stopped at least once because the fielders cannot find the ball in the high grass of the outfield. The procedure is to wait a bit while the outfielders tramp down the grass around where they think the ball finished up. This takes some doing, as past a certain line in the shallow outfield the grass grows at knee height. If they do not find the ball, everyone—the man waiting in the batter's box lays down his bat, the infielders drop their gloves where they stand—goes out to help beat the brush of the outfield until it is found. One day, a truck turns up with a tractor and mower, and precious gasoline is spent to cut the outfield back to the ground. Lord knows how many balls they came across out there.

From the ballpark, my walk crosses the Plaza de la Revolución. It is a vast, open plaza with a 150-foot obelisk at its center, honoring José Martí. The obelisk points up toward where vultures are usually circling against the bright blue sky. I pass right in front of the Ministry of the Interior, with Che's face painted on the side, *Hasta Siempre* (For Always), written beneath it. The plaza is a stop on the sightseeing circuit of Havana, and its vast parking lot is always dotted with tourist conveyances: tour buses rumbling, their engines idling to keep the air-conditioning working so the tourists will have the pleasure of escaping the morning heat and climbing back aboard the cool bus; coco taxis, the little yellow motorized bicycle taxis shaped like a coconut and devoted to the tourist trade, which seat two people behind the driver; and a few impeccable Detroit models from the 1950s devoted to transporting tourists. A state-owned company, Gran Car, provides classic cars with drivers to tourists or to Cubans themselves, who often rent them for a wedding or a *quinceañera*, a girl's fifteenth-birthday celebration. Gran Car drivers at the plaza sit behind the wheels of their American beauties with the windows open and wait, or sit in one anothers' cars and chat, while tourists stand gawking up at the obelisk, taking pictures of it and of themselves in front of it. I walk along the parking lot's perimeter, across the huge plaza, to the plain, rectilinear, fourteen-floor building that houses the José Martí National Library, with more information about the cars in Cuba's past than is to be found anywhere else in the world.

Between 1950 and 1958, the number of cars on the island had risen an average of 13 percent a year, from 70,000 to 167,000, according to National Vehicle Census figures reprinted in *El Automóvil de Cuba*. At the same time, some 30 percent of adults were illiterate and 60 percent functionally so, while a large number of Cubans were too poor to afford even minimal health care. Nevertheless, the island had the largest per capita sales of Cadillacs in the world. The tourist trade was booming, particularly in Havana. By the fall of 1958, thirteen large casinos were going full blast in the capital. Some 350,000 tourists visited Cuba in 1958, according to *Bohemia*, apparently undiscouraged by the contrast of wealth and poverty.

Bohemia itself reflected the same sort of division. Weekly, the magazine's pages were full of advertisements for expensive domestic products like cars, refrigerators, televisions, and washing machines. At the same time, it ran a weekly section called "Arriba Corazones" (Arise, Hearts), written by Guido García Inclán, who passed on to readers the letters that poured in each week from all over the island written by parents making public pleas for money to buy medicine, or crutches, or wheelchairs, or treatments, or life-saving surgeries that their children needed but that they could not afford. Sometimes there were also pleas of desperation on the parents' own behalf. María Dominga Martínez, for example, reported García Inclán in the March 9, 1958, issue, had lost her husband, a newspaper vendor who had been an exemplary citizen. "She is anaemic and asthmatic and cannot work. She has urgent need of the anti-asthma drug, Derchobran, Deltacortene (prednisone). And benadryl cough medicine. ¡Arriba Corazones!" A black-and-white photo of her reveals a skinny, white woman who looks sixty but is probably forty standing against a peeling gray wall, two young kids beside her dressed in dirty clothes.

Or take Señora Mathilde Ramos of Guanabacoa, who has lost her hearing: "What's more, she tells us, she doesn't know how she can suffer this life of desolation and misery any longer. She has an imperative need for a hearing aid. They've told her that hearing aids are expensive and she doesn't even have so much as a place to fall down dead. ¡Arriba corazones!"

A third of the total labor force was virtually unemployed, with great numbers of people in the countryside able to find work only during sugarcane season. Less than half of urban dwellings had indoor plumbing, and a mere 3 percent of rural homes. An estimated 5,000 beggars worked the streets of Havana daily, and government corruption had reached tremendous levels.

By the autumn of 1958, there was little doubt that a change was on the horizon and that Batista's days in Cuba were numbered. A series of rebel actions in both the cities and the countryside made it clear that his army was faltering. Meanwhile, United States support had weakened significantly. Not that the U.S. government was happy with the rebel alternative. Despite Castro's repeated reassurances that he was not a communist, veteran anticommunists like William Pawley, the former owner of Havana's Autobus Modernos, sensed something far too left-wing for their liking.

The CIA decided to send Pawley to talk to Batista, to try to get him to resign before Castro could claim victory. The dictator could return to the luxurious property he still owned in Daytona and live out his days in quiet comfort. Historian Hugh Thomas quotes the testimony Pawley gave on the matter in a U.S. Senate hearing: "I told them that we should now, to try to save the peace, see if we can go down there to get Batista to capitulate to a caretaker government unfriendly to him but satisfactory to us, whom we could immediately recognize and give military assistance to in order that Fidel Castro should not come to power."

Pawley made the trip and spoke to Batista in Havana on December 5, but the dictator was not interested in resigning. He still held out some hope. Three weeks later it was clear that the end had arrived and that Castro was victorious. On New Year's Day, 1959, Fulgencio Batista and his family flew to Santo Domingo and then on to luxurious exile in Francisco Franco's Spain. Che Guevara's forces entered Havana, and Fidel Castro accepted the surrender of Santiago de Cuba on January 2. Castro arrived in Havana on January 8 and entered the city from the airport in a Willys Jeep, later switching to a tank as the parade of victorious rebels made its way through the center of the city.

Outside observers and Cubans alike knew that something of great moment had happened and that things would never be the same, but few imagined that Castro's arrival would herald the end of life as they had known it. Soon, the car business would disappear, because all business, as it had been practiced heretofore in Cuba, was on its way out. The United States viewed Castro's left-leaning philosophy with some concern, but the idea that Yankee influence could be eliminated by anybody, regardless of his politics, was not taken seriously. Governments and leaders might change, but the dollar would always be welcome and business interests from the North would be accommodated. Cubans themselves were uncertain about what the shape of the new government would be, but they were ready for a change and turned out en masse to welcome Castro.

"The streets were full that day," recalled mechanic Juan Carlos. "They came down the street a block away from Relámpago, and all of us who worked there came up the street to see them pass by. People were up on all the roofs; people were everywhere. Everyone shouting, 'Fidel, Camilo, and Che,' and then all of a sudden there they were, the three of them on that tank.

Fidel enters Havana beside Camilo Cienfuegos on January 8, 1959, in a Willys, with Abel Santamaría's name on the front bumper. (Courtesy of the photographic archives, Prensa Latina, Havana)

• • •

"Every year, up until the Revolution, it was incredible the number of cars that came into Havana. Thousands. They'd go out to everywhere else on the island. Some on boats, some on trains, some on special trucks built to transport cars. It never occurred to me that it was all about to stop. It would have seemed impossible. After the triumph of the Revolution, we kept on selling cars, working on cars. Then, the government spent a few months organizing, figuring out how to organize the car

Che's Chevy and Fidel's Olds : 179

business. Gradually, the number of new cars coming in dwindled away. By 1960, there were almost none."

Throughout 1959, the thousands who made their livings along the tributaries of the river of money that was the automobile business continued to trust that a way would be found to reconcile their interests with those of the Revolution. Even most of those who were not so sure sat out the first year, waiting to see what life would be like under Castro's rebels. No one could believe that the *barbudos*, the bearded ones, would go out and purposefully slaughter the geese that had been laying golden eggs for so long.

Gambling and prostitution were different. The Revolution had sworn to abolish them, and little time was wasted. The sex trade was shut down. Some of the casinos lasted a few months before being closed, but by the end of the year the casinos and sex clubs were gone, and so was the lottery. The government had lived up to its word. However, there had been no similar commitment to wipe out legitimate business interests. People thought perhaps private enterprise would be tolerated, or even encouraged. In fact, Castro seemed to like cars as much as the next person. People who did flee usually did so by air, leaving their homes and their cars behind. The rebels were quick to divide up the spoils. Confiscated cars were brought to a lot near a Miramar beach, and high-ranking rebel officials were invited to go and pick one out. Castro wound up with an Oldsmobile and Che Guevara with a 1960 eight-cylinder Chevrolet Bel Air, Series 1600, one of the last lot of new cars brought from Detroit by Ambar Motors. The Bel Air was deep emerald green and had a white roof; with flat fins and a chrome strip on either side, it was shaped like a horizontal rocketship. It had a Powerglide automatic transmission. Camilo Cienfuegos followed Castro's lead and took a 1959 Oldsmobile Rocket 98. It had a big eight-cylinder engine and an automatic transmission, with Hydra-matic and power steering. It was also green, but a more muted shade than Che's Chevy. The cars that belonged to Guevara and Cienfuegos are now in Eduardo Mesejo's Havana car museum, but the fate of Castro's Oldsmobile remains unknown.

In his book about Guevara, Jon Lee Anderson tells a story about Or-

Fidel and a pair of young admirers, in a photograph taken by Uber Mathes that appeared in Bohemia in May 1961. The car, judging from the window frame, could well be an Oldsmobile. (Courtesy of the photographic archives, Bohemia, Havana*)*

. . .

lando Borrego, one of Che's trusted assistants, who appropriated a virtually new Jaguar left behind by a wealthy Cuban who fled to Florida. Guevara was furious and asked him what he thought he was doing driving around in such a car. It was a "pimp's car," ostentatious, not one for "a representative of the people" to be seen driving. He recommended a modest car that would not stand out, like the Chevrolet he himself had chosen. Borrego told Anderson his heart dropped, because he loved the Jaguar on sight, but he told his leader he would return it. "Good," Guevara replied. "I'll give you two hours."

Revolutionary leaders appeared to agree that cars were a necessary component of life, and there was every expectation the automobile busi-

Che Guevara driving a Studebaker, with his second wife, Aleida March, sitting beside him, following their wedding on June 2, 1959. (Courtesy of the photographic archives, Prensa Latina, Havana)

• • •

ness would continue in some form. No sense of impending doom was apparent in the editorial pages of *El Automóvil de Cuba*, for instance. The magazine embraced the change in governments, applauding the ouster of the corrupt and arbitrary Batista administration. Fernando López Ortiz spent the first year after Castro's triumph writing editorials in a sensible, hale-fellow-well-met, let-us-all-reason-together tone, begging to point out to the *fidelistas* some obvious truths, such as how the Cuban auto industry would not survive without installment buying or parts from the United States, both of which were threatened during that year.

Cubans were accustomed to buying on credit, though interest rates were generally high. In 1950, for instance, as credit buying was rapidly increasing in popularity, the interest charged by auto finance companies meant that $1,370 would have to be repaid for every $1,000 loaned, according to Octavio Jordan. This meant a rate of 37 percent—a usurious interest charged on top of prices that were already a third higher than the manufacturer's suggested retail price when the car left the factory in the United States. A standard 1950 Ford 100, for instance, with a suggested sticker price of $1,546 in the States sold in Havana for $3,275.

During the first few months of 1959, the government froze all credit arrangements, issuing a moratorium for debts contracted during the Batista regime and announcing that it would shortly issue new laws regulating credit and installment buying. Hope was widespread that if the government issued a permanent ban on credit terms, it would exempt expensive consumer goods, which Cubans were used to buying on time. In an editorial in August 1959, entitled "Once Again, Sales on the Installment Plan," López Ortiz called for "an equitable law to get up and running again the businesses of automobiles, televisions, refrigerators, washing machines, etc., which are currently nothing more than paralyzed.

"Contrary to what some demagogic critics may say, we, who have always applauded and defended the Revolution, believe that a law of the just kind we are asking for would be one of the best things to be done for the consolidation of the Revolution and the recuperation of our nation's commercial life."

Valiant efforts were made to put a good spin on what was happening. For instance, in September 1959, the *Bulletin of the Union of Auto Accessory Salesmen* lauded the restructured work rules newly in force for garages. "Without a doubt, big steps are being taken to humanize the businesses connected to automobiles. Look at the workshifts in the garages, closing on Saturday all year long, raises in salaries and the new rules about work hours.

"This is what a retired garage worker said. He used to work outside from five in the morning to twelve at night every day of the year, and all he had to show for it was the home he could scrape together and the children God had sent him."

However, garages, along with other automobile-related businesses, were affected by the sudden lack of access to credit. U.S. companies that had been providing credit terms to their Cuban customers for decades began to reconsider their policies. As Cuba started passing new laws affecting U.S. corporate investors in sugar, bananas, and the North American oil companies and refineries operating in the country, banks in the United States became willing to do only cash-on-the-barrelhead business with Cuba, and they advised their stateside clients to follow the same policy.

One company that listened was Champion Spark Plug of Toledo, Ohio. In the spring of 1959, the company announced that its vendors in Cuba would have to pay cash. While Champion was the most popular spark plug in Cuba, alternative brands were available. An agreement to boycott Champion was reached among virtually all the Cuban businesses using or selling their spark plugs. The unions at factories in Cuba like that of U.S. Rubber won a guarantee from management that their vehicles would not use Champion plugs. Effectively, no further orders from Cuban spark plug vendors or users would be forthcoming, and those pending would be canceled.

Champion saw the light. In July, a delegation from Toledo came to Havana, mending fences and arranging credit terms. In August, *El Automóvil de Cuba* ran a photo of two Champion executives at a cocktail party chatting with Fernando López Ortiz. The photo ran at the bottom of a piece entitled "Return to Normality," which reported that the Champion executives toasted "an ample and satisfactory rectification of the situation that recently arose as a consequence of a lamentable error, which has already been corrected." The piece went on to say, in plainer language, that the boycott was called off.

Not all stateside companies were quite so fast to cut credit to their Cuban dealers in the first place. Some chose to support the change in governments, optimistic that things could be worked out. Even Shell Oil, its refineries a point of contention almost from the moment the

Oil companies had been doing business in Cuba for a long time before being nationalized in June 1960. This photograph ran in Bohemia *on May 8, 1949.*
(Courtesy of the photographic archives, Bohemia, *Havana)*

· · ·

Revolution came to power, took a positive attitude in public. Each month it ran a full-page ad in *El Automóvil de Cuba* showing a happy white Cuban couple—she in sunglasses and a scarf, he with his camera to his eye, wearing an olive green Revolutionary army cap—with a map of Cuba beside them. The text beneath the couple reads: "Now that you can travel freely wherever you want, it's time to resume your trips around Cuba. . . . Visit the historic sites, now including those of the Revolution . . . and always travel problem-free with Shell."

In 1959, S. P. Smith, president of Airtex, a Chicago-based manufacturer of fuel and water pumps, wrote a Christmas letter to the company's Cuban dealers. *El Automóvil de Cuba* reproduced it in its December issue. "We really admire the work that is being done by your maximum leader, Doctor Fidel Castro," said the Christmas greeting. "Cuba has always been and will be a free country, happy and hard-working, and with these qualities combined with the honesty and goodwill of its leaders the Revolution cannot help but go forward and triumph."

In addition to credit, the other sensitive economic issue that immediately began to affect Cuba's auto industry was the nation's negative balance of trade with the United States. A dependence on imports weighed down the Cuban economy. The value of foreign imports had grown from $515 million in 1950 to $777 million in 1958. Worse, sugar was the island's only real export, and up to a third of Cuba's sugar went annually to the United States. By 1960, the estimated annual deficit with the States had reached about $30 million, and the United States was cutting back drastically on its purchases of sugar, as retaliation for the nationalization of American-owned properties that had begun.

Cuba's relations with the Soviet Union were expanding. A state bank was established through which all import business had to go and from which licenses for such businesses were issued. Official policy was to allow imports only from countries that were also buying Cuban products, which meant sugar. Castro spoke more and more frequently of the need for new patterns of consumption. It was clear that an economy encouraging expensive imports from the United States would not support health care and schooling for every Cuban regardless of age or race. In a September 1959 speech reported in *Revolución*, Castro explained that people would not have to quit consuming, merely change their buying habits:

> The country must import what it needs in the way of basics, what it needs in the way of food, what it needs in the way of machinery and fuel, because it is not producing these things, but the nation cannot afford the extravagance of importing Cadillacs or luxury items of any kind. . . . The following, for instance, is absurd: in the year 1958, 30 million pesos were spent for cars and accessories and 5 million for tractors, and this is totally absurd from any point of view . . . that in a country that imports rice and other food that they would spend 5 million on tractors and 30 million on cars. This is impossible to keep

doing, impossible. Like it or not, we have to import more tractors than cars.

If there was one thing that Amadeo Barletta understood, it was shifts in power. A man who had worked closely with Mussolini, Trujillo, and Batista did not need to be told that his income from Cadillac sales in Cuba was in jeopardy. Yet even Barletta waited a bit before leaving. He was still in Cuba, and still running *El Mundo*, during 1959. In January 1960, both his newspaper and television station were "intervened," meaning they were placed under revolutionary direction, and he headed to the Dominican Republic to run the Santo Domingo Motor Company he had begun four decades previously.

When Barletta left, he did it without regard for the employees he was leaving behind in Cuba, Olivia Bernabei told me on the phone from her home in Fort Worth, Texas. Her late husband, Anthony, had served as an executive vice president to Barletta's son, Amadeo Barletta Jr. "By the time Barletta and Barletta Jr. left after the Revolution, they had already moved a lot of money out of Cuba. They went to Santo Domingo, and left behind some bad feeling. All Barletta ever cared about was his family. He would always take care of a ne'er-do-well nephew, but not always do the same for an employee.

"He was an industrial tycoon who brought a chef over from Italy to prepare his lunches with celebrities and movie stars. There was a lot of conviviality and a luxurious lifestyle. Then it was finished, completely, all of a sudden."

By the fall of 1959, the Cuban government had put severe restrictions on the import and sale of North American cars. In all of 1959, only 3,264 cars were imported, and most of those in the first six months of the year. The total was half what it had been in 1958. No import restrictions had been applied to the replacement parts business, however, and it was better than ever. The limited number of cars imported from Detroit meant that people needed to keep the cars they had going rather than think about buying a new one. One shipment of 1960 Oldsmobiles left Detroit late in 1959, and a few 1960 Chevrolets. One of the former would go to Camilo Cienfuegos and of the latter to Che Guevara. The annual unveiling of the coming year's new models did not happen. There was no Motorambar; there were no full-page newspaper ads; and the Cuban new car market disappeared.

Tourism was off dramatically during the first year of the Revolution. Sporadic fighting, bombings, and acts of sabotage still flared up in the streets of Havana, as pockets of resistance appeared among the remnants of Batista's army or disgruntled revolutionaries. In addition, a worker's paradise, without gambling or sexual dalliance, had limited appeal to North American tourists. Castro wanted to try to reposition Cuba as a place for people to come with their families to enjoy the tropical climate and cheap prices. The American Society of Travel Agents had scheduled its 1959 international convention in Havana, and it kept the plans, meeting at the Hotel Riviera in October. Castro addressed the group, telling the travel agents that Cuba was prepared to do whatever it took to become their favorite destination.

Another convention—this one three years in the planning—also came to Havana that fall. The first international automobile show ever to be held in Cuba was opened on November 25, 1959, in the Sports Palace, by Castro's handpicked president, Oswaldo Dorticos, dressed in pressed army fatigues and sporting a bushy rebel beard. The show lasted three weeks and came off without incident, drawing favorable attention from the world's automotive press. The U.S. magazine *Automotive World*, in its Spanish-language edition, editorialized: "Cuba's first try at presenting an international automobile show can be considered to have been a success, taking into consideration that it was attended by more than 250,000 visitors and had exhibitions from East Germany, Czechoslovakia, the United States, France, England, Spain and Sweden."

One of the star attractions of the show was a car that converted to an airplane, built by a Massachusetts company. It was driven from New England down to Key West, Florida, from whence it flew to Havana for the auto show. It covered the ninety miles in eighty minutes, which included "several" minutes circling low over Havana before landing, during which "thousands of persons could not believe their eyes," according to the *Diario de la Marina*.

The article in *Automotive World* reported that the aeromobile could attain heights of 12,000 feet and go a hundred miles an hour. Its propeller was mounted in the rear, the wings folded up inside of less than five minutes, and there was room for four passengers. The article was accompanied by a photograph of a smiling U.S. ambassador, Philip Bonsal, sitting behind the wheel of the pod-shaped prototype.

The auto show was a last gasp. Cuba's auto industry was about to be consigned to the same obscurity that awaited the aeromobile from Massachusetts. In November 1959, *El Automóvil de Cuba* was reporting the radical new changes in store for consumers of 1960 model cars—innovations like the distinctive slant-six engines that were being introduced in new Plymouths and Valiants. They were models that would prove tremendously popular in the United States but would never be seen in Cuba.

———

The Astro (Asociaciones de Transportes por Ómnibus) bus station is just a couple of blocks from the National Library. It is a lively public space, as bus stations used to be in the Unites States, before they became the sparsely peopled halls of those too poor to fly. The Astro terminal is a center of community interaction, an urban hub, where people come to eat, drink, or shop, as well as to catch a bus to some other place or to wait for somebody arriving on one.

It can be a long wait. The television monitors flashing transit news throughout the terminal often announce delays in the arrival and departure of the long-distance carriers, the buses for Santiago de Cuba or Holguín or Baracoa. However, hope springs eternal, and the buses do eventually pull in. A number of *jineteros* are always trawling the terminal at arrival time, waiting to pounce on those unfortunate travelers too foreign to know better, eyes glazed from the interminable journey with its excessive or nonexistent air-conditioning and rough ride, packs on their backs looking heavy, indeed, and who are often receptive to the first offer of food and lodging that comes their way. Or *guajiras* overwhelmed by big-city Havana even before their feet touch the bus station's pavement, easy pickings for a smooth-talking man, helpful and sympathetic.

For a period during the 1980s, the Astro terminal fell into such disrepair that even the official media deplored its lack of functioning hygenic facilities and total absence of anywhere to get a little refreshment while in transit. Things have changed for the better. The bus station has a shopping, where cookies, beer, rum, and water can be bought to take away; and there are a pastry shop and a post office as well. Most important for me, on the days when I am working at the José Martí library, there is a little bar with a limited menu in dollars. The basement of the library houses a cafeteria where staff members eat a free lunch of rice and beans with a hard-boiled egg, but the closest place where the reading public can exchange a couple of dollars for a quarter of a desiccated chicken and a few greasy fries, or a piece of pasty pizza and a beer, is the bus station. Though only a handful of tables furnish the cafeteria, a seat is always available. For most of the people passing through the bus terminal, such a meal in any currency is an extravagance that would tax their weekly budget beyond its limits, and they have to find some other way to deal with their hunger.

Across the street from the south end of the terminal, aging Detroit models are parked, long-distance taxis waiting for passengers, their owners crowded up on a couple of stone benches under the shade of a pair of scrawny acacias at the corner. The drivers holler destinations whenever someone coming out of the terminal looks like a potential traveler to another town. "Matanzas," or "Santa Clara," or "Pinar del Río," they sing out. They are driving Chevys, Fords, Dodges, all the mid-Fifties workhorses, beating the broiling road whenever two or more passengers can be gathered. With luck, they will pick up a full load of passengers along the highway, as well as on the return trip to Havana. These cars have not tasted high-octane gasoline for a long time. They have been adapted for hard use with diesel engines, their carburetors modified for economy, tape decks installed in the glove compartments and fans mounted on their dashboards. The drivers all know how to work on their cars, and have to do so on a regular basis. On those rare occasions when something goes wrong that they cannot fix, they have their favorite mechanics.

One of those mechanics is a thirty-eight-year-old Habanero, call him Rafael, the next-door neighbor of someone I met at the library who took an interest in my project and sent Rafael around one day to find me in the reading room. He has close-cropped red hair that is thinning in front, worried brown eyes, a lean face with the skin stretched tight. When he sits down across from me at the reading table and shakes my hand, I know he is the mechanic I was told might turn up, because the skin of his palm is tough and cracked, a mechanic's hand, with lunettes of grease under his nails.

Cars from the United States have fed Rafael since he can remember. His father was one of the small freelance fish that used to swim in pre-revolutionary auto waters. During the 1950s, his father went regularly to Miami and bought a car, bringing it back on the ferry to sell in Havana. Legally. Risking his own money, hoping he could resell it a little cheaper than an agency could but still at a price high enough to leave something for him beyond what he paid for the vehicle and the $80.00 it cost him to bring it over on the ferry. Since the dealers' markup on the Cuban end made the cost for consumers so much higher than the suggested retail price in the United States, a margin existed for an individual to act as a middleman and make a little profit.

Lots of freelance auto dealers operated in those days—some, like Rafael's father, perfectly legally, others less so. Cars stolen in the United States wound up selling in Havana at prices too good to be true. In November 1951, Octavio Jordan wrote about a ring of car thieves that had been uncovered after shipping more than 300 stolen cars on the Miami-to-Havana ferry. In that same year, reports Louis Pérez in *On Becoming Cuban*, twenty Cadillacs stolen in New York City turned up in Havana.

Rafael's father had a successful *chapistería*, a body shop, in Havana, and after the Revolution he kept working on cars. Rafael spent his time after school watching his father replace something on one Detroit model or another. Even when he was in school, he admits, he paid more attention to what he was learning in his father's garage than to his studies, although he stayed in school. Eventually he went to the polytechnic university and studied mechanics.

Of all the cars Rafael's father bought in Miami and shipped over on the ferry, the one he chose to keep for himself was a 1954 Buick Special. When his father died in 2000, Rafael inherited the car. At the moment, he is waiting to get together enough cash to buy a part he needs to get it back on the road. He has, at least, located someone who will sell him the part.

These days, Rafael does a bit of everything—body work, engine work, whatever people need. He is also flexible as to where he works. It may be behind his house, or it may be in a warehouse space where a friend lets him have a small corner. "I have a degree in mechanics, but you can't learn to do it right from a book. I learned from watching my father. There are people who won't let anyone but me touch their cars."

We walk down to the bus station to drink a couple of cans of beer. When we get there, he points to a client's car parked along the curb and raises a hand in greeting to someone under the acacias. Life is not easy, *no es fácil*, he tells me. It is impossible to be happy trying to stay alive in Havana. He has a wife and a girlfriend, each with his kids, each family living in a different house. I met a number of people in Havana who were living in similarly unusual arrangements; families seem to come in numerous configurations and cohabitations.

I point out that many people have trouble just maintaining one family. Rafael raises his eyebrows, shrugs his shoulders, and says he loves them all but keeping everyone satisfied is a constant stress. He feels he's growing old with a lot of possibilities closed to him by the system. "People can't live on their salaries. People can't just go to work, put in eight hours, and get by. They have to put in those hours and have a *búsqueda*, too. How can you live on ten dollars a month, much less get any enjoyment out of being alive? If you want to open up a small business, you can't. If you want to drink a beer, you can't even do that. A beer might cost ten pesos, more than a day's wages. Who can spend a whole day's earnings on one beer?"

The only nonoriginal pieces on his Buick are the carburetor and the alternator, the latter modified to use fewer volts and the former to use less gas, but he has kept the originals, not just for when he might want to sell the car and leave, but for when he might have to get a new license plate, have the car inspected. "If they see a Russian carburetor, they'll ask who I bought it from, and if it was an illegal sale, we're both in deep trouble. After all," he reminds me, "selling meat on the black market can land someone in jail for twenty years.

"Sure things here are going to change," he worries, "but maybe I'll be too old by then to enjoy it or take advantage of it. Ah, well. *Todo tiene arreglo excepto la muerte* [Everything can be fixed except death]."

―――――

Following the Revolution, relations between the United States and Cuba went from Guate-*mala* to Guate-*peor* as Cubans say, from bad to worse. By February 1960, Cuba had agreed to sell 5 million tons of sugar to the Soviet Union over a five-year period in return for oil and a range of other products. In March, President Dwight Eisenhower responded to this Cold War offense by drastically reducing American purchases of Cuban sugar. The Revolutionary government made a point of searching for imports from countries other than the United States. For the myriad of people who had depended on cars to provide a living, the ground was shifting beneath their feet. "The automobile business, which depends almost entirely on the import of vehicles and parts, is one of those that has suffered the most with the rigid control of changes indispensable to remedy the inequality in the balance of trade with the United States and other countries," complained, discreetly, an editorial in the April 1960 issue of *El Automóvil de Cuba*.

When the first shipment of Soviet crude arrived in June, Shell, Standard, and Texaco refused to refine it at their Cuban installations. On June 18, 1960, the government issued a decree that said in part: "The oil companies have continuously defrauded the nation's economy, charging monopolistic prices and distributing huge amounts of cash with the intention of perpetuating their privileges, evading the nation's laws and hatching a criminal plan of boycott against our fatherland, obligating the Revolutionary government to nationalize them."

By July, the refineries had been nationalized. Standard Oil claimed losses of over $71 million, and Texaco put its at $50 million. By the end of July 1960, according to Hugh Thomas, nationalizations of U.S.-owned industries and businesses resulted in losses amounting to $800 million. It was clear that no one was going to return to business as usual anytime soon.

Fidel Castro began to make good on his promises to change the nation's buying habits. A series of measures was passed imposing astronomical taxes on "luxury items." Cars were included among them. An aggrieved Fernando López Ortiz begged the government to reconsider in an August 1960 editorial in *El Automóvil de Cuba*. "Making a detailed and exact calculation of cost and sales price, and taking into account all the charges included in Law 566 and the new taxes, the figures seem incredible," he reasoned, "but they are true. One would have to sell an imported European car that at the beginning of 1959 sold for $2,170 for a few cents less than $6,000."

In response to the nationalizations, on October 13, 1960, Eisenhower announced a complete ban on exports to Cuba, excluding only some medicine and food. The thriving replacement auto parts business was brought to a sudden end. In November, following custom, the annual banquet in the Centro Gallego was held to celebrate the automobile business. However, the trophy for best business of the year was not awarded, because there were no deserving candidates, according to the jury. This edition of the annual banquet was more a wake than a party. The handwriting was on the wall, and it was bad news.

"The United States hopes to paralyze transport in Cuba, but it will not. What it will do for its own industry and export business is lose forever this part of the market, even after they have lifted the prohibition in force," editorialized Fernando López Ortiz in November's *El Automóvil de Cuba.* Many clung to the distant hope that relations would be normalized between the two countries, and that the auto industry would return to how it had been, but prospects for that grew ever dimmer.

On January 3, 1961, the United States severed diplomatic relations with Cuba. The CIA was authorized to orchestrate a range of covert actions against the Revolution. Surely, thought those who still had faith the Yankees would rescue their free-market system, the United States would mount a quick, Marine-led invasion and put someone in power. On April 17, 1961, the battle at the Bay of Pigs, or Playa Girón as the Cubans know it, proved that to be a false hope. In November 1961, two years before he himself was shot in Dallas, John Kennedy authorized Castro's assassination. Over the next few years, everyone had a go at it, from the Mafia to the CIA, with everything from poison pens to exploding cigars. In 2003, the Cuban government put the number of assassination attempts at 625 and counting.

Even the veteran dirty tricks man William Pawley, who had made so much money from Cuban planes and buses, had a last fling at recovering Cuba for the free-market forces. In June 1963, he undertook an elaborate plot to "prove" the existence of undiscovered sites in Cuba where the Soviet Union still had missiles, in contravention of the 1962 missile crisis agreement. He organized a CIA-blessed trip in his sixty-five-foot yacht, the *Flying Tiger*, to bring to Cuba a team that would kidnap a pair of Russian engineers who would swear to the existence of the sites. Military action against Cuba would be justifiable. It was, like all the other assassination and incitement-to-war schemes, a failure.

In fact, the unthinkable had happened. The United States, and its auto industry, were gone from Cuba. No more cars were coming. No more new models would appear on the revolving pedestal under spotlights behind the long plate glass window of what used to be Ambar Motors. And it was not only the business of buying and selling cars that was doomed. The on-hand spark plugs, carburetors, thermostats, brake shoes, fuel pumps, and radiator caps were the last stocks. Goodyear tires or Willard batteries would soon entirely disappear from the shelves. It was the death knell for the parts salesmen who traveled the island and those who maintained shops, the end of the road for the guy with a tire store.

It was also *adiós* to the specialty magazines. It was a long, unexpected fall. As recently as August 1957, an editorial in *El Automóvil de Cuba* had triumphantly announced that the magazine was making its biggest investment in forty-two consecutive years of publishing. A brand-new offset printing press had been bought by the magazine, which would henceforth have higher-quality graphics, a bigger print run, and a more punctual arrival in readers' hands. The magazine was looking forward to a bright, high-tech future. In January 1960, only two-and-a-half years later, *El Automóvil de Cuba*'s big technological announcement was that it was printing on paper made from Cuban *bagasse*, the fibrous pulp left over after sugar has been crushed from cane. The magazine's pages were down from 104 to 48. It had been publishing continuously since 1916, but by July 1961, it was gone. The automotive magazine that lasted longest was *Auto-Cuba*, a monthly published by the Automobile Chamber of Commerce that first appeared in 1948. It made it through April 1963. The editorial in its last issue was self-fulfilling: "The life of our publication is hanging by a thread, so thin and delicate a thread that it could break at any moment, leaving *Auto-Cuba* no choice but to disappear from circulation."

A few branches of the automobile trade, however, did not disappear with the elimination of the profit motive and commerce with the United States. A good mechanic was a good mechanic regardless of the market system, and machines had to be repaired and kept in use. With the sudden fixed quantity of replacement parts, mechanics were more valuable than ever. Initially, before vehicles began to arrive from the Eastern Bloc, the Revolution had to depend on the rolling stock that was already on the island. As factory-made spare parts ran out, the ability to analyze and improvise, which every good Cuban mechanic possesses in abundance, became more and more valuable.

The Revolution meant that Carlos Alonso, who had owned and run Relámpago for four decades, was out of a job and out of a business, but Juan Carlos, the mechanic who had worked at Relámpago since he was twelve, kept right on working after the Revolution. Juan Carlos's skills with an engine were evident, and his low-key but unshakable confidence in his ability to diagnose a car's problems and get it back on the road had not escaped attention.

"I had a little shop that I worked in on the side that I figured would still be there if Relámpago went under. The government intervened, and they sent me, and a lot of other small mechanics, to work on freight trucks. In 1961, I was with the first group of mechanics who went to study in the Soviet Union. I had never been out of Cuba. We went to Odessa. From there they sent us to Kiev, the capital of the Ukraine."

He initially lived with six other mechanics in a hotel room. The Soviets liked them and eventually provided them with a house. They studied at the Gaz factory, learning how to repair Soviet trucks so that they could come back to Cuba and keep the trucks running. "And, we did. We established a plant for the repair of Soviet vehicles in Cuba. It's still here in Havana on Vía Blanca."

In 1994, at sixty, Juan Carlos retired from his mechanic's job with the military. He now works as a freelance mechanic, paying his self-employment tax and finding parts where he can. By the time he left government service, Cuban mechanics were completely familiar with Soviet Bloc vehicles, a lot of which eventually came to Cuba; but for the first few years of the Revolution, Cuba's existing fleet had to bear the load. It took a while before vehicles from the Eastern Bloc, and the know-how to maintain them, arrived.

Among the first new vehicles to arrive in numbers, in the early 1960s, were heavy-duty Soviet-made Gaz trucks from the same plant where Juan Carlos was working at the time. They were mostly for military use. While the Cold War raged in the rest of the world, Gaz trucks teamed up in Cuban fleets with Fords and GMCs and Dodge Fargos. "Military use" in those early years of the Revolution could cover a lot of things, from battlefields to literacy campaigns. By August 1961, nearly a million illiterate people had been identified, and battalions of students and adults volunteered to teach them to read. It was the fleet of available trucks that carried these volunteers to their tasks around the country.

As the Revolution sought to address Cuba's public transportation problems, private taxis became ruteros *under the administration of the Servicio de Transporte Popular; here, a* rutero *picks up passengers in March 1962. (Courtesy of the photographic archives,* Bohemia, Havana*)*

• • •

The Soviets thought of the Gaz as a heavy-duty workhorse. The Cubans, used to Detroit steel and technology, did not agree. A common joke among Cubans is that in Russia a Gaz lasts through three drivers, but in Cuba one driver goes through three trucks. Nevertheless, the addition to the existing fleet was welcomed, and almost immediately mechanics figured out how to utilize one or another part from the Gaz assembly to repair something on a Detroit model, so that the Soviet vehicles soon began to make their first contributions to the parts pool.

It was American cars that moved people and goods during the early years of the Revolution. Petroleum products were flowing from the Soviet Union and were priced within reason. Gas and oil were not out of reach, and people who had cars from before the Revolution kept them running. Those who acquired cars by appropriating them from someone fleeing into exile were also able to keep them on the road. Fidel Castro continued to travel in an Oldsmobile, almost always with a driver. He went to the Bay of Pigs invasion in an Oldsmobile, sitting up front next to his driver, Ángel, according to a *Bohemia* article by Flavio Bravo Pardo, who was also in the front seat as they sped toward the battle at Playa Girón.

Che Guevara also continued to drive his Chevrolet, only occasionally allowing himself to be driven. When Guevara was driving, the journey's outcome was never certain. One of the men who often accompanied him as driver—or passenger, depending on Che's mood—was Eliseo de la Campa. In a 1987 *Juventud Rebelde* article, he recalled one of Che's accidents:

> We left the Ministry of Labor in Che's Chevrolet and with Che driving, when we suddenly came up behind an old guy pedaling his bicycle. The old guy hadn't realized that the hoe he had strapped on behind had slipped and the handle was sticking out toward the ground.
>
> Che didn't see the handle, and trying to pass, his right fender caught it and tossed the old man and his bike. The old man was sitting on the ground, looking at the damaged bike, worried.
>
> Che came up to him and asked if he'd been hit, if he was all right. And the old man lifted up his wrinkled face, looked at the *comandante*'s face, recognized him, and said, "But was it you who hit me?" And Che: "Unfortunately, yes." And the old man: "What's unfortunate? What luck I've had to be hit by you. Do you know what my family will say when I tell them it was you who hit me? . . . If I wasn't on the road, you wouldn't have hit me. What luck for me!"
>
> At any rate, Che later sent him a bicycle.

Even with some supplies of gas and oil flowing from the Soviet Union, public transport quickly became a problem for the Revolution. Buses were harder than cars to keep on the road. It was one thing to jerry-rig an automobile engine, but entirely another to improvise with a GMC bus motor or chassis. The parts embargo began to be felt almost immediately, and nowhere more acutely than at bus stops around Havana and

Santiago de Cuba. Between 1959 and 1966, the nation's urban bus fleet was reduced from 4,300 to 3,300, according to Gonzalo Fundora in his 1985 book, *Transporte Urbano*.

One of the first shipments of vehicles to reach the streets of Havana after the Revolution was a fleet of Warsawas, a sort of minibus with seats for ten, which was built in Poland. In an example of the sort of innovative thinking that predominated in those early hopeful days of the Revolution, when anything seemed possible, the demand for public transport served as a means of providing work to unemployed ex-prostitutes forced by the government to abandon their old profession. Driver training was provided, and the women ran the Warsawas as *ruteros*, running a standard fixed-rate route at five cents a passenger. The Polish vehicles were all painted violet, and the Cubans called them *violeteras* or *polaquitas*, according to transport historian Mercedes Herrera Sorzano. The passenger service lasted until July 1964, with an average of 640 vehicles on the street, annually carrying an average of 24 million people, before being phased out in favor of larger buses.

The first new passenger cars began to appear on the streets in the late 1960s: Skodas from Czechoslovakia. These, and the Soviet-built Ladas that followed, were reserved, like most privileges, for high-ranking military and government officials. As more Soviet oil and Eastern Bloc cars began circulating in Cuba, Ladas and Volgas and Trebants and Skodas were distributed to professionals—doctors and lawyers and university officials.

The utilitarian, boxy vehicles did not excite much aesthetic enthusiasm. But, for most people, by then it did not matter. That they were cars and ran was what counted. It did not take long to expunge the longing to buy a new North American car every few years. Those who had cars kept them. Those who got a car after 1960 hoped to get one that would keep running with a minimum of upkeep, burning as little gasoline as possible. How it looked was relatively unimportant; what mattered was getting from one place to another. Under the circumstances, Cubans plumped down solidly for the Henry Ford consumer standard of durability—now emanating from the Eastern Bloc—as opposed to Alfred

Sloan's concept of a car as a matter of style. Castro had, indeed, changed the country's patterns of consumption.

As the government distributed cars to the deserving, it put narrow restrictions on their use, making sure that even though people might drive the same Ladas or Moskviches or Volgas for five, ten, or fifteen years, they would not consider themselves owners of the cars. Owners of prerevolutionary cars with their *traspaso* papers in order can buy, sell, and bequeath them, but to this day, a Lada, or any other postrevolutionary car, cannot even be passed on as an inheritance, much less sold. People do sell them, of course, but it is a tricky business. Since it is illegal to sell, the seller can never admit to having sold a car, so if the buyer refuses to pay all that is owed after taking possession, there is nowhere for the seller to complain.

The gradual flow of cars into Cuba from Eastern Europe was also good news for the existing stock of Detroit's finest. It did not take Cuban mechanics long to learn how to adapt parts made in one part of the world to cars made in another. Time and again, Cuban ingenuity commuted death sentences for the North American workhorses, keeping them on the road and off the scrap heap. Saved by people like the man Roberto Pérez knew in Santiago de Cuba who could replace a wraparound Chevrolet windshield with one formed in a wooden mold he built in his back yard. The technology to produce wraparound front windshields, rather than two pieces of glass joined at the middle under a protective strip, was introduced throughout the Detroit auto industry in 1951, but it is not easy to do in the back yard, so Cubans have also become adept at replacing shattered wraparounds with two halves of windshields salvaged from somewhere and joined in the middle.

Or rescued by a man outside of Havana who salvages worn-out batteries in his backyard garage, recharging them by using a homemade crucible and a complicated system of his own design. Stephen Smith has written about him: "Before Ángel would let a battery out of his garage, he measured its performance against a collection of coils thrumming in a corner of the garage which made your tongue prickle if you went within a few feet of them."

The names of many of those early mechanics are legendary—people like Delfín Matos Ortiz from the Vista Hermosa neighborhood of Santiago de Cuba, who figured out the metal composition of piston rings from Detroit and taught himself how to reproduce them. He was so well known that Fidel Castro once asked him to come to Havana and install piston rings in a broken hospital generator, according to journalist Frank Smyth.

No less renowned is Eugenio O'Hallorans, a tall man with thinning gray hair, seventy-nine years old, who lives in the small, bustling town of Santiago de las Vegas, seventeen kilometers outside of Havana, and whose stainless steel replacement grillework and bumpers reproduce the originals exactly. Members of his family staff the shop where the metal is worked, under his direction. If the metal around the headlight on a 1955 Ford has oxidized, or the grillework on a 1953 Cadillac is damaged in an accident, it is likely to wind up in his shop to be replaced. O'Hallorans was apprenticed to a tinsmith at the age of twelve and can reproduce a part that will look identical to the original but last lots longer because it is made of stainless steel, not a nickel-chrome alloy of the sort used in Detroit. It may take him months to find the material, but once he does, it will have been worth the wait. O'Hallorans's parts are not built to wear out.

Much of his business, over the years, has come from taxis and cars that are hired for weddings and fiestas. Havana is a big city, and people who live there have always relied, at least occasionally, on use of a taxi for transport. Taxi drivers, like mechanics and car watchers, turned out to be necessary in postrevolutionary Cuba. Early on, revolutionary authorities decided that the best way to control the business and make taxis available to those who needed them most was to establish and enforce a system of taxi stands, or *piqueras*. The two most important functions served by taxis, it was agreed, were to carry passengers to and from hospitals and to take them to and from funerals. When fifty Alfa Romeos arrived from Italy in 1970, they were designated as taxis and distributed to *piqueras* at hospitals around the city.

By the end of 1977, some 16,500 cars had been imported by the revolutionary government. Some of them were working as taxis, according to a *Granma* article by Alexis Shelton published on January 23, 1979. "Nevertheless, this service [taxis] has been seriously affected by the blockade, and a growing number of vehicles have been paralyzed by the lack of replacement parts or tires."

The state-run taxi service, Panataxi, created a fleet of distinctively painted yellow and black taxis, mostly Ladas, that did not run fixed routes but went where the passenger requested and charged by zones. The yellow-and-black taxis can still be seen on the streets of Havana, still mostly Ladas, many showing their age. By February 1990, 3,991 taxis were operating in Havana, according to an article in *Bohemia* by Enrique Valdés. Five hundred of these were free to roam, and the rest were assigned to *piqueras*. After the Special Period, the total number of taxis had fallen to below a thousand. In an interview with *Juventud Rebelde* in 1998, Armando Reyes, the director of Panataxi, said, "There are 720 in the fleet, but only 238 are really working; the rest are unable to because of fuel problems.

"Of these 238, about 120 are destined to lend their services to funeral homes, because here, on average, there are fifty-five deaths per day. Today's taxis have two principal missions: hospitals and funeral parlors. This is what we have to guarantee."

Because they are big and strong and can hold a lot of people, the fleet of surviving North American cars in Cuba has often been used for taxi duty. Cars exist that have been working continually as taxis since before the Revolution. I discovered one when I stopped to talk to its owner, sixty-five-year-old Antonio, who had his head under the hood of the 1956 Chevrolet that he had bought almost new in 1958 for 800 pesos and has been driving as a taxi ever since. Antonio is short and blocky, with thinning white hair and, on the day I met him, grizzled with a three-day stubble of gray beard. "The hours are better now. In the old days I would drive all night. I was twenty-five, I didn't care. You'd drive tourists all night long, take them to fancy expensive places like the Tropicana, or other more reasonable ones like the Mambo Club. You waited all night outside. You had to take good care of the tourists. If anything

An older car requires constant attention, as the owner of this Pontiac, photographed in December 1990, would be the first to acknowledge. Still, he seems to be taking it all in stride. (Courtesy of the photographic archives, Bohemia, Havana*)*

• • •

happened to them, it was on your head. Even the prostitutes had to take good care of them. Now the hours are better, but sometimes it's not so interesting.''

The '56 Chevy is not exactly the same car that waited outside the Tropicana—these days it has a six-cylinder engine from a Chevy built in Argentina and a carburetor from a Lada. The car was parked curbside under the shade of a ceiba tree, along Twenty-fifth Street in Vedado. Antonio gestured toward the engine with a thick, grease-stained hand. ''Before the Revolution, all you had to pay was the gasoline. Now, there are taxes, and you've got to be your own mechanic, too. No one can afford to be bringing their car to be fixed. Those are the changes for the taxi driver. For the taxi, it's also harder than it used to be. When you drive it as a *rutero* you carry as many people as you can, and they're always getting in and out and slamming the doors." He reflected a moment. "At least things have improved since the Special Period. That was terrible, that was the worst."

The Special Period engendered a gypsy cab market in Havana, a black market in taxis. Dollars were illegal but would buy what was not otherwise available. Tourists were the only source of dollars, and someone with access to a car could ferry tourists if he was not apprehended. If that happened, he would be subject to fines, or jail, or confiscation of the vehicle. For many, dollars were worth the risk. Doctors and dentists and lawyers and university professors who had been fortunate enough to receive a Lada or a Volga in the 1970s or 1980s moonlighted as taxi drivers during the 1990s. Two people were necessary to make the business work: one to hang around the hotel and pick off likely tourists before they found a legal cab and the other to wait with the car and drive it.

In 1993, when the government began allowing people to work for themselves, in limited numbers, some people immediately applied to work as taxi drivers. Once this happened, other individuals began putting their cars to work as taxis without waiting to apply for permission. By December of that year, Panataxi was losing $34,700 a month in tourist revenues to gypsy cabs, according to an April 1994 *Bohemia* article by Alberto Salazar. In early 1994, the police began cracking down on people who hung around hotels and fished for tourists. In the first three months of the year, they took 105 cars off the streets.

Another partial solution to the transportation crisis was two-wheeled. Bicycles were not particularly popular in Cuba historically, either before or after the Revolution. The average Cuban's attitude seems to have been the same as that of a North American: why ride a bicycle when you could be in a Buick? or in anything else with four wheels and an engine? Che Guevara inaugurated the first postrevolutionary bicycle factory, in Caibarién, on June 19, 1964. It produced the Gaviota (Seagull) brand. By 1990, at the start of the Special Period, it was still the only bicycle factory in the country, producing some 5,000 bikes a year. In 1991, however, four new factories were built and by 1994, over 200,000 bikes a year were being manufactured in Cuba. The government also distributed more than a million bicycles from China over those three years, and by 1994 more than 2 million were in circulation. The bikes were not just being used to transport individuals. Many were rigged up with an extra seat and an awning to cover passengers behind the bicyclist, rickshaw-style, and used as taxis. Even today, with the island in recovery from the Special Period, most Cuban towns have almost no automobile, truck, or bus traffic. What moves people and goods is either carts pulled by animals or bicycles. The circumstances of transport during the Special Period were described by Margot Pepper in an article in *Granma Internacional*:

> Imagine what will happen if an industrialized nation of more than 10 million inhabitants has its oil reduced by 40% and as a consequence has to cut in half its fleet of metropolitan buses, cut in half the number of state vehicles and cut by 30% the amount of gas distributed to private cars, leaving their owners to wonder how they can resolve their situations with only 10 and a half gallons a month? This is the type of economic paralysis that threatened Cuba after the collapse of European socialism, but which was, in great measure, halted by the introduction of bicycles into the urban transport system.

City buses were, naturally, hit hard by the scarcity of combustible fuel. In 1990, at the beginning of the Special Period, Havana had some 2,614 buses, according to a report from the Ministry of Transport published in 1993 in the *Tribuna de La Habana*. By May 1993, the fleet was down to 1,649, of which 1,058 were temporarily or permanently out of service. In 1989, 225 tons of fuel had been used each day by Havana's buses, and by 1995 that was down to 70, wrote Eloy Rodríguez in *Granma Internacional*. Habaneros made some 800,000 trips a day by bus in 1995, as opposed to 4.3 million in 1985. Another 700,000 people rode bicycles, as opposed to virtually no one in 1985. An estimated 500 buses a year broke down beyond repair and needed to be replaced. When a parts factory burned down in Russia, 160 Kamaz buses were soon idled in Cuba. Donations of secondhand buses from countries like the Netherlands or Spain were

*The state will pay for a wedding cake or a birthday cake, but people still have to get it home.
Photographed in September 1990, these folks didn't want to wait any longer for a taxi,
so they stopped a Lada to ask its driver if he would give them a ride.
(Courtesy of the photographic archives, Bohemia, Havana)*

• • •

frequent, but they rarely included replacement parts, so the buses were vulnerable to being sidelined by breakdowns.

Hay que resolver. If petroleum products are not available, then the weeds, grass, and other silage a horse eats become valuable for their potential as fuel, once again. A well-fed horse can get people from one side of town to the other, as, for that matter, can a donkey, a mule, or a pair of oxen. A Chinese-made bicycle with two seats jerry-rigged over the rear wheel can do the same. Do what can be done, try and stay alive, and wait the shortages out. "Everything can be fixed except death."

It is nine-thirty on a Sunday morning, and with nothing else to do, I walk over to the Astro bus station from my room to buy a can of Bucanero beer to drink with lunch. On a two-block residential stretch of Twenty-seventh Street, the monthly neighborhood cleanup is in progress. Not a teenager is in sight—no doubt all are still deep in Sunday adolescent sleep—but everyone else has turned out to work, from young marrieds to senior citizens. Many kids are also in attendance, still young enough that a parent can command them to do chores. Everyone is out cutting the grass along the curb, picking up trash, pulling weeds, raking, piling. Toddlers pull a weed or two and further their ongoing civics education about how to live with others. It is a typical Sunday morning neighborhood cleanup in Vedado, organized by the block's chapter of the Committees to Defend the Revolution, the *Comités de Defensa de la Revolución* (CDR). The CDR is the government's grassroots organizational and security apparatus, with a chapter in every neighborhood and community in Cuba. The local CDR director keeps a comprehensive eye on everything that happens in the neighborhood, from who sleeps with whom to which neighborhood residents did not vote in the last mandatory referendum or put in volunteer time in the mosquito eradication program. Who participates in the "block beautification" morning and, more important, who does not, will be recorded. The CDR chief is easy to spot—a middle-aged woman moving through the midst of her working neighbors, a clipboard held against her chest. Nevertheless, everyone else seems relaxed, people enjoying themselves. The morning is pleasantly warm, and it does not feel bad to work up a desultory sweat chopping weeds along the curb with a machete or raking up the chopped weeds. It is good to see the block look increasingly trimmed and manicured, cared for, as the morning wears on. A nice easy feeling is in the air as neighbors joke and laugh with each other, lean on rakes, and exchange family news.

In the next block a folding table has been set out on the sidewalk, and a domino game is in progress beneath the shade of a curbside acacia. Four men are sitting around the table on kitchen chairs, and the game will likely continue all day. Players will change, coming and going, but the game will go on, played with a verve and grace that is a pleasure to watch. I dawdle. A Fiat Polski comes down the street, I hear it before I see it, the distinctive high, vacuum cleaner whine of its engine washing across the domino players. The little Fiat-shaped bug is powered by an engine in the rear, and the hood covering the motor is usually left open slightly for ventilation. Built in Poland, it is so small that the roof is barely higher than a person's waist. Roberto Pérez calls the car "a uterus," because by the time someone unfolds his or her body and struggles up out of the front seat it's like being reborn into the world.

Continuing to the Astro terminal, across the street from the south end of the bus station I see a man standing beside a gray 1952 Chevy. When I ask about it, he tells me that he bought it five months ago for 60,000 pesos (about $2,200) and rents it out daily, except Sunday, for a hundred pesos. He rents it to a guy who drives it as a *rutero* and clears 150–250 pesos a day. The driver pays for the gas, but the owner pays for repairs and maintenance. The engine is original and runs on gasoline. The owner would have to have a *permiso* to put in a diesel engine, and if the authorities open the hood and catch him without a permit, they can take the car. He has brought his father-in-law to catch a bus, and his wife is inside seeing her father off. The bus, not surprisingly, is late.

The Chevy owner has fine, sandy brown hair, cut short, balding in front. He's lean, with big forearms. The Chevy is rough looking on the outside, and that's how he likes it, he says. If it looks that way, no one messes with it. He has a 1955 Ford at home, which he bought ten years ago, also all original. He uses it for his personal car if the Chevy is out working as a *rutero*. The Ford looks a lot better than this one, he says. It's a collector's car.

I comment that 60,000 pesos in *moneda nacional* does not seem like too bad a price for a good car. He shakes his head at my ignorance about how things are. "A Cuban depending on a salary of 250, 300, 400 pesos a month can't get 60,000 pesos together in a lifetime—never, absolutely never, no way. Just buying food, paying the bills, keeping a household going, having a little fun on the weekends, he'll never be able to get any-where near that together without something extra on the side, a *búsqueda* to bring in some dollars."

What does he himself do? I ask. "*No importa*, it doesn't matter," he answers. "*Hay que inventar* [You have to invent something]. Without some-thing, no one can get 60,000 pesos together, or even live decently."

His wife comes out of the station, a broad-beamed woman with blonde hair. She comes up, nods a greeting toward me, and sits down in the passenger seat. He excuses himself, we shake hands, and he gets in and starts the car. It sounds good and strong, the engine running without a miss or a stutter. I say so.

He looks up out of the window at me. "You think this sounds good, you ought to hear my Ford. It's a beautiful car. And, it looks good. I've had guys stop me in the street to tell me about this or that old car club. I don't want to join any old car club. My car is nobody's business but mine. I don't want anyone telling me what I can or cannot do with my car.

"See you later." He raises his arm in a half wave, elbow braced on the broad window rest, and drives away, right hand at the top of the large black steering wheel. I buy a couple of cans of Bucanero in the termi-nal, and walk back to my room, stopping to watch a few innings of Little League–level baseball on the way.

He may not want to join a car club, but when he speaks about his Ford, his voice has the same fondness and respect that I heard in the voices of club members talking about their cars. It seems odd that collec-tors and car clubs still exist in Cuba, given the fact that everything needs to be used. To possess something for its aesthetic value rather than its utility is a luxury that few Cubans can afford. Nevertheless, in addition to the club in Santiago de Cuba, administered by Roberto Pérez, two clubs exist in Havana, each with more than fifty members. They meet monthly and organize an annual rally. The hundred-odd members of the Harley-Davidson motorcycle club do the same thing, plus hold an annual memorial service in the Colón Cemetery at the grave of a Harley mechanic considered to have been the best ever.

Some of the old models owned by car club members, if they just hang in there for another few years, may once again gain parity with their North American counterparts and be treated like gems, like jewels, cosseted, buffed, shined, and pampered, kept under cover except for rare excursions. When trade between the United States and Cuba finally reopens, as must inevitably happen, it is impossible to guess what price a pristine 1959 burgundy Ford Edsel convertible will bring on the market. It might be enough money to last quite a while.

Francisco "Paco" Rodríguez has a 1925 Chevrolet in the garage next to his house in Havana's Lawton neighborhood. It is a beautiful car, beige with black fenders and running boards. All its parts date to between 1925 and 1928, a period when the engines stayed the same. His father's uncle bought it new in Havana. He inherited the car from his father in 1990. Because it is a prerevolutionary model with all its papers, private ownership is permitted. He loves the car, but it is also the only one he has, so when there is a trip to be made or something to be hauled, the Chevy is not exempt and has to get out there in Havana traffic. In the States, the Chevy would easily be worth $20,000, but Rodríguez says he would never sell his, even if he could.

Rodríguez is a past president of the Automobile Club of Havana, which has some fifty-five members who meet at the beach with their cars on the third Sunday of each month. This car club is a reincarnation of one that lasted from 1903 to 1956 before disappearing. Today, the oldest car club in Havana is the La Macorina Club, named after the first Cuban woman to obtain a driver's license. Lorenzo Verdecia began organizing the club in 1994. He does not own a car, but he started the club when he had a difficult time finding thirteen pre-1940 cars for a Cuban television program he was directing.

"I couldn't believe how hard it was to find the cars, because there was always a special feeling among Cubans for the North Americans and for their cars," Verdecia told me when I spoke with him one afternoon at a table on the grounds of Havana's Hotel Nacional. "The United States is only ninety miles away, and its cars were always considered the best here. After the Revolution, during the gas and parts shortages, there were people who just put their cars away, kept them, and did their best to maintain them, but did not use them. You still see cars here with the original paint job or seat covers they had when they left the factory in Detroit.

"Others held on to their cars thinking the revolutionary government would fall in a few years. They died waiting, and their cars passed to other people. Then there are some who found another car like theirs and used the pieces from one to keep the other running. The numbers of surviving American cars are diminishing every year and if we don't take care of them, they'll disappear. That's why I started the club."

In the Special Period, when the Cuban government was desperate for hard cash and products to export, officials decided to take advantage of the collectibility factor and sell off North American cars to anyone who wanted to buy them for dollars. U.S. citizens could not buy them directly, prohibited by the continuing economic blockade, but anyone else could take them to a third country, from which they could be sold legally to a gringo. Of course, the government had to acquire them first. The cars were among the few things left from before the Revolution that were still held as private property. They were legally owned by individuals. The government had to pay for them, which it did with a new Lada. That was the offer: a new Lada for an old American car. There were some takers, some practical-minded folks who saw that a new Lada would run lots cheaper and probably last much longer than the old Detroit steel they were driving. A Lada is a perfectly good car, economical and dependable, if plain and small. But a number of owners said thanks but no thanks and hung on to their collectibles.

The government sold the cars pretty much at Cuban prices, often in lots, to foreign dealers who would resell them to collectors. Sometimes the lot would be six *cacharros* and one treasure. The buyer had to spring for a group of cars that would take a lot of investment to bring up to collectible status, but, among the cars, thrown in to make the package worth buying, might be a red-and-cream 1959 Ford Fairlane convertible or a spotless 1951 Nash Rambler Country Club. Eduardo Mesejo, director of Havana's Museo del Automóvil, does not have any firm estimate of how many cars were shipped out, but he believes that the number was in the hundreds and that many of Cuba's rarest and most collectible cars were sold. "Nobody came here to buy a *cacharro* from the government," he said. "They came to buy a car that would be worth having and spending money on to restore it to top condition. It was a mistake that the government made because of an acute need for foreign currency. They bled the country of some of its automotive patrimony. These cars form a part of our national identity, and such things don't have a price. There were people who didn't have that vision, who thought that selling the cars would help the country. It did help from one point of view, but from the other it was not helping.

"It makes me sad, but people contact me all the time, from all over the world, to say they have found cars that came from Cuba that are now in the hands of famous or wealthy people. Fortunately, the sale of these cars was stopped by a man who does have a historical vision of them, Havana's city historian, Eusebio Leal. He does not have a profound knowledge of these cars, but he does have a lot of sense, and he realized what was happening and stopped it."

After all, the same chord is struck in the chest of a Cuban who glimpses a 1957 Plymouth Belvedere swooping by in the open street as strikes a North American of a certain age—mine—who grew up with these cars in the driveway. The sight of a 1954 Chevy with its hood up was once familiar in North America, in the countryside or on a city street, and to see it repeated fifty years later in big-city Havana, or in the smallest hamlet, a *pueblocito*, arouses a profound sense of nostalgia and a pleasing sense of continuity. Unfortunately, neither this shared nostalgia, nor a common devotion to baseball, nor numerous other ties that once bound have proven strong enough to bring the United States and Cuba into a civil relationship of reconciliation. The occasional baseball game between teams from the U.S. and Cuban big leagues has drawn sell-out crowds but has not led to an overall thaw in relations—any more than has the admiration of car collectors from the States for the extant Cuban fleet done much to remove the chill between the island and the United States.

While much Cuban ingenuity has gone into keeping old American vehicles on the road, some of it has been deflected into turning them into seagoing vessels. The twelve Cubans fleeing the island in this floating truck—with its drive shaft rigged to turn a propeller—were intercepted forty miles from the Florida coast in July 2003. (Photograph © Gregory Ewald/U.S. Coast Guard)

· · ·

A group known as TailLight Diplomacy, formed under the aegis of the United States–Cuba Sister Cities Association, hopes to promote the island's surviving U.S. cars as a Cuban cultural asset, according to the group's spokesman, Rick Shnitzler, a Philadelphia urban planner. The Americans want to ship parts, from door handles to carburetors, down to Cuba by the containerful, along with repair manuals, paint specifications, and other information that would ensure that restorations are carried out following internationally accepted collectors' standards, according to an article in the *New York Times* in June 2002.

"How these cars survived is like, How did they build the pyramids?" Shnitzler is quoted in the *Times* piece. "[Cuban mechanics] are just magicians and wizards, pure and simple. They just take stuff from Russian vehicles and adapt parts, but the quality of the work is outstanding."

The North American auto collecting community has a high regard for Cubans and the way they have preserved their cars, Schnitzler told me in an e-mail, and this admiration is shared by grassroots Americans of every demographic stripe. But for all the group's good intentions, it cannot actually do much, primarily, Schnitzler told me, because it is illegal for his group's members to ship anything to Cuba.

Communication between the United States and Cuba is not easy. E-mail transmission can be sporadic. Paper mail is problematic, to put it mildly, as it is all routed through an intermediary nation. Calling on the phone from the States requires an Olympian patience, as the few existing circuits are busy for hours on end. The only way to make certain a package will arrive is to send it with someone traveling to Cuba. As anyone who tries to communicate with the island knows, *no es fácil*, it's not easy, as the Cubans themselves say about so many things.

While most Cubans scuffle to put food on the table daily, a new car market also exists there. A certain amount of money is spent by the government on new cars for state rental agencies and for high-ranking officials. Mercedes-Benz has an agency in Havana, as do Peugeot, Mitsubishi, Toyota, and a number of other European and Asian car manufacturers. Just as Cubans took to Detroit's fins and flash before the Revolution, their eyes now follow the newest European models as they pass in the street. When Cuba and the United States are finally reconciled, a market for sport utility vehicles will be waiting, and new cars will once again flow from Detroit to Havana. It is also likely that a traffic in cars will flow the other way. It is widely believed in Havana that a number of the finest North American cars have been taken out of circulation by speculators in Miami who pay someone in Cuba to garage and maintain these classics, to keep them hidden somewhere out of harm's way, lubricated, polished, and started once a week, betting that when Castro dies and the regime changes, the car can be recovered and brought to the States.

But what will happen to those 60,000 or so *cacharros* now plugging away in Cuba, the vast majority of which are in Santiago de Cuba and Havana? It is hard to imagine a favorable future for these multitudinous beasts of burden. When collectors from the States can visit Cuba, perhaps they will pay high prices for the chance to bring an old car home. It is possible that some venerable vehicles will once again feel U.S. pavement beneath their tires before they go to the scrap heap. Even so, when people finally can travel freely between the two countries again, gringo car collectors will be interested only in the jewels, those few with unbent frames, with unbashed doors, with original parts inside and out.

A pampered old age is not what awaits the vast majority of North American cars in Cuba, the *cacharros* with their battered bodies and smoking modified engines, their Lada carburetors and Fiat Polski points, or tubing coiled around the tailpipe to heat kerosene as it passes through on its way to a mongrel engine. Who will want them? Likely, no one other than their owners, who will keep them working until they cannot run or will not start. The cars will keep on doing what they have been doing on a daily basis for over half a century already, playing a key role in moving people from one place to another. They will run out their lives along the steamy streets of Santiago de Cuba and Havana. As the years pass and the actual number of Detroit's cars on the road in Cuba grows ever smaller, their iconographic status will rise. They will come to evoke the Fidel Castro years, revolutionary relics that will gradually disappear, absorbed into the collective memory of *compañeros* and *compañeras*, as new Cubans are born and old cars fade into the world's pool of recycled steel.

BIBLIOGRAPHY

General

Anderson, Jon Lee. *Che Guevara: A Revolutionary Life.* New York: Bantam Press, 1997.

Arizala, Aurelio. *Verdades vs. Mentiras: Ilegalidades "Legalizadas" en El Affaire Pawley.* Havana: Editorial Zarcotipicos, 1950.

Baker, Christopher. *Cuba.* Moon Handbooks. Emeryville, Calif.: Avalon Publishing Co., 2000.

Beadle, Tony. *The American Automobile.* New York: Barnes and Noble Books, 2000.

Fagiuoli, Martino. *Automoviles del Sueño Americano en Cuba.* Bologna: CV Export Divisione Libri, 2001.

Feijoo, Ángel. "Medio Siglo de Automovilismo." *Carteles,* May 18, 1952, 134–37.

Hatchwell, Emily, and Simon Calder. *Cuba: A Guide to the People, Politics and Culture.* New York: Interlink Publishing Group, 1999.

Hinckle, Warren, and William W. Turner. *The Fish Is Red: The Story of the Secret War against Castro.* New York: Harper & Row Publishers, 1981.

Hirsch, Jay. *Great American Dream Machines.* New York: Macmillan Publishing Co., 1985.

López Ortiz, Fernando. "50 Años de Automovilismo." *El Automóvil de Cuba,* May 1951, 42–121.

Miller, Tom. *Trading with the Enemy.* New York: Atheneum Publishing Co., 1992.

———, ed. *Travelers' Tales: Cuba.* San Francisco: Travelers' Tales Guides, 2001.

Morrison, Allen. "The Tramways of Havana (Habana)." On the Web site: www.tramz.com.

Pérez, Louis A., Jr. *On Becoming Cuban: Identity, Nationality, and Culture.* Chapel Hill: University of North Carolina Press, 1999.

Ripley, C. Peter. *Conversations with Cuba*. Athens: University of Georgia Press, 1999.

Smith, Stephen. *The Land of Miracles*. London: Little, Brown and Co., 1997.

Stanley, David. *Cuba*. London: Lonely Planet Publications, 2000.

Thomas, Hugh. *Cuba or The Pursuit of Freedom*. London: Eyre & Spottiswoode, 1971.

Chapter 1. Locomobiles and Model T's

Alfonso Gallol, Berta. *Los Transportes Habaneros*. Volume 3. Havana: Instituto de Investigación del Transporte, 1991.

"El Automóvil en La Habana." *El Fígaro*, December 10, 1901, 542–43.

Breese, James. "Motoring in the Cuban Republic." *Motor*, May 1904, 1–8.

Carrobello, Caridad. "Autos Viejos: A Toda Maquina." *Bohemia*, November 20, 1998, B4–B7.

"Cien Años de Velocidad." *Granma*, July 10, 1998, 5.

"Cuban Automobile Trade Shows Marvellous Increase." *Motor Age*, February 15, 1906, 21.

"The Cuban Road Race." *Motor Age*, December 29, 1904, 3.

Estep, Ralph. *El Toro*. Detroit: Packard Motor Car Co., 1909.

Forment, Carlos E. *Cronicas de Santiago de Cuba: Continuación de la Obra de Don Emilio Bacardi*. Volume 1. Santiago de Cuba: Editorial Arroyo, 1953.

Goodman, Walter. *Un Artista en Cuba*. Havana: Editorial Letras Cubanas, 1986.

Grenet, Emilio. *Musica Popular Cubana*. Havana: Ministry of Education, 1939.

Herrera Sorzano, Mercedes. "Los Primeros Automoviles en La Habana." *Transportes*, July–August 1981, 44–45.

Memorandum from Secretary of Public Works of Oriente Province to the Provincial Governor, Nov. 27, 1915. Archivo Historico Provisional, Santiago de Cuba 1915, box 2827, no. 16.

Mota, Francisco. "El Automóvil Llegó a Cuba en 1898." *Bohemia*, February 18, 1966, 104.

Post, Augustus. "The Cuban Motoring Invasion." *Motor*, March 1905, 49–50.

Sexto, Luís. "Cuando por La Habana Andaban Dos Siglos." *Juventud Rebelde*, September 10, 2000, 9.

Sherman, E. C. "Memorandum to the Home Office, Dec. 14, 1916." Benson Ford Research Center, Dearborn, Mich., acc. 76, box 67, Foreign Branch Dealer Agreements.

Tuttle, M. Letter to provincial governor and reply. Archivo Historico Provisional, Santiago de Cuba 1915, box 2827, no. 16.

Williams, Ramón. "Cuba Sets the Example for the United States." *The Horseless Age*, December 20, 1899, 15.

Chapter 2. Tudores *and* Fordores

"¡Adelante Los Primeros!" *Automovilista*, April 1928, n.p.

Arni, C. Edison. *The Art of American Car Design: The Profession and the Personalities*. University Park: Pennsylvania State University Press, 1988.

Céspedes, Carlos Miguel. "La Carretera Central." *A.C.C.* (Automóvil Club de Cuba), February 1930, n.p.

"Cuba, Primer Mercado Automóvil de la América Latina." *El Automóvil de Cuba*, November 1919, 17.

"Cuba Puede Tenir Cien Mil Automoviles." *El Automóvil de Cuba*, December 1936, 17.

de Abad, L. V. *Problemas de los Transportes Cubanos*. Havana: Editora Mercantil Cubana, 1944.

de Zendegui, Guillermo. "Biografía de los 'Guagua': Un Siglo de Transporte Cubano." *Bohemia*, October 24, 1948, 50.

A Future without Child Labour—May 2002. London: International Labour Organization, 2002.

"El Gran Desfile de los Ómnibus el Día Primero de Mayo." *Diario de la Marina*, May 23, 1928, sec. 2, p. 27.

"La Habana Se Ofrece los Ojos de las Turistas como un Enorme Peligroso Lugar de Accidentes." *El Heraldo del Chauffer*, March, 1925, 24.

"Havana Imports G.M. de Mexico's G.M.O.O. Bus." *General Motors World*, January 1950, 10.

Heilman, Paul. Letter to R. I. Roberge, October 4, 1940. Benson Ford Research Center, Dearborn, Mich., acc. 49, box 11, folder C-5.

Martínez, C. A. Letter to H. L. Moekle, December 8, 1939. Benson Ford Research Center, Dearborn, Mich., acc. 49, box 11, folder C-5.

Memorandum Regarding Movement to Obtain a Moratorium on Time Sales of Buses, Trucks in Public Service and Rental Passenger Cars. Benson Ford Research Center, Dearborn, Mich., acc. 49 box 11, folder "Pedro Junco."

Minutes of provincial council meeting, March 31, 1930. Archivo Historico Provisional, Santiago de Cuba 1915, box 2827, no. 16.

"Nuestra Habana." *El Heraldo del Chauffer*, May 1924, 25.

Packard, Vance. *The Waste Makers*. New York: David McKay Co., 1960.

Quintana Bermúdez, Ángel. "Un Accidentado Viaje Que Hizo Historia." *Bohemia*, August 5, 1983, 11–13.

Raban, Jonathan. *Soft City*. New York: E. P. Dutton, 1974.

Ramet, Simonne. "Entrevista." *A.C.C.* (Automóvil Club de Cuba), April 1930, n.p.

Sloan, Alfred. *My Life with General Motors*. New York: Doubleday Publishing Co., 1963.

U.S. Department of Commerce. "Imports of Motor Vehicles." *Automotive Foreign Trade Manual*, Vol. 1. Washington, D.C., 1940.

"Vehículos Inscriptos en Cuba." *El Automóvil de Cuba*, May 1951, 138.

Whitney, Robert. *State and Revolution in Cuba: Mass Mobilization and Political Change, 1920–1940*. Chapel Hill: University of North Carolina Press, 2001.

Wright, Richard A. *West of Laramie: A Brief History of the Auto Industry*. On the Web site of the Antique Automobile Club of America, <www.aaca.org/autohistory>. (This is an "on-line book" published by the Communications Department of Wayne State University in Detroit.)

Chapter 3. Buses and Trolleys

"Adiós a la Tranvía." *El Oriente*, January 28, 1952, 13.

Ads during the war years. Benson Ford Research Center, Dearborn, Mich., acc. 44, box 16.

"La Ambar Motors Corporation." In *Libro de Cuba: Una Enciclopedia Que Abarca las Artes, las Letras, las Ciencias, la Economía, la Política, la Historia*. Havana: n.p., 1954.

Automobile Manufacturers Association Whole Sales Report—12 Months 1947. Benson Ford Research Center, Dearborn, Mich., acc. 713, box 12, folder 4-60.

Castro Ruz, Fidel. *Fidel: My Early Years*. Melbourne: Ocean Press, 1998.

Castro Ruz, Raúl. "Durante Aquel Amanecer del 26 de Julio Se Inicio el Fin del Capitalismo en Cuba." *Bohemia*, July 26, 1963, 66–71.

"El Censo de Vehículos Motorizados de 1953." *El Automóvil de Cuba*, May 1953, 22.

Cerviño, J. M. Letter to P. M. Heilman, June 19, 1940, Benson Ford Research Center, Dearborn, Mich., acc. 46, box 129, folder "Havana Exec."

Cirules, Enrique. *El Imperio de La Habana*. Havana: Editorial Letras Cubanas, 1999.

"Datos Estadisticos de la Inscripción de Vehículos en Junio 30 de 1951." *El Automóvil de Cuba*, September 1951, 41.

De la Fuente, Alejandro. *A Nation for All: Race, Inequality, and Politics in Twentieth-Century Cuba*. Chapel Hill: University of North Carolina Press, 2001.

Doolittle, C. M. Letter to R. I. Roberge, September 22, 1947. Benson Ford Research Center, Dearborn, Mich., acc. 713, box 6, folder 2-41.

"Facts, Data and Statistics on Cuba." In *Investment in Cuba: A Handbook of Basic Information for United States Businessmen*. The Truth about Cuba Committee: Washington, D.C., 1956.

Gómez, Juan. *Ultraje a la Constitución*. Havana: Editorial Zarcotipicos, n.d.

"Importación de vehículos automotrices." *El Automóvil de Cuba*, April 1960, 44.

Jordan, Octavio. "Con El Tanque Lleno." *El Mundo*, November 21, 1951, 6.

———. "Con El Tanque Lleno." *El Mundo*, July 25, 1953, A-4.

———. "Con El Tanque Lleno." *El Mundo*, April 23, 1955, A-4.

López Ortiz, Fernando. "Insistimos en la Supresión de los Matusalémicos Tranvías." *El Automóvil de Cuba*, July 1951, 24.

Mende, Tibor. *América Latina Entra en Escena*. Santiago de Chile: Editorial del Pacífico, 1953.

Merle, Robert. *Moncada: Premier Combat de Fidel Castro*. Paris: Robert Laffont, 1965.

"Miami-Dade Transit History." <www.co.miami-dade.fl.us/transit/history/1930.html>.

Miguez Deus, Gabriel. "Automovilismo en Cuba: Su Desarrollo y sus Asociaciones Imperfectas." *El Automóvil de Cuba*, May 1951, 149.

Miranda, Fausto. "La Gran Tragedia de Comprar Un Cacharro." *Bohemia*, October 1, 1950, 40–42.

Montané Oropesa, Jesús. "La Generación de Primeros Combates." *Verde Olivo*, July 29, 1962, 8–12.

Morejón, Carlos, ed. *Moncada: Antecedentes y Preparativos*. Havana: Editora Política, 1980.

Moreno, Enrique. "90 Años Dura La Tranvía." *Bohemia*, December 21, 1953, 17.

Pacheco, Judas. *Abel Santamaría y El Moncada*. Havana: Editorial Política, 1983.

Parjón, Mario. "El Automóvil Es Una Necessidad." *El Mundo*, November 19, 1954, D-2.

Payas Madlum, Teresa. "Biografía de Abel Santamaría Cuadrado." (unpublished manuscript, 1984).

"Resumen de la Circulación de Vehículos Motorizados en la Republica de Cuba." *El Automóvil de Cuba*, February 1953, 25.

"Rinde la C.O.A. Homenaje de Gratitud a los Señores Amadeo Barletta y Amadeo Barletta, Jr." *El Automóvil de Cuba*, January 1952, 42–44.

Rojas, Marta. "La Quinta Vista." *Bohemia*, July 24, 1964, 24–29.

Tejada, Rafael. "Cuentamillas." *El Crisol*, July 30, 1952, 7.

————. "Cuentamillas." *El Crisol*, August 27, 1952, 7.

"300 GMC Coaches for Havana." *General Motors World*, April 1950, 5.

Chapter 4. 1957 Chevys

Arenas, Reinaldo. *Before Night Falls*. New York: Viking Penguin, 1993.

Borge, Tomás. *Un Grano de Maíz*. Havana: Oficina de Publicaciones del Consejo de Estado, 1992.

"El Censo Nacional de Vehículos de 1958." *El Automóvil de Cuba*, June 1958, 57–59.

Chaumón, Faure. *El Asalto Al Palacio Presidencial*. Havana: Editorial de Ciencias Sociales, 1969.

Cirules, Enrique. "La Gran Ofensiva y El Monte Carlo de America." *Bohemia*, July 10, 1992, 11.

Dan, Uri, Denis Eisenberg, and Eli Landau. *Meyer Lansky: Mogul of the Mob*. New York: Paddington Press, 1979.

Fangio, Juan Manuel. *My Twenty Years of Racing*. London: Temple Press, 1961.

Giancana, Sam, and Chuck Giancana. *Double Cross*. New York: Warner Books, 1992.

Gutiérrez, Pedro Juan. *Dirty Havana Trilogy*. New York: Farrar, Straus and Giroux, 2000.

Jordan, Octavio. "Con El Tanque Lleno." *El Mundo*, February 21, 1950, 36.

————. "Con El Tanque Lleno." *El Mundo*, March 18, 1951, 38.

Marquis, Christopher. "U.S. May Punish Cuba for Imprisoning Critics." *New York Times*, April 17, 2003, A-10.

Masjuan, Miguel. "Mis Amigos Secuestradores." *Bohemia*, October 9, 1981, 36.

"Menelao Mora Morales." *Revolución*, April 26, 1965, 7.

Messick, Hank. *Lansky*. New York: G. P. Putnam & Sons, 1971.

Montenegra, Emma. "Como Fue Secuestrado Fangio." *Bohemia*, January 7, 1959, 79.

"El Motorambar 1957." *El Automóvil de Cuba*, December 1956, 83.

Padron, Pedro Luís. "Amadeo Barletta, Representante en Cuba de Los

Negocios de La Pandilla Yanqui 'Cosa Nostra.'" *Granma*, March 30, 1971, 2.

Ragano, Frank, and Selwyn Raab. *Mob Lawyer*. New York: Charles Scribner's Sons, 1994.

Rodríguez, Arnold. "Como y Por Qué Secuestramos a Fangio: Más Que un Secuestro Fue una Retención Patriótica." Part I, *Juventud Rebelde*, February 21, 1988, 8–9; Part II, *Juventud Rebelde*, February 28, 1988, 10–11.

Schwartz, Rosalie. *Pleasure Island: Tourism and Temptation in Cuba*. Lincoln: University of Nebraska Press, 1997.

Selser, Gregorio. "Lansky y La Historia Política de Cuba." *Bohemia*, March 11, 1983, 8–13.

Valdespino, Andrés. "Cuba Se Nos Llena de Hampones y Tahures." *Bohemia*, February 16, 1958, 63.

Vega, Jorge. "Economicos Autos de Liliput y Gigantescos Carros de Ensueño por Las Vías de Cuba." *Carteles*, January 27, 1957, 38–39.

Velie, Leslie. "Suckers in Paradise." *Saturday Evening Post*, March 28, 1953, 32.

"Venta de Automoviles Nuevos de E.U.A. por Marcas y por Provincias." *El Automóvil de Cuba*, June 1958, 80.

Vincent, Mauricio. "Subsistir in Cuba." *El País*, May 11, 2003, Sunday Supplement, 1–3.

Xiquer, Delfin. "Objectivo: Palacio Presidencial." *Granma*, March 13, 1975, 2.

Chapter 5. Che's Chevrolet and Fidel's Oldsmobile

"Boletín de La Unión de Vendedores de Accesorios de Automoviles de Cuba." *El Automóvil de Cuba*, September, 1959, 136.

Bravo Pardo, Flavio. "Pasajes de Una Victoria con Fidel." *Bohemia*, April 18, 1986, 12–17.

Castro Ruz, Fidel. "Comparencia de Fidel 'Ante La Prensa.'" *Revolución*, September 19, 1959, 12.

"Che Cumple 59 Años." *Juventud Rebelde*, June 14, 1987, 9.

Cuban Transportation Ministry. "Sobre la Situación del Transporte

Urbano en el Capital y las Nuevas Medidas Necessarias de Aplicar."
Tribuna de La Habana, May 16, 1993, 4.

Estrada, Ulises. "Difícil . . . pero Se Mueve." *Granma Internacional*,
April 27, 1994, 7.

"Una Exposición Automovilística de Caracter Internacional." *Automotive
World*, February 16, 1960, 48.

Fundora Ayuso, Gonzalo. *Transporte Urbano*. Havana: Editorial Pueblo y
Educación, 1985.

Herrera Sorzano, Mercedes. "Las Abuelas de las Cuarentiñas."
Transportes, January 1987, 40.

Jordan, Octavio. "Con El Tanque Lleno." *El Mundo*, February 5,
1950, 36.

López Ortiz, Fernando. "El Automóvil: ¿Es Un Lujo?" *El Automóvil de
Cuba*, August 1960, 9.

———. "No Hay Mal Que por Bien No Venga." *El Automóvil de Cuba*,
November 1960, 9.

———. "Otro Vez Las Ventas a Plazos." *El Automóvil de Cuba*, August
1959, 17.

"Llegó un auto con alas desde K. West, Florida." *Diario de la Marina*,
November 27, 1959, 1.

Mastrasana, Francisco. "Tras el Día de la Bicicleta." *Juventud Rebelde*,
October 23, 1994, 14.

Mexidor, Deisy Francis. "Taxi Virtual." *Juventud Rebelde*, June 28,
1998, 10.

Mota, Francisco. "20 Millones de Pesos Cuestan a Cuba Los Accidentes
de Transito de Cada Año." *Bohemia*, August 13, 1961, 6–9, 127.

Navarro, Mireya. "Cuban Wizardry Keeps Tail Fins from Drooping."
New York Times, June 5, 2002, E-1.

Pepper, Margot. "Revolución obligada del transporte en Cuba." *Granma
Internacional*, January 10, 1993, 5.

Rego, Oscar. "Contra Los Accidentes del Transito." *Bohemia*,
December 17, 1971, 5–9.

Rodríguez, Eloy. "Un Desafío Cada Día." *Granma Internacional*, April 12,
1995, 6.

Salazar, Alberto. "Patente de Corso sobre Ruedas." *Bohemia*, April 15, 1994, 31.

Shelton, Alexis. "Veinte Años sobre Ruedas." *Granma*, January 23, 1979, 4.

Smyth, Frank. "Heroes of the Revolution: Cuban Ingenuity Keeps American Classics Running." *Automobile*, March 1999, 109.

Valdés Pérez, Enrique. "Las Piqueras Si o No?" *Bohemia*, February 23, 1990, 40–43.

ACKNOWLEDGMENTS

It is always a pleasure to thank by name those who have assisted me in my work. But people in Cuba can suffer consequences for helping a foreign writer. Some of the nearest and dearest of the people who put up with me in Cuba are not named here, nor in the text. I am deeply grateful to them nevertheless.

As anyone who reads this book can tell, I am not a mechanic. A number of mechanics I spoke with in Cuba were convinced that their skills were rooted in a genetic predisposition, developed at an early age by hanging around other mechanics, usually fathers or uncles, and watching them work. If so, I was born without the requisite DNA. It didn't happen in my family. Instead, my role has been that of the guy a mechanic always has around, close to hand, who stands by the mechanic's side, peering down into the engine, or crawls under the car to observe the work and listen to explanations, handing over a $3/16$-inch wrench when asked, lighting a cigarette to pass, or going in the house to bring out a couple of cold beers from the fridge. In short, I have spent a lot of time as a mechanic's assistant, gofer, or sycophant, call it what you will. A mechanic spends a lot of hours working on cars but actually gets something accomplished in the end. A mechanic's sycophant has nothing more to show for his time than the present moment's pleasure of the mechanic's company, a warm day, and watching something get fixed. I'd particularly like to thank a couple of good mechanics who have tolerated my presence for long periods over the years: Robin Barksdale and Michael Gies.

When I began researching this book, I contacted major car companies for assistance. Only one of them, Ford, seems to have any sense of the company, or the automobile industry, as a part of social history. Ford maintains an extensive historical archive at the Henry Ford Museum and Greenfield Village Research Center in Dearborn, Michigan. My thanks to the staff of the Benson Ford Research Center there. The other companies keep no public records, leave no paper trails. William Pelfrey, director of General Motors' communications department, assured me his staff had spent "several" hours trawling for material about Cuba but found less than a half-dozen items, which they photocopied and sent to me, since I would not be allowed to search for myself. The material included a page from a 1950 company magazine with a photo of Amadeo Barletta visiting the GMC bus factory in Detroit. At least someone answered my inquiry at GM. Try even finding someone to ask about locating company papers at Chrysler or Plymouth or Packard.

A number of people helped with this book in one way or another. In many cases they helped me get things right, and, if in spite of that I still got some wrong, it is certainly my fault, not theirs. Thanks to Elaine Maisner for her keen editorial sense, to Circles Robinson for reading an early draft and saving me from some bad mistakes, to Ron Maner for his careful editing, and to the rest of those to whom I am indebted: Olivia Bernabei; John Bowen; Sara Epstein; Suitberto Goire Castilla; David Hines; Richard Neill; Adele, David, and Jean Schweid; Keoki Skinner; Juan Carlos Subiza; Bridget Vranckx; Ron Watson; the staff of the José Martí National Library; the photo department at *Bohemia* magazine; the staff of the City Historian's Office in Santiago de Cuba; and the staff of the Detroit Public Library's National Automotive History Collection.

Special thanks are due to Roberto Pérez Mirabent, director of the National Transport Museum in Santiago de Cuba, for being kind enough to let me consult the bibliography he has worked so diligently to put together over the years.

INDEX

Aeromobile, 189

Airtex, 185

Alfa Romeo, 202

Alfonso Gallol, Berta: *Los Transportes Habaneros*, 45

Alonso, Carlos, 112, 158, 196

Ambar Motors, 108, 143, 157

American Society of Travel Agents, 188

Anderson, Jon Lee: *Che Guevara*, 68, 162, 180, 181

Andreu, Carmita, 59

Arazoza, Rafael, 27, 29

Arenas, Reinaldo: *Before Night Falls*, 136

Arizala, Aurelio: *Verdades vs. Mentiras*, 45, 46

Astro buses, 73

Astro bus terminal, 189, 190, 208, 209

Astudillo, Francisco de P., 27

Autobuses Modernos, S.A., 107, 110, 177

Auto-Cuba, 196

Automobile Chamber of Commerce (Camara de Comercio de Automoviles), 116, 196

Automobile finance companies, 183

Automobile racing, 34, 37

Automotive World, 188, 189

Auto Universal de Cuba, 72

Banes, 64–65, 162; and public transportation, 49

Baobab tree, 173

Baracoa, 189; and public transportation, 49

Bar Detroit, 129, 131

Barletta, Amadeo, 110, 111, 157, 166, 187; and Ambar Motors, 107–9; and Batista, 120; and Motorambar, 143; and the Mafia, 164

Barletta, Amadeo, Jr., 187

Baseball, 41, 42, 174, 213

Bassart, Luis, 120, 122

Batista y Saldívar, Fulgencio, 81, 122, 124, 143, 146, 149, 162, 177, 183, 187, 188; and Detroit automakers, 82–83, 87, 118–20; race of, 117; and Moncada, 127–28; and Cuban Grand Prix, 157–60; and casinos, 163, 166;

and parking meters, 167; end of government of, 178

Bayamo, 19
Bay of Pigs, 195, 199
Benz, 32
Bernabei, Anthony, 187
Bernabei, Olivia, 187
Bicycles, 205–6, 207
Bock, Gustavo, 29
Bohemia, 147; 1948 poll in, 103
Bonano, Joe "Bananas," 164
Bonsal, Philip, 189
Borge, Tomás: *Un Grano de Maíz*, 136–37
Borrego, Orlando, 180–81
Bosch, José, 106
Bravo Pardo, Flavio, 199
Brooks y Galo, Charles, 16, 19
Bugatti, 59
Buick, 5, 21, 67–69, 88, 129, 146, 193, 205; in Santiago de Cuba in 1915, 19; Special, 21, 192; Abel Santamaría's, 123; at Moncada, 124, 126
Buick, David Dunbar, 92
Bulletin of the Union of Auto Accessory Salesmen, 183

Cabrera Hernández, Juan, 86
Cacharros, 9, 138; definition of, 7; government sale of, 212–13; future of, 216
Cadillac, 5, 10, 65, 67, 68, 129, 131, 140, 141, 147, 191, 202;

1905 model, 60; sales in 1939, 83–84; and Harley Earl, 92; and Amadeo Barletta, 107, 108, 187; Castro on, 186
Caibarién, 205
Calvo y Nodarse, María. *See* La Macorina
Camellos, 50
Campo, Eliseo de la, 199
Carricaburu, Ernesto, 30, 33, 35
Carsi, Higinio, 72
Carteles, 141, 146
Castelli, Leo, 66
Castro Ruz, Fidel, 5, 6, 97, 141, 146, 147, 158, 161, 182, 185, 202, 216; and cult of personality, 12, 152; announces Special Period, 20; and Ortodoxos, 45; and September 11, 2001, 98–100; assassination attempts, 99, 195; and Moncada assault, 122–28; Chevrolet of, 124; and homosexuals, 136–37; as threat to United States, 177–87; and consumer habits, 186–87, 194, 200; and Oswaldo Dorticos, 188; Oldsmobile of, 199
Castro Ruz, Raúl, 141, 146; and Moncada assault, 5–6, 125–27
Ceiba tree, 173, 204
Central Highway (Carretera Central), 63, 71, 73, 76, 161
Central Intelligence Agency (CIA), 99, 177, 195

Cerviño, J. M., 120
Céspedes, Carlos Manuel de, 137
Céspedes, Carlos Miguel, 70–71,
    81
Chalmers, 19, 33
Champion Spark Plugs, 113, 184
Chase National Bank: and Central
    Highway financing, 71
Chaumón, Faure, 147
Chevrolet, 5, 19, 20–21, 33, 40,
    65, 66, 120, 129, 131, 157,
    161, 167, 190, 201, 209; 1957
    Bel Air, 6, 7, 138, 144, 151,
    156, 173; and middle class,
    10; and Santiago de Cuba, 19,
    140; trucks, 47, 107; sales in
    1936, 84; and Amadeo Barletta,
    107–8; Fidel Castro's, 123, 124;
    role in Revolution, 146; Che
    Guevara's, 181, 199; post-1959,
    187; as taxis, 203, 204; 1925
    model, 211
Chibás, Eduardo, 45
Chibás, Eduardo, Jr., 85
Chrysler, 5, 146; percentage of
    1957 market, 144
Chrysler, Walter P., 92
Ciego de Ávila: and Ford, 141
Cienfuegos: and public trans-
    portation, 49
Cienfuegos, Camilo, 5, 60, 141,
    178, 180, 188
Cirules, Enrique: El Imperio de
    La Habana, 108

Clark, Sergio, 106
CNN, 98, 132
Coco taxis, 175
Committees to Defend the Revolu-
    tion (CDR), 208
"Con El Tanque Lleno" (With a
    Full Tank), 109, 113, 145
Conga, 40–44; and baseball, 41;
    and batá drum, 41, 44; and
    Chinese cornet, 41, 44
Conill, Enrique J., 35
Constancia Sugar Mill, 122
Cooperativa de Ómnibus Aliados
    (COA), 107, 110; formation of,
    80; 1933 strike by, 81; and Ford
    Motors, 85–87; and Menelao
    Mora, 106; and General Mo-
    tors, 108
Credit buying, 183
Créditos y Descuentos Mercantiles,
    85, 87
Cuba: and housing stock, 12;
    and infant mortality rate, 12;
    and women's rights, 59; ve-
    hicle ownership in 1917, 62;
    registered cars from 1931 to
    1938, 72; and litter, 90; and
    classroom size, 99; registered
    cars in 1941, 100–101; post–
    World War II, 101; middle-
    class population in 1953, 102;
    cars sold in 1952, 111; census
    figures for 1952, 118; traffic
    accidents in 1952, 131; homo-

sexuals in, 136–37; European car sales, 144; Ministry of the Interior, 150, 175; and dollars, 153; and health care, 155; vehicles imported in 1957, 161; rural area of, 162; Cadillac sales in, 164, 176; cars registered in 1958, 176; balance of trade with United States, 186; relations with USSR, 186; cars imported in 1959 and 1960, 187; relations with United States in 1960, 193–95; disappearance of auto industry in, 195; Soviet vehicles in, 197; old car clubs in, 210; and sale of old cars in 1990s, 212; and communications with United States, 215

Cubana Airlines, 106

Cuban Credit Automobile Company, 62

Cuban Grand Prix, 157–60

"Cuentamillas" (Odometer), 111, 120

Darracq, 35

De la Fuente, Alejandro: *A Nation for All*, 117

De Soto, 7, 23

Diario de la Marina, 189

Dion Bouton, 29

Directorio Revolucionario, 147

Dodge, 33, 157, 190; and Santiago de Cuba, 5, 19; as *ruteros*, 50;

role in Revolution, 146; Fargo truck, 147, 148, 149, 161, 197; sales in 1957, 161

Dodge brothers, 92

Doolittle, C. M., 103

Dorticos, Oswaldo, 188

Driver's licenses: requirement of, 30

Durant, William C., 92

Earl, Harley, 92

Echevarría, José Antonio, 5, 147, 149

Eisenhower, Dwight, 193, 194

El Acusador, 123

El Automóvil de Cuba, 27, 28, 37, 116, 184, 189, 193; ranks auto markets, 62, 111; and trolleys, 105–6; and 1957 Motorambar, 141, 143; and revolutionary government, 182, 185; disappearance of, 196

El Bodeguito, 65

El Capitolio Nacional, 6, 7, 51, 71

Electric buses, 105

Electric Light and Traction Company of Santiago de Cuba, 44–45

El Fígaro, 25, 27, 57

El Garaje de Mi Tío, 129

El Libro de Cuba, 112

Encrucijada, 122

Estep, Ralph: *El Toro*, 30

Estrada Palma, Tomás, 29, 30

Fangio, Juan Manuel, 162; kidnapping of, 157–61
Fernández, Justo, 30
Fernández Hurtado, Fermín, 18
Fernández Mell, Oscar, 162
Fernández y Miranda, Roberto, 167
Ferrari, 160
Fiat, 17, 18, 19, 32
Fiat Polski, 15, 208, 216
Flying Tiger, 195
Ford, 5, 23, 103, 129, 131, 146, 157, 167, 190, 202, 209; Edsel, 7, 173, 211; buying on credit, 10; as taxis, 19, 144; 1956 Thunderbird, 22; Model-T, 33, 62; trucks, 47, 85, 197; 1954 station wagon, 50–51, 173; 1926 repair manual for, 68; sales in 1936, 84; bus sales, 85, 87; sales in 1924 and 1931, 92; ads during World War II, 101; and Relámpago agency, 112; relationship with Batista, 118, 120; sales in Ciego de Ávila, 141; percentage of 1957 market, 144; Prefect, 146; Fairlane, 147, 212; sales in 1957, 161; higher price of in Cuba, 183
Ford, Edsel, 93
Ford, Henry, 92, 200
Forment, Carlos E.: *Cronicas de Santiago de Cuba*, 16, 17, 18, 44, 45

Fundora Ayuso, Gonzalo: *Transporte Urbano*, 200

Gambling, 165; post-Revolution, 180
Gaz trucks, 47, 197
Geli, José, 17
General Electric, 103
General Motors, 123, 143, 164; Chevrolet exports in 1936, 84; bus sales, 85, 107, 108; truck sales, 85; car sales in 1924 and 1931, 93; and concept of styling, 93; and Amadeo Barletta, 107; and Relámpago agency, 112; and Batista, 120; and Jesús Montané, 122–23
General Motors World, 78
GMC: buses, 197; trucks, 199
Gómez, Juan: *Ultraje a la Constitución*, 110
González, Ernesto, 124
Goodman, Walter, 17
Goodyear Tires, 113, 195
Gran Car, 176
Granma (boat), 128, 143
Granma (newspaper), 132, 164, 203; *Granma Internacional*, 206
Grau San Martín, Ramón, 81, 163
Grenet, Emilio: *Cuban Popular Music*, 40
Grinasy, Pepe, 17
Gua-gua, 53, 56
Guajiros, 153, 172

Guantánamo, 19, 150

Guayanaba, 112

Guevara de la Serna, Ernesto "Che," 5, 141, 175, 181; Chevrolet of, 60, 180, 188, 199; sleeps on office floor, 68; drives for first time, 162; takes Havana, 178; inaugurates bicycle factory, 205

Gutiérrez, Pedro Juan: *Dirty Havana Trilogy*, 149

Havana, 64, 124, 125, 156, 172, 179, 197, 216; cars and climate in, 7, 19; as first city to have cars, 24; early dealerships in, 34; public transportation in, 49–51; La Rampa, 57, 108, 173; Automobile Museum, 60, 212; condition of streets in 1925, 63; cars and tourists in, 66; buses in, 78, 80, 107, 111, 199, 206; streetcars in, 103, 105–6; voters' priorities in 1948, 103; parking in, 114–15, 167; during 1950s, 131; bars on windows in, 132; new car sales in 1956, 141; new car sales in 1957, 144; working cars currently in, 149; and Cuban Grand Prix, 158; and organized crime, 163; Plaza de la Revolución, 173; sightseeing circuit, 175; beggars in 1958, 177; Che Guevara enters,

178; and international automobile show, 188; contemporary life in, 192; and taxis, 202, 203; Harley-Davidson motorcycle club in, 210; old cars hidden in, 215

Havana Automobile Club, 35, 211

Havana Automobile Company, 29

Havana Automobile Transfer Company, 25, 27

Havana Electric Railway, Light & Power Company, 45, 105, 106

Hawkins, N. A., 33, 34

Haynes-Apperson, 25

Heilman, Paul, 85, 120

Heraldo del Chauffeur, 63, 64

Hernández, Melba, 127

Herrera Sorzano, Mercedes, 200

Hinckle, Warren: *The Fish Is Red*, 107

Hitchhikers, 76

Holguín, 162, 189; and Mercurys, 141

Horseless Age, The, 25

Hotel Melía Santiago, 98

Hupmobile, 19, 32

Inclán, Guido García, 176, 177

International Labour Organization, 53

Iveco trucks, 47

Jaguar, 181

Jineteros/jineteras, 137, 189

Jordan, Octavio, 109, 111, 113, 115, 144, 145, 183, 190
José Martí National Library, 173, 176, 189, 190
Juventud Rebelde, 132

Kaiser, 7
Kamaz: trucks, 47; buses, 206
Kapok, 173
Kefauver, Estes, 163, 164
Kennedy, John F., 195
Korenda, Peter, 149

Lada, 9, 15, 98, 146, 205, 212, 216; as taxis in Santiago de Cuba, 138; among first post-Revolution cars to arrive, 200; distributed by government, 201; as taxis in Havana, 203; carburetor for used in Chevrolet, 204
La Estrella, 64
La Floridita, 65
La Gaceta, 27, 29
Lainé, Dámaso, 28, 35
Lainé, Honoré, 28, 35
La Macorina, 60, 62
La Macorina Club, 211
Lansky, Meyer, 163, 164
Larcher, Roy, 143
Lasalle, 92
Leal, Eusebio, 213
Leyland Motors, 107, 108, 110
Lincoln, 82–84, 146, 147
Locomobile, 15, 19, 27, 33

López, Germán, 17, 18
López Ortiz, Fernando, 27, 28, 32, 34, 35, 62, 63, 72, 105, 182, 183, 184, 194
Luciano, Charles "Lucky," 163, 164, 168
Lusso, Rodolfo, 35

Machado, Gerardo, 6, 70, 71, 80–81
Mafia, 163, 164
Malecón, 27, 34, 57, 144, 157, 160, 163, 167
Mambo Club, 203
Manzanillo, 19
Marmon, 35
Marquis, Christopher, 153
Martí, José, 13, 97
Martínez, C. A., 83, 85
Marx, Luis, 29
Maserati, 157, 159
Masjuan, Miguel, 159
Matanzas, 162, 190; new car sales in 1957, 144
Matos Ortiz, Delfín, 202
Mende, Tibor, 118
Menocal, Mario G., 63
Menocal, Raúl, 120
Mercedes, 25
Mercedes-Benz, 67, 161, 215
Mercury, 141
Merle, Robert: *Moncada*, 122–24
Mesejo Mestre, Eduardo, 60, 61, 62, 212–13

Messick, Hank: *Lansky*, 167
Miguez Deus, Gabriel, 111
Milanés, Pablo, 136
Miranda, Fausto, 101
Mitchell, Teodulio, 124
Mitsubishi, 215
Moncada military barracks, 6,
    124–28, 146
Montané Oropesa, Jesús, 122–24,
    126, 127, 146
Montenegra, Emma, 160
Mora, Menelao, 85–87, 106, 147,
    148, 149
Moreno, Enrique, 110
Morrison, Allen, 106
Moskvich, 9, 201
Moss, Stirling, 157
Motor Age, 29
Motorambar, 141, 143, 188
Muñoz, José, 24, 25, 28
Museum of the Revolution, 149
Mussolini, Benito, 108, 164, 187

Nash Rambler, 7, 212
National Automotive Federation
    (Confederación Nacional Auto-
    motriz), 116
National Transport Museum, 17–
    18, 140
Neill, Richard, 40–41

O'Hallorans, Eugenio, 202
Oil refineries: nationalization of,
    194

Olds, Ransom F., 92
Oldsmobile, 29, 33, 65, 120, 129,
    146; and Amadeo Barletta, 107,
    108; in Camagüey, 141; post-
    1959, 187
Oriente, 13, 63, 124, 143, 161
Ortodoxos (Cuban People's Party),
    45, 85

Packard, 7, 15, 30, 33, 71, 73, 129,
    146, 173
Packard, Vance: *The Waste Makers*,
    92
País, Frank, 5
Palo Mayombe, 173
Panataxi, 203, 205. *See also*
    Havana: and taxis
Panhard Levassor, 29
Parisienne, 24, 28
Parjon, Mario, 128
Paseo, 53, 173
Pawley, William, 108, 177–78, 195;
    and Autobuses Modernos, S.A.,
    106–7, 109–10
Peerless, 19
Pegaso trucks, 47
Pentagon, 98
Pepper, Margot, 206
Pérez, Louis A., Jr.: *On Becoming
    Cuban*, 56, 62, 191
Pérez Mirabent, Roberto, 17, 18,
    19, 20, 21, 22, 140–41, 201,
    210; and Fiat Polskis, 208
Peugeot, 215

Pinar del Río, 67, 71, 190; new car sales in 1957, 144
Piñera, Virgilio, 136
Piqueras, 202, 203
Planned obsolescence, 92, 93
Playa Girón, 195, 199
Plymouth, 5, 7, 66, 150, 156, 159, 189, 213
Polaquitas, 200
Pontiac, 120, 122, 124, 127, 129, 146
Presidential Palace, 147, 149, 158
Prío Socarrás, Carlos, 103, 108, 117
Prostitutes, 118, 169; post-Revolution, 180

Quintana Bermúdez, Ángel, 65

Radio Bemba, 10, 132
Radio Reloj, 147
Rambler, 5, 160
Ramet, Simonne, 59
Rauschenberg, Robert, 66
Relámpago agency, 112, 113, 129, 157, 158, 178, 196, 197
Renault, 32
Replacement parts, 187. *See also* Spare parts
Revolución, 186
Riviera Hotel and Casino, 164, 188
Roberge, R. I., 85, 103, 120
Rochet & Schneider, 25, 29
Rodríguez, Arnold, 160, 161

Rodríguez, Francisco "Paco," 211
Rojas, Marta, 127
Rolls razor, 92
Ross, Lawrence, 33, 34
Ruteros, 9, 50, 51, 174, 200, 204, 209

Salazar, Alberto, 205
San Antonio de Blanco, 111, 112
Sans Souci Casino, 157
Santa Clara, 190
Santa Coloma, Boris, 127
Santamaría Cuadrado, Abel, 5, 122, 123, 124, 126, 127, 146
Santamaría Cuadrado, Haydée, 122, 123, 127
Santería, 6, 173
Santiago de Cuba, 13, 64, 189, 216; public transport in, 13, 44, 49; Plaza de Marte, 13–15, 18, 22, 47, 98, 136; first car in, 15; 1902 population of, 17; old car owners' association, 19, 210; Parque Céspedes (Céspedes Park), 21, 42, 45, 137; auto racing in, 37; first taxi fleet in, 37; first trolleys in, 45; *camiones de uso particular* in, 46; provincial council, 71; French Beach, 88, 91; *casas de la trova* in, 96; Elvira Capé Library, 96–97; Calle Heredia, 97; and terrorist attacks, 100; and streetcars, 103, 105; Santo

Domingo Motor Company, 108, 187; bars on windows in, 132; Aguilera Street, 135, 137; Plaza Dolores, 135–37; Plaza de Armas, 136; sexual tourism in, 138; and Chevrolets, 139–41; new car sales in 1957, 144; street food in, 153; neighborhood clinics in, 154; International Bolero Festival, 169, 171; Casa de las Tradiciones, 169–70; Vista Hermosa neighborhood, 202

Sarrá, Ernesto, 25, 61

Sarrá, Tina, 59

Sarrá family, 131

Schumacher, Michael, 157

Schwartz, Rosalie: *Pleasure Island*, 157, 165

Scovel, Silvester, 28

Sexto, Luís, 25

Shell Oil, 184, 185, 193

Shelton, Alexis, 203

Sherman, E. C., 33, 34, 37

Shnitzler, Rick, 214, 215

Sierra Maestra, 143, 147, 154, 158, 161

Skoda, 15, 200

Sloan, Alfred, 92, 200–201

Smith, S. P., 185

Smith, Stephen: *The Land of Miracles*, 201

Smyth, Frank, 202

Snap-On Tools, 113

Son los Mismos, 122

Soviet Union, 186; cars of, 13; and petroleum, 193, 198, 199

Spare parts: embargo on, 9, 195, 199; value of in 1952, 103. *See also* Replacement parts

Special Period in a Time of Peace, 47, 152, 154–56, 205; announced in 1990, 20; and crime, 132; and taxis, 203; and buses, 206; selling collectible cars during, 212

Sport utility vehicles, 215

Squiers, Herbert, 35, 56

Standard Oil, 120, 193, 194

Steinhart, Frank, 45

Studebaker, 5, 7, 19; 1951 Champion, 21, 22, 174; 1956 Golden Hawk, 173

Sugg, H. L., 86

TailLight Diplomacy, 214

Tejada, Rafael, 111, 120

Telemundo, 157, 166

Texaco Oil, 193, 194

Thomas, Hugh: *Cuba*, 102, 126, 161, 177, 194

Tourists, 165, 166, 176, 188, 203, 205

Toyota, 215

Trafficante, Santos, 163, 164

Traspaso, 13, 174

Trebant, 200

Tribuna de la Havana, 206

Trolleys, 78
Tropicana nightclub, 203, 204
Trujillo Molina, Rafael Leónidas,
    108, 164, 187
26 July Movement, 146, 159

United Fruit Company, 120
U.S. Rubber, 184

Valdés, Enrique, 203
Valdespino, Andrés, 166
Valiant, 189
Vedado, 50, 52–59, 116, 122, 156,
    160, 173, 204, 208; and car
    business, 129; Colón Cemetery
    in, 123, 210
Vega, Jorgé, 146
Verdecia, Lorenzo, 211–12
Vía Azul buses, 73
Violeteras, 200

Volga, 9, 138, 200, 201, 205
Volkswagen, 146

War of Independence (1898), 13
Warsawa, 200
Welles, Sumner, 81
White, 28, 29, 33
Whitney, Robert: *State and Revolution
    in Cuba*, 81
Willard Batteries, 113, 195
Willys Jeep, 6, 161, 162, 178
Willys Overland, 7, 19, 33
Wood, Leonard, 28
Woods Electric Automobiles, 27
World Trade Center, 97–98, 99
Wright, Richard, 92

Zaldívar, Santiago, 65
Zendegui, Guillermo de, 53